EVEN MORE
VOICES FROM
PRISON WALLS

by
WILLIAM CAWMAN

Author of
Voices from Prison Walls
More Voices from Prison Walls
Yet More Voices from Prison Walls
Still More Voices from Prison Walls

SCHMUL PUBLISHING COMPANY
NICHOLASVILLE, KENTUCKY

COPYRIGHT © 2021 BY SCHMUL PUBLISHING CO.
All rights reserved. No part of this publication may be reproduced or used in any form or by any means—graphic, electronic, or mechanical, including photocopying, recording, taping, or information storage or retrieval systems—without prior written permission of the publishers.

Churches and other noncommercial interests may reproduce portions of this book without prior written permission of the publisher, provided such quotations are not offered for sale—or other compensation in any form—whether alone or as part of another publication, and provided that the text does not exceed 500 words or five percent of the entire book, whichever is less, and does not include material quoted from another publisher. When reproducing text from this book, the following credit line must be included: "From *Even More Voices from Prison Walls* by William Cawman, © 2021 by Schmul Publishing Co., Nicholasville, Kentucky. Used by permission."

Published by Schmul Publishing Co.
PO Box 776
Nicholasville, KY USA

Printed in the United States of America

ISBN 10: 0-88019-638-6
ISBN 13: 978-0-88019-638-3

Visit us on the Internet at www.wesleyanbooks.com, or order direct from the publisher by calling 800-772-6657, or by writing to the above address.

Contents

	Foreword	4
1	God is Not Finished Yet	7
2	Real Men – Real Stories	27
3	And Then?	43
4	Growing Spiritually	61
5	Victories and Disappointments	79
6	Extra Blessings	96
7	In Spite of Politics	113
8	Why So Many Dull Ears?	130
9	And Still He Tarries	148
10	Will It Work When They Get Out?	165
11	Life's Changes Continue – But God!	184
12	"Let Brotherly Love Continue"	202
13	Jesus is Working Still	219
14	A Whole New Approach	238
15	Even in Troubled Times	254
16	Carry On!	271

Foreword

AT THE CLOSE OF the fourth volume of these letters I really did not anticipate publishing another one, but such has been the continuing delay of the return of our Lord, that another four years has slipped into history—four years of God's faithful Holy Spirit working in answer to many prayers among precious men in a State Prison.

For the first three years of these four (2017-2019) it could be said that they were a continuation of the seventeen before them, but with the opening of a new decade (2020) everything took on tumultuous changes, and almost continual re-directions of former procedures.

If our Lord delays His coming for another four years, God alone knows what will be the future of ministry among men in prison. All I know at this point is that He is nothing short of miraculously keeping a door open for His Word to reach a few more souls and transform them from society's outcasts to Bridehood Saints.

I take this opportunity to render heartfelt thanks to God for giving me this small corner of His great harvest field to labor for Him. It has been filled with joys, heartaches, disappointments, and rewards. I gladly offer up to the Sacrifice of Calvary all credit and praise for any eternal good accomplished. I humbly and repentantly take full responsibility for any shortfall, error, or failure to see anything short of His full desire accomplished in this ministry. I lay it all at the blessed feet of Jesus. It has all been for Him.

As I pen this introduction to the past four years, I wonder how long God will keep this door open. Then I look upon the faces of men who have had hardly any of the wonderful privileges to live the good life that I have had, and I wonder how I could ever walk away from them.

And so, knowing nothing except that He knows all, I look up into His smiling face and say in the words of an old song:
Shall I empty-handed be

When beside the crystal sea
I shall stand before the everlasting throne?
Must I have a heart of shame
As I answer to my name,
With no works that my Redeemer there can own?

What regret must then be mine
When I meet my Lord divine,
If I've wasted all the talents He doth lend,
If no soul to me can say,
"I am glad you passed my way;
For 'twas you who told me of the sinner's Friend."

If my gratitude I'd show
Unto Him Who loves me so,
Let me labor till the evening shadows fall;
That some little gift of love
I may bear to realms above,
And not empty-handed be when comes the call.

When the harvest days are past,
Shall I hear Him say at last,
"Welcome, toiler, I've prepared for thee a place?"

Shall I bring Him golden sheaves,
Ripened fruit, not faded leaves,
When I see the blessed Savior face to face?

When the books are opened wide,
And the deeds of all are tried,
May I have a record whiter than the snow;
When my race on earth is run,
May I hear Him say, "Well done,
Take the crown that love immortal doth bestow."

Your unworthy fellow-servant,
WILLIAM CAWMAN

1
GOD IS NOT FINISHED YET

January 1, 2017

Didn't we just start using the digit of 6 at the end of our dates? So quickly it has turned to 7. Life is most certainly what God's Word describes it to be: "For what is your life? It is even a vapour, that appeareth for a little time, and then vanisheth away." Oh God, did I do my best for Thee this past year? I don't feel any degree of confidence that I can claim that, but let it only compel me more for the coming year, if Jesus tarries.

These letters are not about me, but about the dear brethren in prison, yet I know and do appreciate all of your prayers and love for me, their chaplain. Some of you have heard that I had a heart attack. Well, let me explain just what did happen. I had a day of uneasiness in my lower abdomen and so paid a visit to the emergency room and there they discovered that I had stones in my gall bladder. The doctors were very sure that since I go out of the country quite a bit, I should have it removed. It could make the difference between having it removed by a robot or a butcher knife, so I submitted and on Thursday, December 9, went in to have it removed.

The surgery went fine but as I was in recovery and just gaining what meager sense I usually have, I suddenly felt a pain hit my chest. I looked up and here my cardiologist was sitting right across the room from me! I said something about it and people started flying all around and within about three minutes they had me in the Cath lab and were unblocking a clot of blood from around the stints they had put in a year before. Going off of the blood thinner for the surgery caused it to happen. They acted so fast that no damage at all was done to my heart. "His eye is on the sparrow, and I know He cares for me." Enough about me, except that I love Him!

No, God will not let that be enough, and so a bit more for His glory alone. When I left the Cath lab they sent me to ICU so that they could observe what my heart was going to do. I see now that God had some others that He wanted to observe my heart as well. When the time came for me to step down to lesser care, there were no beds open and so I stayed there from Thursday night through Sunday afternoon. The room was way down at the end of the hall and very quiet and I had a good time with Jesus while there.

One morning He just flooded my soul over and over with Psalm 23. Truly my cup was running over. Was that for me? Yes, thank God, but not just for me. I soon became conscious that two or three of the nurses would just come down to my room and seem to want to hang around and talk. I did not put my running-over cup under a bushel, and the more I opened up the more they seemed to want to be there. Why am I telling you this? Because I discovered that this world about us is sick with sin, and the only answer is that which makes someone's cup run over with goodness and mercy.

Dear Praying Friends, may God help us to serve the present age. We have no more important business here on earth than to be His voice, His hand, His love extended to a world reeling under the disease of sin. Fade, fade every other attraction—Jesus is all the world to me, and others need Him, too.

It was Tuesday, December 20, 2016. I had scheduled some

interviews for the morning and had two classes in the afternoon. Early into the first interview a fight broke out down in the educational wing and my client had to be put into security until it was finished. This is not unusual at all, especially this time of year. All the attention I give it is to sort of keep track of the time involved, for the sooner it's over, the more minimal the disturbance. At any rate, it was soon over and my man returned.

The next one to come I had never spoken to before and he greeted me with the observation that he didn't believe in anything. Of course, when a statement like that is made, one easily conjectures that if such is true, he doesn't believe in his own statement, either. And so, we began to probe around a bit. He said he came from England and was oriented toward a loyalty to Odin or some other pagan deity, but he wasn't stuck on that as he really didn't have any belief. He was in a four-man cell and one was a Muslim, one was a Catholic, and the other a Protestant— he thought. He wanted to know what the difference was between Catholic and Christian. I gave a minute briefing on that and then went to the point. I asked him if he believed that a God existed that created him. He said he definitely did. I asked him if He didn't think he had a right to know Him? He did. I began to testify to him and tell him what a change Jesus makes when one really lets Him come into their heart.

All of the sudden he was believing, and I could see him believing. He was struggling to not let the tears run down his cheeks. He said that for five years in prison he had pretty much just ignored this whole issue, but of late it was really claiming his attention. I told him that was because Jesus was knocking at his heart's door because He loved him. That really touched his heart and he promised me after we had prayed that he would earnestly go and seek for the Lord to reveal Himself to him.

The old song came with force to me: "Heartaches, broken pieces, ruined lives are why You died on Calvary..." Please pray for him. I will not leave him alone; I will follow up on him very soon.

One of the men who is enrolled in the Bible college courses was working in the hallway with the buffer and I had a couple of books to give to him, so I asked the officer to send him in to me in the office. He came in and I gave him the books and then just bowed my head and prayed for him. When I finished he said, "Wow! I really felt that!" I don't want to ever take prayer for granted, do you?

Are you tired yet of hearing from our former Mormon? I just received another six-page typed letter and I just cried as I read it. While he claims I have helped him so much, I'm quite sure he is helping me even more. Listen a bit more:

> I'd like to discuss how the Lord is working with me regarding doctrine, and perhaps get your guidance. When I'm asked about my doctrinal approach, and I let the Holy Spirit respond, it usually comes out of my mouth that I belong to God. When they then say that I'm not making any sense, or not answering the question, I ask them if they are looking for the perfect path, or the perfect destination. In human terms, in the flesh, I think we emphasize paths rather than gates. We think we do the work, we walk this path to Jesus, we find it, we walk it, He's at the end of it. We earned Him, or whatever reward we imagine.
>
> To break us out of such thinking (based, at its core, on self-salvation), He starts His Word in Genesis and John with "In the beginning, God..." "In the beginning was the Word, and the Word was with God, and the Word was God." Jesus is THE beginning of the path, the gate itself. He's the only possible beginning. Once the Father has called us to Jesus, and we've come to Him and believed, and surrendered (taken the yoke), why look for a path instead of a person? The "narrow way" is simply staying now with Jesus forever, through eternal life.
>
> Spiritually speaking, I believe doctrine will only make sense after we don't need it. Perhaps better said, "Flesh and blood has not revealed it to thee..." The Spirit initiates, creates; doctrine

can only describe what happened. When we know that HE is what we (desperately) need; Him alone, the Holy Spirit reveals to us who He is, so we turn to Him. That which is born of Spirit is Spirit. If I start with the learning of the flesh, I'm doomed already. That's actually the order of events in His invitation: Come to Him, He will give us rest (His person, love and forgiveness), we can surrender in love to His yoke, THEN learn of Him.

For me, that's not a developed theory, but rather a simple description of my experience. Remember how He did this with me? Cult life meant I'd missed Christ and been lied to about (and kept out of) the Bible. Which problem did God solve first? Through your efforts, my dear brother, you helped me gain Christ. God drew me to Christ, and the Holy Spirit revealed Christ. It was over a year later, when I was in another state in a cell by myself, that He told me to read the Bible. I fought with Him for three days over that because of how the Bible had previously been misused in my life, but I couldn't resist Christ once He was working in me. So the yoke took over, I started in Genesis and finished Revelations four months later—astounded. (And He's never removed that directive, I'm still in the Bible.)

But if I'd gone to the Bible first, without Him, without His Holy Spirit, how would that have been any different than the road I'd already traveled? How would that be any different than Satan himself who knows the whole Bible and missed Jesus; missed a submitted relationship to the Father? You can gain the Bible and miss Jesus Christ, but you can't gain Jesus Christ and miss the Bible (He won't permit that, and it's simply not possible). Doctrine will come. When I'm in love with Jesus, and He's shown me my desperate need of Him, I will learn of Him, voraciously. My motivation is then to fill myself with Him, and to adopt His priorities and become transformed to His image. But if I'm not in love with Him first, if I want to be my own god, then my motivation for doctrine is, at best, to feel a little better about my guilt, or (more commonly) to contend with others, judge others, and promote myself...

So what's my doctrine? What can I tell a person? I say: "My

doctrine is to be fully God's. Love Jesus and be His. Learn of Him by the power of the Holy Spirit..."

But...when I'm asked about this or that FALSE doctrine, the Holy Spirit works a little differently. He smiles through me, and I ask them if the person I love most, Jesus, has asked me to spend (waste) my time exposing every false gospel, or did He give me the great commission of exposing HIS gospel?...

Wouldn't the enemy laugh at our waste of energy on what we really know already (thank You Holy Spirit) in our spiritual heart is just a rabbit trail that goes nowhere? In studying finance, I learned about "opportunity cost." Any financial option I pursue precludes me from taking advantage of the other options currently available. My profit on any pursuit must consider the preclusion of the other options for my money... In the spiritual realm, what is the opportunity cost of following false doctrine rabbit trails? What will I miss that God has for me if I waste my time and energy in that manner? Frankly, I'm not interested in being the enemy's entertainment. And I'm very, very certainly not interested in missing what God has for me. So I'll spend my precious time with Jesus, and let the "opportunity cost" of THAT be whatever Satan had wanted for me with false doctrines. Let the dead bury their dead.

...love Him and surrender and learn of Him. Then hold onto your hat because His blood is going to go to work. He's also going to teach you. That's my best shot at doctrine. The Holy Spirit will show you the scriptures, and the Lord will show you full salvation—BUT NOT from a safe distance as a scholar—He'll grab your right hand and show it to you from the front row, as a participant. Then, if you feel like you have the anointing to write it down, okay. That may happen. But most of the blessed men and women who I've read about or know, once they've been there, they look at the Bible and say, "Yup, that's it, it's all over the Bible. How could you miss it? Read That."

I can also testify to people that the path to doctrine doesn't lead to Jesus, it starts with Jesus. So let Him in! Let His love change us. See where He takes us when our love for Him is white hot! Let that be our testimony first, and then see if the Holy Spirit leads us to ways of describing it that prove helpful to others. He might. That's up to His purposes. Once we're in His gate, He'll lead us all the way.

(Isn't that good? Do you see why it's impossible to not share it with you?)

And now let's go back to that December 20th. After my morning interviews I went to my first class for the afternoon. Our subject was, "What it Means to Be a Christian," taken from 1 John 3:1-14. As I stood there teaching the men I suddenly felt very clearly and unexpectedly a warm mantle settle down from heaven all over me, and with it a fresh renewed call to minister to these men. Between meeting with such a hungry needy man in the morning and a fresh call of God in the afternoon, it was a red-letter day on my calendar. I've often been overwhelmed by a sense of fresh love for these dear men, but this was straight from God. I heard Him. I will gladly obey Him. I am serving a life sentence!

Thanking you for your prayers, I am yours in Him,

W Cawman

February 1, 2017

PERHAPS I SHOULD BEGIN this letter by telling you of the changes that God is allowing and even making in my life. On December 29th after I had sent out the last letter, I flew to Sucre, Bolivia to preach twice a day in the conference there from Tuesday to Sunday. I left my home, which is minimally above sea level, and landed at an altitude of nine thousand feet. I hadn't anticipated that my heart, having so recently been through some dramatic stress, would not enjoy that altitude at all. In a few days I was prostrated with altitude sickness and after four hospital visits was flown out of the country to the lowlands wherein I was born. All this caused me to realize that I had been pushing too hard for too long, and it was time to listen to advice and slow down. I cancelled all meetings for a couple of months and then thinned out my evangelistic schedule for some time to come, and felt very clearly that I was doing the right thing in it.

Then, right on the heels of that, I went back into the prison and when I walked into class a round of clapping and applause went up from men that I love so much. They began calling out, "Chaplain, you're back! Please stay here. We need you. Don't leave us!" We had a good time in class and then I went into the administration building. The superintendent, a man that I have known for the whole nearly nineteen years in prison, grabbed me coming down the hall. "Mr. Cawman, your supervisor tells me that you are going to lighten your travels and spend more time here with us. I want you to know that I very much approve of that. We need you here more. We need more of what you are doing here." That is the first time I ever heard something like that in all these years. Later one of the other staff members told me he had been asking different ones, "What do we need to do to get Chaplain Cawman here more?"

I looked up and said, "Lord, I hear Your Voice. I will gladly obey." And so it is that God has so clearly made it known to me that there is more work to be done right here in this prison. I told the men in one of the Bible Studies that I was making plans to be with them more than before, and I told them I would be there for business. I would not be playing around with them. The serious minded among them really grabbed that with visible satisfaction. I don't know how many more of these men God will save and sanctify before He returns, but I am committed afresh to burn out for Him and do it right where He pleases. Now will you help us pray that God will send a real revival and awakening among the many men here in prison?

I will also tell you that since all of the above happenings in my own life, I have noticed very conspicuously an upswing in the working atmosphere all over the prison. You see, on any given day there are approximately five thousand souls inside the prison compound. With thirty-five hundred inmates, around six hundred officers, and about nine hundred civilian workers it adds up to that number. Within any composite of *homo sapiens* there is inevitably a wealth of gossip, whether for good or evil. Whatever has been spread around through the whole compound regarding my personal role there and the intent to put in more time there, I have encountered everywhere I go a very warm reception than I have never known in the almost nineteen years I have been there. While that is certainly more desirable than ill will, I have felt very strongly the words of that old hymn, "My soul, be on thy guard..." I have known and felt for years the animosity of Satan to us being in there. Without a doubt he may counterattack even this upswing in "approval rating." (And you know how vain and fickle that is!)

In all of these happenings I have felt my own heart just drawn closer and closer to the God I love. I have literally marveled at how intricately God works things out when we leave them up to Him. What a micromanager He is! I cannot put into words how rich His providences and direct dealings in my life have been just of late. If you look closely at me I know you will see me bearing some pretty conspicuous stretch marks, for He has been enlarging my vessel to my own amazement! I love it, too; so I do!

A very young-looking man who is half Peruvian and half Ecuadorian has been such a bright spot for some time now. I have watched him grow in grace and he is very promising. He enrolled in the Bible college classes and has been making good progress. When I returned to the unit I was informed that he was transferred to a northern prison. I was very disappointed, but since God allowed it, we will just have to pray for him. I trust he will continue his studies from where he is, but I have little control over that.

Now I must tell you that it is so good to see a few of these men who have definitely entered the walk of a holy life, growing and becoming established in their everyday lives. One of them came to me and said, "Chaplain, I want to tell you something. First of all, I have the victory! But here are the particulars of it. About three years ago I heard you say that television watching was not at all conducive to the Christian life. I respect you and believe it right that I would follow your example, for God has set you as a leader to us, so I got rid of it. Then when this election was coming up, I got very interested in how it was going to all come out and I asked the sergeant for a TV. He gave me one, but somehow, I just didn't really feel right about it but couldn't exactly see why. I wasn't looking at anything evil, but still I had this feeling that all was not right. After a while God began to open my eyes. Now I have always concluded that the besetting sin was unbelief, and indeed that is a great sin. But God showed me that for me, the greatest besetting sin was robbing Him of His time in my life. The TV was doing exactly that. I got rid of it and I have the victory. But as much as I respect you, it is not because you told us it was harmful, but because God told me." Thank God for listening ears and willing hearts!

And then another one (our man from Colombia) came in with a glow all over his face. When I asked him how the journey with Jesus was, he just beamed and said, "It is absolutely wonderful!" Then he went on to tell me of an occasion where it would have been so much to his advantage as far as saving face would be to have covered up a truth about something that happened. He could not, and he did not. By the way, do you remember that I enrolled him in our four-year theological course within just a few months of him coming out of five years of Islam, after a lifetime of Catholicism? It has been just about a year or slightly over since we enrolled him, and he is almost finished with all four years! His work is impeccable.

He brought back one of the books, *Our Own God* by G. D. Watson. He laid it down and said, "Reverend, I started to read this book and after about twenty pages I hadn't run across a single Bible reference and I was about to lay it aside. Then I thought, wait a minute; the Scripture says we are to respect our teachers and so there had to be some reason why it is in the course of study. I picked it up again and noticed the title of one of the chapters was, 'Go Slow With God.' I started reading it over again carefully and it opened up to me as one of the best books I have read."

Could I insert a thought here at no extra charge? I wonder if some people who have long been discontented with their pastor would earnestly pray for him and then open their ears with a fresh outlook, if they might find... maybe I'd better stop there lest I be accused of preaching rather than reporting.

And now please permit me to reflect a bit on the importance of your prayers for just one inmate. I would have to go to my filing cabinet in my office and look back into my records to find the first visit I had with the man I am now going to tell you about. As I have told you before, I cannot use names in these letters, per state regulations. But one day, no doubt in answer to prayers that were offered by those who did not know him by name, he made a choice. He felt God knocking at his heart's door and this was his response: "If I am going to be a Christian, I'm going to be a real one!" He earnestly asked God for forgiveness and was genuinely born again. He went straight from a Bible study and cleaned house. His rotten magazines and cigarettes went in the trash. A pile of CDs went in the trashcan, but as they did a voice suggested that he could sell them for quite a bit of money. "No," he responded, "if they're no good for me, they're no good for anyone," and he dug to the bottom of the trashcan and hid them.

Shortly after that I first met him and recognized a new creature, hungry for all of God he could get. He heard the light on holiness of heart and went to the Scripture and began to search it out. Guess what? He found it everywhere he looked. When he first started out, he was almost illiterate, but wanted to be able to read the Bible and so he enrolled in literacy classes, and in no time at all was reading his Bible. He doesn't realize to this day what a miracle that was, but God was just as eager to let him into His Word as he was to get into it. He began in earnest to seek for a pure heart. Week after week for a while we would sit together and talk and pray. There were times when I went home and told my wife about him and I remember saying, "I sometimes wonder if he is already sanctified!" Never, never underestimate the power of the new birth; it is power over ALL sin, and power to live a righteous life.

One Friday we were having a heart-warming visit when all of the sudden he just got up and walked out. On Monday he came back and apologized but said he just had to go pray. Then he looked at me and said, "I don't know what to think. Three times this weekend as I have been seeking for a pure heart the Holy Spirit has said to me, 'Son, the work is done!'" I looked at him for a moment and then asked, "Do you think then that it is time that you acknowledged that it is?" All of the sudden his face resembled that of a man coming out into the light from a dark cave. "I think it is!" he said. From that moment until now there has not been one single backward look.

Some time went by and he was moved out into the minimum security camp. He was enjoying the studies out there, but of course the holiness ones more than the sinning ones. I had been gone to a meeting and when I returned my supervisor said, "I think you need to talk to the other Bible teacher out in the minimum camp, because there seems to be some conflict in teachings out there."

The next time I met the volunteer I said, "Brother, I hear there is some conflict out in the minimum camp."

"Yes, there sure is!"

"What seems to be the point of contention?"

"Well, it's over this issue of sinlessness." You see, that teacher had told the men that after we are saved we still have a sinning nature down inside that we will always struggle with. Our dear brother with great joy and excitement raised his hand

and said, "I got rid of that!" Whoops! I don't remember what I said to the other teacher; I only remember what I wanted to say. "Oh, that is a problem to you? Are you enjoying your sinning?" Whatever I did say, I know I didn't say that.

I went out to the minimum camp and sat down with our dear brother and explained to him that it would not really help our class any if someone got up and said there was no such thing as what we were teaching, and that it would be better if he didn't agree with someone to just pray for them.

"Oh! Could we pray?"

"Sure we can pray."

Down on our knees we went and he began, "Now Lord, you have saved me and given me a pure heart. Now can You help my head?"

Upon release from prison, the lieutenant came to him and shook his hand. They had all heard his prayers and devotions, for like Daniel, the window was not closed on them. When he stepped outside the prison gates, Satan jumped an imp on both shoulders at once and said, "Now look what you can have!" It appealed for a moment and then the Blood spoke. He looked old Satan in the eye and said, "Satan, I told you in prison that you can go to hell by yourself, and I mean it now." He did mean it; he still means it; he is now our Sunday School Superintendent.

Now I am relating all this to show you the far-reaching influence of one answered prayer, which our brother certainly is. He had not seen his father since he was fourteen years of age and had beat him up in a park. Now he wanted to reach out to his father and so at the first opportunity he took him a Spanish Bible in a brown paper sack and sat down to visit with him. His father sensed what was in the bag and said he would look later. Then he returned to Puerto Rico. After a time he became ill with Lou Gehrig's Disease and had to come back to the US. Every Saturday our brother would faithfully go see him and pray with him. One Saturday as his father sat there in a wheelchair with oxygen, his son began reading to him from John chapter one. He would read a bit and his father would say, "Give that to me in Spanish." After a bit he just said, "Go on, I'm getting it." At about verse eight, his son said, "Dad, if you want God to do for you what he has done for me and your grandchildren, He will, but you will have to ask Him." Never before had he ever seen his father pray, but with that he tilted back his head, looked up to heaven and with a strong voice asked God to forgive him. And He did! Two days later his father's two sisters came in bringing him a television. He looked at them and said, "Get that out of here; I don't want that!" Twenty-two days later he died and went to heaven.

Our brother prayed on for his mother and within a couple of years and after too long an interesting story to relate here, she also prayed through and was saved. She went on and was fully sanctified and has been a blessing to our church ever since.

For a time now, our brother's oldest sister has been fighting a battle with cancer. Our brother has faithfully visited and prayed with her. The whole church has been praying for months for her. Her mother has prayed for her. A few days before she passed away on January 22, she told her brother that she was forgiven and staying that way. She left a clear testimony of forgiving grace and went to heaven. On the Wednesday following we had a memorial service in our church and the four front pews on both sides of the center aisle were packed with our brother's family who listened to our pastor preach a very clear message on what it takes to be ready for the heaven that their loved one had just gone to. Now we are praying that God will follow that message and bring some more of them to the same clear forgiveness.

Now do you understand just how important your prayers for some man in prison that you don't even know by name are? All because one inmate in a state prison said a "yes" to God and never took it back, half a church full of souls came to hear a message they would never have heard. Cain asked a very self-centered question: "Am I my brother's keeper?" Yes, Cain, you certainly were and you let him down. Oh God, please help us not to let any soul slip through our fingers that You are dealing with! That soul may be the salvation of many more. And with that, thank you for your every prayer!

William Cawman

March 1, 2017

> *There's a new name written down in Glory, and it's mine; oh yes, it's mine;*
> *And the white-robed angels tell the story: "A sinner has come home!"*

OH, THAT WE COULD sing it more often! But let's sing it now, for another sinner has come home. I am writing this immediately after mailing the February letter. A couple weeks before, a young man had come to see me who gave me a rundown on his past life that was anything other than beautiful. He had been involved in pagan religions and bears a huge tattoo on his chest marking him as an Odinist.* He had belonged to the gangs and had given little thought to his eternal outcome, but obviously the Holy Spirit was at work. He made it clear that he was not satisfied and that he was doing some serious thinking about the future. I did my best to direct him to seek for a real relationship with Jesus. A couple of weeks went by.

I called him in again, and he seemed so glad of it. He began to tell me how life was taking on a whole new meaning and enjoyment to him. He said he felt sure his sins were all forgiven and that he was conscious of the presence of God in his heart. God had graciously allowed an older Christian man to move into his cell and they were talking much about the Christian life.

Then he asked me what he should do about the fact that many of the men knew his former life and would come around

*A follower of the pagan religion of the ancient Scandinavians. —Ed.

wanting to talk gang talk or else talk about Odin. He said, "I don't want to be rude, but I don't want anything to do with all that anymore. They see the tattoo and want to relate me to that old life. How do I handle that?" I told him that a Christian never has an occasion to act rude, but that he needed to keep the tattoo covered up at all times and then when someone approached him to just tell them nicely that he was now a Christian and he didn't want to discuss his former life anymore. That seemed to relieve him greatly.

Then he enrolled in Christian Living Class. At the opening of the class after we had prayed and sang our choruses, I told the men that we were always open for good news and that there was a young man among us for the first time who had been other than a Christian, and that we would not talk about what he had been, but that now he was a Christian! A round of applause went up. I then ventured to say that I thought he was enjoying this new life far more than anything from his past. With a beaming face he called out, "I sure am!" And Heaven's presence in the room testified to it. In the next Bible study as we were singing the chorus *Into My Heart* his eyes were closed, his face was upturned with a glow, and his hands were stretched up to heaven.

Do you remember the man who was having trouble with his face hurting from smiling so much? Well, you should see him. The smile just gets more and more intense, and as he walks around one can hear him just bubbling over out loud, "Praise Him! Praise Him!" I just had a visit with him and he is living in the heavenliest atmosphere, notwithstanding he is locked up in a state prison for several years yet to come. Believe me, his is not some charismatic "let's just praise the Lord anyway;" he is literally dwelling in the secret place of the Most High, and all the promises made to one who will do that he is a partaker of.

I received a request from a man I had not known before. He is in his twenties and is a native of Cuba, although I believe he has been in this country for most of his life and has no accent in his language. He had become involved with a young Cuban girl who lied to him about her age and now he is of course under supervision for the rest of his life and if any rule is broken, back into prison he goes. He is tired of his life of sin, but does not know how to turn from it. As I began to try to point out the way of God to him, I realized that he is as ignorant of the Bible and spiritual things as though he had been born in a far-off jungle. I marveled at how a person living in this country could be so absolutely ignorant, but obviously he is.

I did my best (I trust) to point him to seeking God and will follow up with him. He did enroll in my class and Bible study and I hope it will not be so over his head that he will become discouraged and fall away. He certainly needs prayer.

I went over to the prison hospital and found a twenty-two-year-old with such a bad case of Cystic Fibrosis that I wondered how he could go on much longer. He was spitting very thick sputum into a basin and had to have oxygen periodically. He possibly also has some infection because they had put an IV into his arm into which they were sending antibiotics. I asked him if I could pray with him and he thought a few seconds and then said it would be all right. When I finished he said "Amen," but again I wondered how much he had ever known of God. The poor young chap has a most dismal prospect indeed.

Every so often over the years of ministering in prison I seem to face in full force the teachings of John Calvin, resurrected all over again. I can tell you after many such encounters that it is far easier to lead a man out of Roman Catholicism than out of Calvinism. Nearly every case that I have had to deal with has been accompanied by arrogance and total unteachableness. The arrogant contestant can sit back and accuse the one teaching of condemning those who do not agree with him, while he is doing in far greater degree what he is accusing the other of.

In case you didn't know that the Holy Scriptures have already covered an exceptionally accurate description of such a one, just read Romans 2:1, 21, 22. When such a false teacher rises to the foreground, it is with something more than human logic or human intelligence; there is markedly an evil spirit behind it. Satan loves the theology of John Calvin. I tell you he does. There is a reason why it has so profoundly annexed itself to the majority of "Christian" churches.

After many an encounter, I have decided it best to ensconce myself behind the purpose of the coming of the Son of God— "For this purpose the Son of God was manifested, that he might destroy the works of the devil." I then follow up that Scripture with the observation that if we would put forth as much effort to let Him destroy sin in us as we do in finding supposed Scriptural loopholes to make provision for sin, we would not miss heaven. A man actually circulated a pamphlet in the prison entitled, *Sins Christians Commit*. There were a lot of them, too! But the Scripture clearly states that "Whosoever is born of God doth not commit sin; for his seed remaineth in him: and he cannot sin, because he is born of God." Thank God for the way of Holiness that Isaiah saw way back in his day!

I have a very urgent prayer request. Two men who have been doing so well in their walk with God are being released this summer. They both ardently want to attend our church. Will you help us pray that we can find provision for them so that they will not be sent elsewhere for a lack of an address?

Now I must tell you something that is always painful to tell or hear, but this ministry as well as any other has its disappointments as well as bright spots. It has been over two weeks since I wrote the first part of this letter about the young man who I truly believe was brightly saved. He did so well for a while, and then something happened, and I don't know what as yet. I noticed he did not appear at the Bible study. Then when I put him on the appointment sheet for an interview, he came down and told the officer that he did not need to see me. I began to have some concerns over him as I had been standing by him faithfully, trying to make sure he got his feet established before some false teacher would get to him. After the next Bible study and not seeing him, I asked his cellmate, who had also been very helpful to him. He said, "I need to talk to you about him. He's not doing well." That was on Friday night and so on Tuesday morning I had a visit with his cellmate.

He came in the room and just broke down and cried. He said that he, too, had felt it was a genuine conversion, but that all of the sudden he just turned and let the old demons back in again, except now it was far worse. He began to tell me how he himself had battled over snoring at night and had even sought medical help with it, but couldn't seem to conquer it. His cellmate had the bunk below him and even though he had every right to know the man above him couldn't help it, he just took both feet and kicked him up through the mattress, bruising or hurting him in the side quite badly. Then he just cut loose on his cellmate and used abusive language on him and turned into a raging bear.

I said to his cellmate that we were witnessing a classic example of what the Bible warns of, that if a man has had the unclean spirit go out of him and then allows it back in, it will be sevenfold worse. He agreed that was exactly the problem, but then went on to tell me that in the midst of the fire he had felt unclean things trying to rise up in his own heart. I said, "Yes, often God allows us to pass through the fire to show us what yet remains in our hearts that He wants to deliver us from. Don't ignore or get used to it. Take it to the same Blood that forgave your sins and stay before God until He cleanses you from all that would rise up unlike Himself." He cried again and assured me that he wanted that. I wondered if perhaps that was the first light on holiness he had ever received, as he has not been in the classes very long. I will certainly follow up on him, too, and would you pray that he will not back up but go all the way through?

Last night as I was greeting the men in the 7:30 Bible study, a good brother who has been walking in the beauty of holiness for several years now, handed me a small scrap of paper with a man's name and number on it. With a beaming face he said, "Chaplain, put him in everything; he got saved today out in the courtyard!" Dear friend, could I ask you a personal question? How long has it been since you experienced that kind of joy? Next to a clear, definite witness to our personal relationship with God, there is nothing in the entire world more rewarding than to be used of God to lead another soul to Jesus. The look on our brother's face could not have been duplicated by any material substance or reward whatsoever. I'm eager to meet our new "brother." Please pray for him. It is understandably Satan's most pungent thrust to trip a soul up who has just entered the way to heaven. Pray that what happened to the man above will not be duplicated here.

By the way—I hate Satan! I will mince no words about it either, no matter what counterattack he brings against me. I hate to see him snatch a soul away from Jesus, but he does it way too often.

Please let me thank you once again from my heart for your prayers for us.

In love,

William Cawman

2
REAL MEN – REAL STORIES

April 1, 2017

L ET ME TAKE YOU BACK to Thursday, March 2, and I will try to share with you what I really struggled to absorb myself. A man had begun to claim my attention in class as he was obviously and vocally struggling in his relationship with God. He would raise his hand and say something to this effect, "Chaplain, I know I am having trouble there, and it makes me question where I really am with God..." Sensing his honest heart searching for something that was eluding him, I put his name on the appointment sheet to talk with him. He was glad, and in a few words unfolded such a story of his life that I wondered at his having any sanity. As he told me of how he was battered and abused as a child, I was fighting with my own tear glands. Even though the man sitting in front of me was fifty-nine years of age, all I could see was a precious little boy that I wanted so badly to wrap up in my arms and take him away from all that he had known, but it is too late now. Believe me, however, it's never too late, and my arms are wrapped about him now and I will do my very best to rescue him from the past and lead him to the love of Jesus.

He has never been to school, except that is, for prison school. Some compassionate women on the street taught him to read and write, and so please let me have him tell you his own story as I type it out from a paper he wrote it on.

He places this title on his short autobiography: "Now Jesus knew that they were desirous to ask him, and said unto them, Do ye enquire among yourselves of that I said, A little while, and ye shall not see me: and again, a little while, and ye shall see me?... And ye now therefore have sorrow: but I will see you again, and your heart shall rejoice, and your joy no man taketh from you."

> I come from a family of fifteen. Both my mother and father were alcoholics who spent most of their time arguing with one another to the point that they could no longer live with one another anymore. My family was broken beyond repair as a result of no godly home structure.
>
> My mother and father spent most of their time going out to bars at night, leaving me and the rest of my brothers and sisters at home alone with much of nothing to eat, if we ate at all! Upon returning from the night out in bars my mother and father would often fight with each other almost all the time. She hated my father for reasons only she herself knew, and would not hesitate to show him this by being abusive to me and the rest of my family; but not as much as me, for I was her reminder of him, as well as his first son and her reason to get back at him.
>
> One morning at the age of five years old, my mother picked up a rocking chair, hitting me across my left leg; breaking it! Realizing that she had some explaining to do, I was asked or told to say that I had tried to fly off a table because I thought that I was superman, and she promised never to hurt me again. So I lied to the doctors out of love for her, only to be laughed at. I was placed in a laundry bag and put in a closet just because she didn't want to see me crawl around while her and her lady friends were playing poker.

Many times me and one of my brothers had to eat out of garbage cans, or go to our next door neighbor and lie, saying that our mother sent us to ask for food, only to regret it later. Sometimes she wouldn't even feed me and one of my brothers, so we would wait until everyone was asleep and try to get anything that we could out of the refrigerator, but to no avail, for she had locked it; and trying that, my hands were placed over the fire of the stove.

At the age of eight, I had started a fire in a garbage can and was placed in the Youth House awaiting the judge's judgment, and it was that I be sent to a place called New Lisbon State Colony. There I stayed for some years without ever seeing anyone from my family and for the duration of my time there I only received one letter in all those years.

Oh how I yearned for the love and comfort from them, only to find out that they didn't know how to love even themselves! I often cried silently to myself, and would ask God why was I ever born and the answer that I found to be so fitting now, but was beyond my understanding then, is that His grace is sufficient, 2 Cor. 12:9.

I was later moved to another institution called Johnstone* which was somewhat better but no place to be called anyone's home. I remember it as the type of an army setting; I guess because a lot of ex-military personnel work there. But anyway, I felt free and not like a castaway. I stayed there for about three years and was released to the Youth and Family Services where once again I wanted to try to unite with family members but it just wasn't meant; for all that they cared about was the S.S.L. money that I was receiving at the time, and so I wandered off in despair. You know, I really wanted to kill both my parents, and if not for the love placed in my heart, I would have done the unthinkable. If it wasn't for God's love and understanding; for He intervened and His judgments are just as it is written in Romans 12:19,20. Hebrews 2:18.

---

* This institution no longer exists. —*Author*

I am fifty-nine years old and in all my days I have only spent five years total in society; mainly because of the fact that John 15:18,19 states that. "If ye were of the world, the world would love his own: but because ye are not of the world, but I have chosen you out of the world, therefore the world hateth you." Yet no matter what I suffer, it could never be compared to the suffering Jesus Christ suffered for me and I love Jesus regardless of all opposition!

And yes, I have done many wrong things in life, that the accuser thinks to justify himself in condemning, the forgiven of God.

Can you see the reason why this man has told me he has never known love? He grew to hate women because of the way his mother treated him. Stabbing and killing one is why he is serving a sentence which reads "seventy years to life."

Now, I want to ask you something: What do you think you would be had you been raised in his shoes? He has not even told it all by any means in the above short autobiography. Doesn't it make you hate Satan and all his works? And yet men still hug sin to their bosoms and defend a "Christian's" committing it every day.

I have been raised all of my life in the holiness circles, hearing and learning the terminology that is common among us. Among the terms I have heard many times over is the term "playing God," or in other words, trying to do God's work for Him. The other day I was listening to our dear tattooed and sanctified brother as he was telling me that a friendly officer had given him permission to use the dayroom on his tier for an hour morning and afternoon for anything he wanted it for, knowing of course that he would use it for Bible studies and leading other men to Jesus. And so our dear missionary had been zealously fishing and going after men and then he said that God began to talk to him and he saw that he "had too much Holy Spirit junior in him." He needed to simply give them the Word and then let the Holy Spirit do His work. I immediately burst out laughing and then he began, too, and finally said, "That tickled you, didn't it?"

This man and one other are soon to be released and both want very much to be a part of our church on the outside. Please pray for them. Satan is ever so ready to lay heavy artillery against a person starting a new life in Jesus Christ, and unfortunately it seems that many of the parole people are in sync with Satan rather than the redeeming grace of God. Please pray that the combined forces that would come against them will fall before the God who has saved and sanctified them and is now giving them new desires so opposite to their old lives.

Last month I mentioned the recurring problem, or battleground, of the teachings of John Calvin rising up in conflict with the truth of the Bible. We have had just such a man for the last few months in classes and Bible studies. His hand is up way oftener than I want to see it, and invariably the most of the time it is to counter the truth being taught. There is a hard look on his face, even when he tries to smile. But far worse, there is an evil spirit that emanates from him constantly. When the other good men in class began to name it out to me as just what I had felt it was, I knew I needed to address it. I scheduled him for a one-on-one interview. He came to the appointment with a large note pad upon which he had listed points that he wanted to correct me on. I kindly explained to him that I was well aware of the teaching and theology that he had been taught, but that in that particular class I was the teacher, not him. I told him that it was disrupting to the class and other good men for him to be constantly countering the truth being taught. He responded that not everyone in class was in agreement with me and some had even dropped out because of it. I wondered how he knew and just what part he had played in it.

After over half an hour of trying to work with him, he shook his head and pointed to his note pad and told me that he had prayed and came hoping "to win a brother." In the class time just before the interview he had brought up Paul's "thorn in the flesh," and said that he had studied the Greek word for "thorn," and found that it could include a moral defect. I responded that just because a word could include something, it didn't do so of necessity and that he was in deep conflict with Paul's testimony to surmise that he might have had a moral defect. I brought this up to him again and told him that if he could point out a way for me to live a holier life and get farther away from sin, he could expect to win me in a moment, but that if he was constantly trying to convince me to a lower pathway that made provision and excuse for sin, there was not a chance in the world that he would win me to that. Upon that we parted. Oh, the viciousness of the "doctrines of devils!" Pray for him; please do!

Your Brother in the harvest field,

William Cawman

May 1, 2017

LITTLE DO WE KNOW, that is, unless we ask, who it may be who lies hidden behind the façade that a person carries before his fellow men. Let me tell you a specific example of this. For several months now, a man in later life has been attending my classes and Bible studies. His looks and bearing would not match that of a hard-core criminal, but then looks can be very misleading, can't they? Recently I set up an appointment to visit with him. I found that he is sixty-five years old and was raised in an old-time Nazarene church in Indiana. He remembers well the glory days when God came down and people were filled with it and ran the aisles and shouted the victory. Life has led him far away from that, but now he is in prison for a short bid.

As he told me this, he burst into tears more than once. He laid his hand on my elbow and said, as his tears flowed, "I thank God I met you here. You have taken me back to that and now I believe God has restored me and I believe I'm saved and sanctified. Oh, I am so sorry I walked away from Him at all." He will not be long in prison and now he wants to come to church, since he found to his joy there is still such a church as he knew long ago.

Several men who are doing well spiritually are soon to be released and are planning to attend our church outside of the prison. Please help us pray that they will have the strength to overcome every snare Satan most certainly has laid for their feet, for he ardently hates losing any soul he thought he had.

Let me insert something right here that I am so very thankful for. A number of months back when God in His great care and loving-kindness opened a door and brought into my heart and life a precious wife to be, I did not know what I do now, and that is, she loves the prison ministry! She wants to be involved in it and that makes my heart rejoice all the more over God's wonderful gift to me. And so she went in with us and a group for the Good Friday services in all areas of the prison. Our pastor and his family took two of the areas and we did the other two and God really helped us. Perhaps I should insert that the pastor's daughter, however, was with us and not them as she felt we might need a chaperone, bless her noble concern!

Then on Easter Sunday night, several volunteers from other churches called out, so again my future and present helpmeet went in with me and I took two services and the pastor's son and his fiancé took two more.

At the close of the Easter Sunday night service a man on about the third row of seats back called out and said, "Chaplain, you don't have to wait until June 20; we're all here right now!" The room broke into applause! They are very eager for her to join their chaplain, and... and... well, he is too!

I have but one more scheduled meeting abroad as a lonely, single vagabond. After that I intend to most joyfully accept God's wonderful gift to me and take her with me from there on. God is continuing to give His best when the choice is left with Him. What a wonderful Jesus!

The Good Friday services went well and I believe many men's hearts were touched. It is remarkable that there seems at times like there's more good will and happiness than in many people outside of prison. As the men came in greeting us, many of them said with obvious joy, "Happy Resurrection Day!" They really appreciated the Sunday night services and thanked us so feelingly.

Interestingly, three or four, and maybe a fifth, inmates who have been enrolled in the four-year theological course from one of our Bible colleges, are finishing the entire course all about the same time. They have done very good work and they have really enjoyed it too. The record was set by our man from Colombia, who enrolled in the course immediately after getting saved and sanctified right following five years of very disappointing practice of Islam, and that after a lifelong disappointment with Roman Catholicism. He is now settled and grounded in Wesleyan Arminian Holiness, not only in doctrine, but in experience. Now having finished the required courses, I am endeavoring to keep him supplied with good holiness books which he devours with relish. He is also taking some secular college work offered by Rutgers University here in the prison.

It is so wonderful to watch these men growing in the Biblical grace of Romans 6:11-23. I am firmly convinced that God did not inspire the early apostles to write out a theology and then endeavor to live up to it. Nay, rather, He allowed them to pen with joy what they found grace to do for them. And that grace still does everything they wrote about in spite of all that the devil and evil carnal minds have done to undermine it. Hallelujah for the grace of God! Hallelujah for the power of Jesus' blood! Hallelujah for the faithful and intense ministry of the blessed Holy Spirit!

And with that, oh how I long that our Calvinist who is being so vocal in the classes would taste and see the beauty of that holiness he is fighting. Please continue to pray for him. He was moved to another Facility and so wanted to be enrolled in the classes there. He approached me and asked that we could continue to visit and continue whatever it is that he has in mind. I will. I will not dodge him, but neither will I argue with him. I will testify to him! I will do my best to point him to the better way. Please pray for me, and for him.

After an all-night in prayer by some Salvation Army soldiers, about six o'clock in the morning Samuel Logan Brengle arose to his feet. Eager ears were tuned in to hear what the great teacher of holiness would say after an all-night of prayer. He opened his mouth and simply said, "Brethren, if you would retain the blessing of perfect love, don't argue." That was it! Wise man indeed! Job said to his three comforters, "How forcible are right words! but what doth your arguing reprove?" He dug in a bit deeper yet and said, "Do ye imagine to reprove words, and the speeches of one that is desperate, which are as wind?"

But there is one thing that an adversary cannot refute, and that is this: "Hear what the Lord has done for me!" Buddy Robinson was accosted by a man at the back of the church after he had told his most interesting hospital experience and how he was carried by the angels up into heaven and then brought back down onto his hospital bed. The man rebuked him sharply for telling that, saying that no one had ever gone to heaven and come back. Uncle Buddy replied, "You ain't the man that went there; and furthermore, if you don't clean up, you never will!" We'll leave the going to heaven or not with Uncle Buddy. All I know is that I ain't the man who went there, either, so who am I to argue with him?

That is one of the distinctive marks of errant religion; its propagators are expressly adroit at arguing. And it is (what word shall I use?) to watch a man become so hot in arguing his theological point to be the correct one, that he gets as mad as the devil trying to prove it. One of Wesley's early preachers became involved in a showdown with an errant teacher and after a bit the Wesleyan said very calmly to his opponent, "Sir, whether you be right or wrong, the spirit that you are now manifesting is not that of Christ and so we must desist."

For a number of years after our son was married and moved out, we covered many miles with our two girls on the back seat of the car. It seemed they had an endless repertoire of songs and ditties out of the many books they devoured. Some of them are fastened upon my mind to this day, so let me share one of them with you as making the point at hand: "Here lies the body of Jonathan Gray. He died while defending his right of way. He was right; dead right; as he sped along; but he's just as dead as if he was wrong." I do firmly believe that the theology I am endeavoring to teach to the men is Biblical; it is tested; it is sound; it has produced the most holy people that have ever lived. But I do not intend to become wrong while promoting it as opposed to that which leaves one a victim of what Jesus came to deliver from. Old Satan cares very little how he gets us to miss "the mark for the prize of the high calling of God in Christ Jesus." God will take care of His truth; I must take care of my spirit!

On Sunday evening, April 23rd, I took for a Scripture the account of Jesus regarding the ten virgins and then told the men that I stood in great doubt as to whether there would be any talking back at the Great White Throne Judgment, but that according to Scripture there are many answers now that people have in mind they are going to offer to God. I took the two Scriptural phrases: *many will say...* and, *then will I profess...*, and then told them that once there was a ball game where the last play was a very close call. Both sides immediately began shouting their version of who won. The rabble sound grew stronger and stronger until suddenly there was a booming announcement from the umpire: "The game is not won until I call it!" I told them that no matter what they think now their answer to God will be, the final call will be His.

I then began to expose some of the secret reasons why people do not get down to business in knowing that they are ready for that Great Day. In treating the answer the five foolish virgins gave, "Lord, Lord, open to us...", I had no mercy on Tim Lahaye's "Left Behind" series. Some pretty serious thinking was going on, I could tell. At the close of the second service I said, "My prayer is that this circle will be unbroken on that Day." I had no sooner said it than the men got up and formed themselves into a huge circle for prayer. I don't think I ever joined a larger circle in my life. Is that too big a miracle to ask for?

I stayed a few minutes after the service to record the number and attendance in the office and when I stepped out onto the compound an officer said, "Hold back a minute, Chap, they're taking another one out. It's too late at night for this!" And so I waited with him until another handcuffed sad soul was taken into lockup. Isn't it so true that "the way of transgressors is hard"? And yet Satan has so many so deluded that they keep right on like a wild bull with a ring in its nose, just grinding away under the wages of sin. There is absolutely nothing funny, or cute, or comical, or smart about sin, yet it has to be acknowledged that for a season it must have some degree of pleasure. It has no charms for me! I've found a Treasure that has made every bit of it look utterly repulsive!

I am happy in Jesus!

William Cawman

June 1, 2017

GREETINGS TO YOU EACH one and that with an excited heart, as it is now but twenty days until I marry the precious treasure God has so lovingly given me. I will share with you that apart from my own relationship with Him, which I treasure above all else, I have never experienced a clearer witness to anything than this upcoming change in my life. I am excited to find all that God has planned for us if Jesus tarries a bit longer.

I want to tell you about a man and request prayer for him,

but I must be careful how detailed I write about him as he is a very well-known gangster whose name would be recognized all over the country. Movies are out about him as his life has been that which attracts what the Bible properly terms "certain lewd fellows of the baser sort." But let me first tell you how I came to meet him.

A female psychiatrist who has worked in the prison almost as long as I have, has more than once detected that a man needed help from a chaplain and has referred him on to me. I appreciate that quality which is more than rare in that field. This man was requested by her to see me. I am not, and never have been, and never will be (just to be very clear in this) a watcher of either television or movies of any type whatsoever. And so I had never heard of this man, who was very surprised that I had not. His father and uncle were the founders of Hells Angels a year or two before he was born into it. He followed suit, as did his son and grandson. One unacquainted with the horror movies so prevalent in our day (and again, I identify myself as such) would have not the faintest idea of the depths of abject degradation and cold blood found in these men. But now he was sitting in front of me.

I have had two visits with him thus far and will definitely be having more. The reason for his visits to the psychiatrist is that he wakes up with horrifying nightmares in which faces of those he has sent into eternity are looking up at him. Can I crawl inside of him and look out through his windows? Never; but I know One who can understand him, for He carried all those heinous sins to the Cross and nailed them there. I am happy to tell you that this highly profiled man is now seeking God in deep contrition and humility. He is determined to come out the other end of this with a clean conscience, notwithstanding the horrifying scars on his memory. He testifies that he is finding God's presence precious to his heart in spite of the nightmares that plague him. He has already confessed in several states and by the mercy of God, not one judge has added any time to his sentence for what he has confessed. I believe he is going to stay with it until not one dirty footprint remains. Please, will you pray for him?

And then let me tell you something else that happened on the morning of April 25. A young man had come to a few classes and that morning he raised his hand. I acknowledged him and he held up his Bible and asked an honest question: "I just want to know, how can I be sure that this Bible is reliable? It has been translated so many different ways, and it seems it has been altered down through the years, and so many Christians interpret it differently. How can I trust it?" I had not had a chance to respond when I saw fire and joy flashing from our Colombian brother's face. "Can I testify to you, Brother?" He held up his own Bible and with face aglow, launched in. "On October 16, 2015, at 2:30 in the afternoon, I, a confirmed Muslim and one who believed this Book was just the fabrication of men and was badly altered, was in my cell alone. At 2:30 that afternoon I met Jesus Christ! From that moment I had no questions about this Book! I knew it was the truthful Word of God, and it has been so ever since!" Can you imagine the clearing in the atmosphere by then?

I had another visit with the man who was raised in an old-fashioned Nazarene church. He had drifted away from his boyhood teachings when he went into the military and had never gotten back, but neither had the memory left him. He looked at me with tears and said, "Chaplain, I am not happy that I had to come here, but I am happy that I met you! I'm now finding such joy in walking with Jesus again." I asked him how his wife felt about it and he said she is very happy for him. Certainly God is not finished with this man, is He?

And now let me update his situation a few days later. He came in for another interview and I asked how he was doing. He told me that Satan was attacking him from every conceivable angle. He had a cellmate who was absolutely impossible to get along with, and other issues were cropping up besides. I told him I was not surprised at all, but then went on to point out that trials either strengthen us or else they reveal some hidden sediment of remaining sin that needs to be confessed and removed. With that he said with tears, "I know, Chaplain. I listened to you in class the other day and then I went to my cell and just opened up my heart and said, 'Oh God, search my heart. I want what the chaplain has!'" I encouraged him to earnestly seek to be completely filled with the fullness of God that would cleanse out anything unlike Him.

The young man who wanted to know if the Bible could be trusted came back the next week and as we were discussing the reality of being saved and having power over sin, he suddenly blurted out, "Then I'm not saved! If being saved gives you power to not sin, then I'm not saved!" I stopped and said as kindly as I could, "Then the solution to that is—get saved! God wants you to be saved. Let's pray right now." We went to prayer and the other men were really feeling it, too. I trust he will not stop short of the real thing, for no substitute or imaginary experience will work.

For several years now I have written every so often about a man who is very dark skinned, very heavily tattooed, and very conscious of a dark and horrible past life. He was once so hardhearted and unfeeling that he clubbed a woman to death with a hammer and felt no remorse. He is now a marvelous specimen of God's redeeming grace. He is as loving and gentle as a lamb, and is ravenously hungry for everything God can give him. He just recently finished all the work connected with the four-year theological course offered by one of our Bible schools. He brought the final work to me with evident satisfaction as he said, "This is the first thing I have ever finished in my life."

No sooner was he finished than he asked me with a facial hunger, "Can I have more books?" As quickly as I could I rounded up about four more good holiness books and loaned them to him. In a few days he met me and said, "My, Chaplain, you're really feeding me! Those are powerful books!" Is this kind of hunger and love for truth a sample of what Jesus meant when He said that they to whom much is forgiven, love much? I see a rare hunger for the things of God here that is sadly missing among many who have been raised in this beautiful way of holiness. If they who hunger and thirst after righteousness are "blessed," then he is a blessed man indeed!

Just outside my office door as I am typing this letter, the weekly Muslim prayer service is in session. It is called "Jumah Prayer." The inmate speaker is talking to them about the day of resurrection for those who have a clean heart. He is evidently reading excerpts from the Quran and then describing what that day will be like when some are resurrected and others are not. As he is going on about it, he is doing something I have never heard one of them do before. He is testifying to them about his own experience. He is telling them that some time back he was almost gone with kidney failure. They wanted to put him on dialysis and he didn't want it. A Muslim doctor came in and told him that if he didn't take the treatment, he was going to hell. He prayed to Allah and his kidneys started working again, and so he is exhorting them to pray to Allah before it is too late for them. Isn't it pathetic beyond words to think of hearing of such a hope and then missing it on that great day?

I mentioned earlier in this letter the fact that a female psychiatrist has several times referred a case to me and she did so again right after the last one. This man came to her frustrated because he had received no answer as to his ability to procure a rosary. He came to see me and began to unfold his story. He had been raised a Catholic, but had wandered into a nonbeliever while in the military and had all but forgotten about God. Now that he is in prison he has been thinking about his state and had decided to try the different religions and see what worked for him. After being disappointed in much of what he found, he decided the thing to do was to return to his original faith and so decided to be a Catholic again. He tried to obtain a rosary, but no chaplain was getting back to him. Please remember that God makes no mistakes, even in His providences.

I suggested to him that perhaps God had withheld a rosary from him to lead him into something better. If he had obtained a rosary, he just might settle down to say the prayers associated with it and end up in a lost world forever. He nodded assent and then I suggested that he take his Bible and begin to really seek through it and through prayer to find God for himself. He said he would do that. I had prayer with him and told him I would follow up with him in a few days and he said he wanted me to.

And so the other morning I had put him on the list of appointments, but he didn't come. I waited about a half hour and soon the sergeant came looking for me. He said, "Were you supposed to see —— ?"

"Yes, I was."

"Well, we have him handcuffed in a holding cell because he was acting out about coming down. Do you want to go visit him in the holding cell?"

I said I would just wait until they had done what they needed to do, but he said he wanted me to determine what they should do with him, so he asked me if I would go see him and then tell them what I thought.

I was let into the cell with him as he sat on the steel bench handcuffed. He immediately began to cry and told me that he felt so sorry over what he had done. His eleven-year-old son had been very sick and he was concerned about him and really wanted to come and see me, and they were not opening his door and he was afraid he would miss his visit. He began to make a scene over it and now he said he was really sorry about it. I talked with him for a bit and then had prayer with him and told him he needed to commit his son to God and really ask Him to change his nature so that would not act out like that. He humbly agreed to do so and then I told the sergeant that I thought it was safe enough to let him go back to his cell. Please pray for him to become a *new creature!*

In His love,

William Cawman

3
AND THEN?

July 1, 2017

AFTER THE SECOND MESSAGE on Sunday night of June 25, an inmate in leaving the chapel said with a big grin, "Married men preach better!" The men were very exuberant over our wedding the Tuesday before. Guess what? We were, too! God has been so good to us and we thank Him that He came to our wedding just as we desired Him to. Since that day we have just hugged up closer to Him as we draw closer to each other. Outside of the witness of the Spirit to my heart's relationship to Him, never in my life has anything carried clearer witness with it that we are in the very center of God's precious will. We belong first of all to Jesus, then to each other, and it will ever stay that way.

It has been often said that God never runs out of anything. I agree completely with that, but I have found out that His giving of any certain grace may run out. For five and one-half years God so graciously poured into my heart and life the grace to live a single life. But He allowed it to run out! It was marvelous and wonderful as long as that was His will for me, but I am now saturated with gratitude that He let that type of grace run out for me and is blessing me so utterly beyond description with a new kind of grace. You ask what that new grace is? Come to my house and see!

We have been having some very lively class discussions of late. I find it a joy and delight to teach these eager men. Admittedly there are many times when I have to channel the discussion and bring it back into the subject at hand, but then I try to remember that the questions they ask may be at the moment more important than the agenda that I had planned, so I do not discourage the open discussions.

Recently, however, a very disappointing area of discussion came up and I found once again that man cannot convince man; only the Holy Spirit can do that. Two of the men who had been in class for several months began to hold their own Bible studies on the tier. They pulled in another young man and felt they really had a fish on the hook, so started bringing him to class. As this man listened to the discussions he suddenly blurted out, "Do you mean that if a person is saved, they quit sinning?" We assured him that the power to stop sinning is exactly what salvation is. He then said, "Then I'm not saved, 'cause I still sin." I responded to him that the best thing to do about that was to get saved. I suggested we go to prayer right then and there. It was a good time of prayer indeed and yet I am sure he did not get saved. The next class or two, he was again trying to figure this out and the two "teachers" who had converted him began to get very defensive of their new convert. They were trying to argue that he was saved but that he wasn't as far along as some others—but nonetheless, he was saved!

I went straight to the Word of God and to the very purpose that Jesus came and emphasized that if a person is living in known sin, they are not saved at all. He then opened up and said, "Well, I know I can't stop sinning, and really I don't want to. As soon as I get out I plan to sin with my girlfriend and I know I'm going to do it. There's no question about it; I'm going to sin." Even this did not change the two men who had "saved" him, and as much as I fled to the Scripture and common sense, they held to their position that he was saved. I actually felt sick over such flagrant doctrines of devils as have been taught to the multitudes of today's "Christians."

For years now I have tried off and on to help another man. The reason it has been off and on is that he comes to see me off and on. He comes to my classes off and on. The rest of the time he goes where he is comfortable to live in known sin and still think he can gain heaven. I have dealt plainly with this man over and over. There have been times when he has broken down and admitted he was wrong. There have been times when he even prayed into at least a measure of desire for the true way of God. But then he would drift back again into his comfortable sinning religious feelings.

He had left prison for a time, but his lifestyle brought him back with a fresh charge. While out he had gotten acquainted with a woman about twenty some years his senior and when he came back to prison she was sending him $100 a month which was pretty attractive to him. He knew full well that his relationship with this woman was wrong because he had been a married man. Furthermore, the woman had lupus and would more than likely not live that long, but he couldn't seem to break with her to find clearness in his soul, so he stopped coming to see me again.

Just the other day he sent in a request to see me. He told me he was getting out in just a few weeks and wanted to just see me again and thank me for helping him. I began to face him with the shabby state he was living in. I told him that I had watched him mess around with God the whole time he had been there and that I was concerned about him. He began to break down and before long was weeping and we went to prayer. He promised me that he would not stop until he knew he was changed on the inside and truly saved. He said he wanted to keep in touch with me after he left, so I told him he could write to me in the prison and then we could arrange further contact as in his coming to church.

Do pray for this miserable man to whom Satan has sold a bill of goods, as he has many others. What a cheap substitute he pawns off on people for their eternal welfare.

One morning on my way to the prison I came up behind a school bus and a father was putting his children on the bus and then took a moment to talk to the bus driver. A few mornings later the same thing happened. As soon as it was clear to go again, I pulled over next to his car which was parked out at the end of their long driveway and motioned for him to come over. He did so, wondering what I was up to, and when he neared my rolled down window I said, "Sir, I have a few words of wisdom for you." "Good," he said, "I like words of wisdom." I said to him, "I am a chaplain at South Woods State Prison, and we have 3500 men in there. If there were more fathers like you, we wouldn't have a lot of them in there." He thanked me very feelingly.

This year, as Ramadan came on for the Muslim population, there was more attention given it than ever I can remember. The numbers are growing and the demand for their right is also growing. When it came time for it to start, the prison began cutting the evening Christian services short so that the Muslims could be served their meal, which has to come right after sundown. I began to hear murmurings and then some of the men just blurted out in class that they were very unhappy that their services had to be cut to almost nothing so that the Muslims could have theirs. I immediately sent a note to my supervisor to the effect that as employees we are advised that if we see something we are to say something. I said I was hearing that the Christian inmates were not happy with having their service times cut short for the Muslims. He immediately sent the note to the superintendent and they ordered it to be corrected.

However, I cautioned the Christian men that they were only seeing the tip of the iceberg of a Muslim takeover in this country. I pointed out to them that thirty-eight hundred years ago, old Isaac laid dying (or so he thought) and ordered his son

Esau to go and get him some venison. Rebecca heard it and put Jacob up to stealing the blessing that was to be given to Esau. When Esau came in he began to weep and asked his father if he didn't have a blessing for him also. His father asked what he could give him seeing he had given to his brother the patriarchal blessing, including dominion over him, but then he uttered a most remarkable prophecy. "...by thy sword shalt thou live, and shalt serve thy brother; and it shall come to pass when thou shalt have the dominion, that thou shalt break his yoke from off thy neck."

I told them that we were watching that yoke break and Esau rise up against his brother. Now I told them that this was a wonderful opportunity to prove the grace of God and to act like Christians no matter how much persecution and pushing aside we may yet encounter. They began to nod assent as they knew that was what a true Christian should do. Nevertheless, I did feel it my responsibility to make the situation known to the administration, as it is not right.

Let me just insert here that one of the strongest elements of wrong is its aggressiveness. Sin is an ugly pushover! Satan has no manners, no respect, no decency—in fact, nothing of the beautiful virtues that stem from God's creative pattern. The only perfect element of Satan and sin is its perfect antithesis of all that is God. Oh sin! When wilt thou cease from the earth?

We are thanking God that a man recently released is coming faithfully to church and seems to have it settled to obey God no matter what it costs him. Please do pray for him. Satan will not leave him alone and will definitely have his traps set for his feet, but so far the grace of God is keeping him because he is choosing for it to do so.

Another gets out next month, and he, too, has his heart set on being a part of the church. He has been walking in the beauty of holiness for several years now and we are anticipating having these new brothers among us. They are a support to each other, which is a great advantage against the tactics of the devil. Perhaps in few areas is the Scripture more literally exemplified which says, "Two are better than one; because they have a good reward for their labour. For if they fall, the one will lift up his fellow: but woe to him that is alone when he falleth; for he hath not another to help him up....And if one prevail against him, two shall withstand him; and a threefold cord is not quickly broken."

And then, once again this coming month, we plan to have a week of in-house classes from the faithful brother and his wife who have been giving this four-year theological course to a number of the men. This year four of them are finishing the work. I will probably have a couple of new ones to sit in on the classes and see if they want to pursue them and become enrolled.

I would also like to close this letter with a prayer request that is not altogether new. Every so often it appears that the state government officials are making changes that could drastically alter the open door to this ministry that God has opened up. I have requested prayer before and God has answered. I do so again without stating just what areas are appearing distressing just now. God started this—please pray that He will keep the door open.

William Cawman

┼┼┼

August 1, 2017

DEAR PRAYING FRIENDS,
Praise be to God, another soul has been washed in the Blood of Jesus! A twenty-five-year-old Hispanic man came to visit me for the second time. He very openly told me that he had been reading his Bible and trying to pray, but that he couldn't say he was finding anything. I looked at him and said, "No, and you won't either, unless you trust completely in the Blood of Jesus to save you. It's good that you are reading and praying, but if that could save you Jesus would not have died for you. You must trust completely in that Blood he shed for you."

Then I asked him if he really believed that Jesus shed His blood for him; not just for the whole world, but for him. He answered that he absolutely believed that. I said, "Then I will give you a very simple prayer that you can pray. Here it is: 'Jesus, I believe You died for me. Whatever it was that you saw I could become that made You willing to die for me, I want to become that. So here I am.'"

He looked very longingly at me for a few seconds and then said, "Can we do that right now? I want that. Will you help me pray that?" I immediately began to pray for him, and it was very easy to believe that God was hearing the prayer. When I finished, he looked up and said with wonder, "Oh my, I felt that go all the way through me! Chaplain, thank you! Could I give you another hug?" He jumped up just as I did and as he hugged me I said, "Did you let Jesus come into your heart?" "He came in all over me!"

He then wanted to be enrolled in the classes and Bible studies, and when he appeared in the first one and I told the men we had a new brother, there was rejoicing among them all. I am sure the angels are rejoicing, too. Do pray for him that he will get his feet down and go right on with God.

In the June letter I told you some about a very high-profile criminal whose father and uncle were the founders of Hells Angels. I told you how it appears that he has genuinely gotten saved and is straightening out his past life as much as he can from within prison. He wrote me a very touching and precious letter filled with love for my helping him. Knowing his past and the however many souls he brutally sent into eternity, I was very moved by it. All I can say is already said in the words of a songwriter: "It gives us access to God on high, from 'far-off places' it brings us nigh…" Thank God for the Blood that has never and will never lose its power!

As he continues to confess in multiple states to the crimes he has committed, he is awaiting extradition to a western state to stand trial there. I asked him if once that was finished he would be clear from all the past and he said with a sad look,

"Oh no! I'm not sure if that will ever happen." I do believe that should he die before he can get all confessed, God will take the will for the deed, but what a mess Satan can make out of a life!

One day in class we were discussing various areas of temptation. He suddenly raised his hand and said, "I hear all that you men are saying, and I understand it; but I would have to say that with all that my past held, I am not facing those temptations at all. I'm running from all of that!" That led into another area of discussion as to how, when one particular temptation loses its power, Satan will turn his artillery in another direction. He acknowledged that where temptation is strong to him is to take a wrong attitude toward those who know his past and will not forgive or believe that he is changed. Even his own family refuses to believe that he has changed. They simply want to think it's a new scheme of crime he is up to. But then, it is only reasonable that confidence doesn't come quickly, after the trail he has left behind.

I had another visit the other day with the man who was raised a Nazarene. As he talked about how God is continuing to work with him, he again went into tears. "Chaplain, I can't believe that, after all these years, I would have to come to this prison to meet someone who still has what I knew in my early life. I just thank God that I ever met you!"

Then he told me something from his childhood. I don't remember whether he said they were in a camp meeting, or where this happened, but he became very ill with an undiagnosed internal bleeding. It was finally decided that he must have exploratory surgery to find where the bleeding was occurring. Before he went in for the surgery two preachers came and prayed over him. He remembers that one of them had the last name of Griffith. I stopped him. I said, "Was his first name Glenn?" He thought for a bit and said, "I can't remember what his first name was, I only remember that his last name was Griffith."

After prayer he went into the operating room and they explored for the source of the bleeding and found nothing. He never bled again. This would probably have occurred in the late 1950s or early 1960s.

This past month we were blessed again to have the teacher who is giving several of the men a four-year theological course come in for a week of teaching. When he arrived he began to relate how Satan had fought him getting here, and I was fully aware of how much he was fighting on our end. First of all, the clearance papers for he and his wife did not arrive until Wednesday of the week before the classes were to start on Monday. My supervisor came and told me and said that it would never get cleared in time. I went and picked up the forms and decided to hand carry them up front to the special investigations department to save all the time we could, but we all know that it sometimes takes up to three or four weeks to get them cleared. The department has been very touchy about not giving them a month's notice to get them done. I walked in and went to the secretary's desk. I said, "I come with a deep apology. This couple comes in every year to teach an in-house class to men who are enrolled in their college, and we just got their clearance forms." She looked up and waved her hand and said, "Give them to me; I'll get someone to run them tomorrow!"

Whew! I breathed a deep sigh of relief, but the following day I learned that the room in the visit hall that we have used for several years has now been assigned to lawyer visits which can be scheduled at a moment's notice. There were already two sessions slated and then officers and administrators started calling and wanting to know what was going on, and again things were getting tense. It was decided that we could at least use the room for the first morning and my supervisor and I were prepared to seek out other options for after that, but when I escorted them to the visit hall, the officer in charge of it was one I had known for almost twenty years. He asked how many men were in the class and I told him six. He said, "Oh, that's not a problem; I can find a spot for them for every session." Another wave of relief, but that didn't stop more calls from administration as to how it all happened, etc. God provided and they were able to have each session. Does He still have the ability to prepare a table for us in the presence of our enemies?

One of the assignments the teacher gave to the men was to paraphrase the twenty-third Psalm in their own words. Would you like to read a sample of them?

"The Lord God is my keeper, and He has my back. He feeds me, and takes me places where only He can make me feel absolutely wonderful. He refreshes my soul, and gives me the guidance and leadership to do the things that please Him. That's right; I'm a fallen creature, and an alien as I write this verse, but I have a spiritual life through Jesus Christ and death has no sting for me. Knowing that You are Sovereign over all I have the weapon of Your Word. I know that Your word gives me the peace of God that surpasses all understanding. All Your enemies are my enemies, and I will partake of Your table and I will sup with You. I am blessed and it is full; measured and shaken together and running over. My life is not only here for now but eternal, and when I complete my walk through the valley of the shadow of death, I will be with You forever. Only You make me dwell in safety."

"The Lord is my Protector; my Leader; I have need of nothing. He provides all I need for daily living! He puts me in a quiet place; peace with Him. He keeps me lifted up and full of joy. He keeps me on the straight path because I represent Him and not myself. Each day the devil will try and make me stumble; but I know that greater is He that is within me than he that is in this world. I am not afraid of Satan or his demons. I am protected by God for the battle belongs to Him. Once again, You Lord, provide all that I need, even in front of all that hate me. Your favor is not fair. You have placed Your hand upon me. You will never leave me nor forsake me. You give me more than I need so I can share with others. Your love, grace, mercy, peace, and goodness will always be with me. I would rather be a door keeper in the house of the Lord, than to dwell in the tents of the wicked. In Your presence is where I want to be."

"God is my Father; He provides everything. He formed me, called me by name; saved me and sanctified me. His Blood and living water are my refuge. He teaches me how to be with Him and how to worship His name. Even when I walk through dangerous worlds I am not afraid. My Father's life, deep in me, gives me comfort. He protects me and celebrates my life. He anoints me and separates me to Himself, right in the sight of the enemy.
—That's right Satan; I am His. All good and mercy gracefully belong to me; because of that grace, I am welcome to live forever in His presence."

As the men were returning down the compound from one of the class sessions I met them coming the other direction. As I approached them there was a shine of joy on their faces and so I called out, "This looks like a bunch of Christians coming!" Pray that many more will find the same joy in living for Jesus.

Four of the six men have now finished the four-year course, so please also pray that whoever should be taking advantage of this wonderful opportunity will be made clear to us in the days ahead.

I pray that the Lord will protect the publication of what I am about to tell you. I tell it only as an indicator of the strength of evil that has been turned loose in our God-rejecting nation. The Muslim chaplain continues to become more evil with the passing of time. Yet in spite of that, he has gained clout to an unbelievable measure among staff and officers. He jokes and laughs with them and shares their sin without convicting them of anything. Recently a female doctor wrote a complaint against him for his foul language. A couple of days later my supervisor heard a special investigations officer (these are the police of the police, and are not supposed to be showing favor to anyone) passing by, say to the Muslim chaplain, "Don't worry Doc, we've got your back covered!" My supervisor spoke up and said, "You're on pretty shaky territory!" No response. The floodtide of antichrist is gaining momentum at a logarithmic rate, and we had better not be burying our heads in the sand, either. I'll leave it at that.

Please do continue to pray for the men who have gotten out of prison, especially for those who are endeavoring to walk right and are coming to our church. Satan has them in his crosshairs, but God is greater. Please pray for them, for if one of them fails, the waves of that will ripple right back into the prison with a tidal wave of discouragement and disappointment. We are our brother's keeper!

Thank you for your prayers. Your Brother,
William Cawman

┼┼┼

September 1, 2017

Dear Praying Friends,
Let me tell you another bit about our brother who was raised in early life in the Nazarene Church. He had been in the military for over twenty years and had attained some rank when he was placed under the command of a young female officer. She was a very difficult person to get along with and rather than encounter what might happen, he resigned. Immediately after his resignation the terrible conflict broke out over "Desert Storm" and all that followed that, and he has a strong feeling that Providence got him out just before he might have lost his life. How many times, when we finally look back from eternity, will we see the intricate workings of a loving Heavenly Father who spared us and guided us until He could get our attention.

And then do you recall our dear brother who had a problem with his face hurting from smiling so much? Well, the problem has become persistent, with no hope of a letup. The other day he sat joyously in front of me and testified more clearly than I have ever heard him before to being saved and sanctified. He is well along in his studies in the four-year course of theology and what he is studying just rings a bell with all that God has done for him. When he left the office after the visit, I went down the hallway one direction and he the other, and I could hear him literally bubbling over as he went: "Praise Him! Oh, hallelujah!" It was coming from a living well way down deep within him. Oh God, give us more like him!

This past Sunday night I preached to them from the first verses of Galatians chapter four on whether they were a servant or a son. I took the liberty to say to them that from that very pulpit they were hearing many different standards of what it meant to be a Christian. I asked them what could possibly be wrong with picking out of God's Word the highest standard of Christ-likeness and the highest standard of being free from sin that they could find and asking God to give it to them. I then told them that the reason many of them were trying to comfort themselves with preaching and teaching that leaves us still victims of sin, is that they are not yet sons, but only servants. I exposed a few other often-taught errors and asked them if it would not be safer to aim for the highest goal promised in the Bible.

As they were leaving the service our dear brother with face aglow shook my hand and said, "I am a son!" How could I even begin to doubt it? All through the message he had been sitting over to one side with evident joy and often with his hands raised. A servant works for wages; he as a son is finding a rich inheritance.

There is a Biblical phrase that sinning religious teachers have used to literally damn souls under their care. The phrase is found in Romans 3:23— "For all have sinned, and come short of the glory of God..." They misapply the second part of that to every transgression and sin they commit, as if it was just an inevitable accident that is to be expected throughout the

"Christian" life. I get so sick at heart at the ever-so-frequent and ever-so-flippant demonstrations of absolute irresponsibility over downright sin in the life.

Such was another case just a few days ago. A man who is in mid-life and had been in the classes and Bible studies until he was released on parole in 2015 reappeared again in class. He seemed very broken and humbled by being back again, but the reason was the trite "I fell short!" This falling short seems to require no rectification except to try to not do it again. It does not even seem to break one's standing with an imaginary god; it is simply an unfortunate bump in the road— "I fell short again!"

Sinning religion has filled the world with struggling souls. Some hardly even feel bad about it. Others do, but they have been given no alternative to the pathetically low expectation of ever rising above this "falling short" malady. Satan loves it, too!

Some time ago I had written about a man I had met in the prison hospital who was saved only a short while back, out of one of the most horrible cesspools of sin imaginable. This man would break into a house and tie everyone up or kill them as opportunity presented itself, just to rob money or drugs. He seemed to be entirely devoid of any fear whatsoever.

One day, completely sick of such a life, he walked out onto the Ben Franklin Bridge in Philadelphia and was going to throw himself down into the river to his death. Suddenly he heard a voice behind him saying, "Don't do this!" He left the bridge but still was so determined to end his life that he found a junkie who was shooting himself up and asked him to give him a shot. The man looked at him and said, "I can't. I have the black plague." (That was the street term for AIDS.) He told the man he had it too, so the man gave him a syringe of the potion and he injected himself with it to try to hasten his death. That is where he contracted AIDS.

About a year ago perhaps I had asked him if he would write his story in order to magnify the miracle God had done for him, as well as to help others. He said he would, but so far has not done it. The other day I was visiting with him again and I asked him about it. He told me he still had the notebook but had written nothing in it. He then said that he was afraid to write his story. I asked him if he was afraid that it would get him into more trouble if he wrote it. He said very emphatically that it wasn't that. He let me know that his sins were all confessed and he had nothing to hide, but that he was afraid to go back and face again the terrible things he had done. He mentioned the people he had killed; the one he was serving time for; and all the rest of his horrible life. He shuddered as he told me that he was a horrible person back there, and that he was afraid to think about it.

It suddenly came to me to ask him if he didn't realize how much Jesus had suffered to help him. Wouldn't he be willing to suffer to help others? He looked at me and said, "Yes, I do know that, and I do know, too, that God wants me to do this. I will do it." Please pray for him, that God will use his story, not to magnify or glorify sin, but to show what a pit God can rescue a soul from.

His cellmate then came to visit with me. He is an illegal from MX and a Roman Catholic. As he sat visiting with me he told me how his cellmate and he had been talking and how much he needed God to help him. He told me that he was a Catholic and then took out his rosary and kissed it. He said when he prays to Jesus while holding his rosary he finds a sweet presence come to him that causes him to reject all that is sinful and want to get closer to Jesus. He seemed so sincere and so broken that I did not even mention anything about his rosary. I just emphasized praying directly to Jesus, which he seemed to be doing with result.

He has lived with an American girl for ten years and has two children by her. He now wants to get things right and marry her, and she wants it, too. He asked me if I would marry them. I asked him if either of them had ever been married to anyone else before and he said they had not. I called for one of the social workers and she brought a marriage request form for him. I guess it remains to be seen whether a license will be granted to an illegal in prison???

I opened last month's letter with praise for a new soul being born into the family of God. A few weeks have gone by and he seems so bright and happy with the change in his life. But I must tell you something to the glory of God and the power of the Living Word. Now, remember that this young man is coming from a totally heathen background. He told me that he had gotten into a conversation with another inmate and the subject matter was not good, nor was some of the language used. He went away feeling bad about it and went to his cell. He thought he would lie down and take a nap.

Suddenly he dreamed that a hand was touching him on the shoulder and he saw something like a banner before his eyes which said, "James 3:5." He has barely begun reading his Bible for the first time, but he thought he knew where the Book of James was. He opened it up and read, "Even so the tongue is a little member, and boasteth great things. Behold, how great a matter a little fire kindleth! And the tongue is a fire, a world of iniquity: so is the tongue among our members, that it defileth the whole body, and setteth on fire the course of nature; and it is set on fire of hell." He immediately told God he would stay away from such conversations and language as that from now on. Let's pray he will continue walking in the light and walk right into holiness!

This past Sunday night as he came into the chapel I asked if he was staying in love with Jesus. "Oh yes! Of course! All the time!" And that with a clear shining countenance. Why do so many want to continue living in such a struggling state when the real thing works so well? There have been several times when speaking about this that I have used the following illustration.

"Suppose, men, that at the close of the day you found me out at the curbside sitting in an old 1972 Nova with several windows broken out, springs sticking up through the upholstery, paint all worn and rusting through, driveshaft broken off at the universal joint and lying down on the road, and I'm turning the key over and over in the ignition. You watch me for a while and then walk up and ask me what I'm doing. I reply that I'm trying to go home. You tell me I'll never get there in that thing, but right behind me is sitting a brand-new BMW with a clear title and a tank full of gas. You hand me the key and tell me I am welcome to take it and go home. I look out at you through the cracked window of my Nova and ask you why you are being so critical of my Nova. Just give me more time and I'll get where I'm going all right. It just takes time, you know, and eventually I'll get there.

"You would probably wonder if I had gone into Alzheimer's or had slipped a cog or two and you would probably be right. So why would you get upset and angry at me when I tell you that if what you think you have is not keeping you and giving you power to not sin, there is a real work that God wants to do in you that will get you where you need to go?"

Sadly enough, heads nod to the undeniable truth of this and many of them go right on cranking the Nova. After all, it takes time to become a perfect Christian. And that is absolutely the truth. It takes more than the lifespan of Methuselah to make oneself a Christian, and no one has ever attained it. But every once in a while, some hungry soul opens the door and lets Jesus come in and is born again, and he is immediately a Christian, for he is born into the family.

Now you might be tempted to ask, "Why, Chaplain, is that so rare that you see a genuine new birth with the promised power to become a son of God?" I ask in return, "Why is it that you see it so rarely in your church?" We are certainly in a battle royal for the remnant of souls that Jesus is delaying His coming for, but let's be faithful and true, for they are not all in yet, and heaven rejoices over every last one of them that really touches the sin-cleansing Blood.

Apparently, some higher power in Trenton has a Jewish friend or relative who is presently incarcerated, for we are experiencing an extremely heightened attention to the Jewish inmates. One obviously would-be Jew recently came from another prison and within two days sent a complaint all the way to Trenton that he was not receiving his kosher tray. The executive called my supervisor and wanted to know what was going on. My supervisor told him that was the first he knew of it and so he called the man down and addressed his lack of protocol. Then he asked the inmate if he also needed a Tephillin for his prayers and the man did not even know what one was. Isn't it amazing what our top executives are troubled about while weightier matters slip under the wire? I just thought that little bit of realism from prison chaplaincy might be of interest to you.

Thank you so much again for your faithful prayers.

In love, William Cawman

4
GROWING SPIRITUALLY

October 1, 2017

U PON ENTERING THE PRISON one morning the first thing I saw was a very old man shuffling across the compound with a very cheap walker. His steps were labored and small, his head was bent over nearly on his chest, and his remaining hair was as white as snow. I could have cried as I began to think thus: "Dear man, what was it that Satan held out to you that made you choose it? Is this it? Did he let you know that this was how you would end up your last days?"

How stark the life-size drama of those warning words: "The thief cometh not, but for to steal, and to kill, and to destroy..." And how contrasting the words that follow: "I am come that they might have life, and that they might have it more abundantly." Oh, the shocking power that lies within our free moral choice, whether used for good or evil. But God was so good to give it to us, for it takes the same moral choice to become a saint as it does to become a sinner.

Listen to our Dear Colombian Brother: "Chaplain, it's amazing how God gets His witness through, no matter what!" He then went on to relate how varied is the voice of

God as He guides us through every new arena of our life here on earth. I couldn't help but agree ever so wholeheartedly with him. I remember that for a good while after God had led my own heart into His holiness, it just seemed He witnessed to His work in so many ways. One day I said to my dear sanctified mother, "Mother, I knew theologically that the Holy Spirit would witness to His work, but I didn't know He loved to do it like this!" I love this clear pathway of the highway of holiness!

And so does another of our brothers in prison. Just recently we were visiting and he was glowing with the presence of God in a greater measure than I have ever seen before. The very next best thing to growing in grace is to watch another soul grow.

But there are so many who oppose and fight against the very best thing they could ever know in both worlds. It is so sad to see so many men cheated out of such wonderful grace that others are conspicuously enjoying, because they want to believe a lie and hold onto their sin.

For a couple of years or more there has been in some of my classes and Bible studies an internal medicine doctor from Dominican Republic. The other day he was visiting with me and said, "Every time I draw closer to God, I immediately enter into attacks from somewhere or other, and they are so severe." I quoted the Scripture to him, "Beloved, think it not strange concerning the fiery trial which is to try you, as though some strange thing happened unto you: But rejoice, inasmuch as ye are partakers of Christ's sufferings; that, when his glory shall be revealed, ye may be glad also with exceeding joy." He immediately brightened up and said, "Ooooh, I see, so it's not that I'm doing something wrong?"

"Oh no, that is to be expected, for the devil does not want you to draw closer to God." Then he told me that in the Spanish services the teacher will often ask one of the men who are living right to give a message. He said he declared plainly that there is the danger of losing what God has done for us. The teacher of the class agreed with him fully, but a number of other men came to him and said, "You are just following Chaplain Cawman; he doesn't know what he is talking about!" Well, supposing I don't know what I'm talking about? I still feel it safer to live as though one could lose it than to lose it because one thinks he can't. So that settles that!

One morning recently I was entering the gate into Facility 3 and the institutional dietician was coming out. He asked if my supervisor was in and I told him that he was not as yet. He said, "Well, maybe you can help me." Then he cautiously began to present a situation and I could tell he was feeling me out somewhat as to how freely he could make his point. He said that there was one Jewish inmate who had sent in a request that for the salad on his kosher tray he be given onions and peppers along with the lettuce and tomatoes. The dietician had written back to him that the institution did not have access to kosher onions and peppers. A written dialog had ensued as the inmate had enquired of a rabbi and the rabbi said that peppers and onions would be acceptable in his salad.

At that point I knew where he was going and so I replied, "Well, if I could answer him as I would see best, I would ask him how long it was going to take to realize that he was in a state prison." I saw the hesitancy melt down and he just plainly said, "I'm fed up with this!" But the reality of this scenario is this: anything at all which can be remotely related to some religious belief system is soundly within the rights of a violator of the law of the land—except, that is, it be something related to Christianity. We are deeply into the workings of the anti-Christ; not anti-religion: anti-Christ! We may as well be aware of it.

Let me tell you some encouraging news. Our Calvinist friend, who has been so vocal and confrontational in classes for some time, is finally opening up. He has been sitting long enough now under truth to recognize that it is the truth, and he is examining it. He sent out and ordered a book written by an Arminian who has undertaken to contradict the false claims that Calvinists make against Arminians, and he seems far less controversial as time goes on. Please pray that this will be a deeper change than just his mental theology, but that he will really get a change of heart, for there is quite obviously a deep lack of the Spirit of Christ in him. The Scripture cannot be bypassed which declares so bluntly, "Now if any man have not the Spirit of Christ, he is none of his."

I must tell you a refreshing incident about a man who has just been released from prison and is enjoying the family of God in church. When he was released, his stepdaughter gave him a smart phone and told him he would need it. He found it quite interesting and after all, he could call his pastor on it, etc. Then she put an app on his phone so that he could use it for purchasing something or other and he began to feel a cloud come over him. He went to prayer and God showed him that some of his time that belonged to God was being occupied by that phone. His violent love for Jesus and clearness with heaven sent him straight to his room where he took the smart phone in both hands and crushed it to death. Bless his heart! That is exactly the violence Jesus was referring to when He said, "And from the days of John the Baptist until now the kingdom of heaven suffereth violence, and the violent take it by force." Daniel Steele said, "If anything brings a veil of the thinnest gauze between me and the face of my Savior, I henceforth and forever give that thing a tremendous letting alone."

Thank God for a personal Savior who loves us enough to bring a cloud over us when something begins to take His place. No matter what others may do, blessed is that man who will stay in the clear with God at any cost. Heaven will open wide to that man, and that someday soon.

It has been a while now since giving you an update from our former Mormon brother who has been in one of the northern prisons for some time. A recent letter says,

Dear Brother Cawman,

Greetings in the name of our Lord and Savior Jesus Christ. He fills us up every day with more than we can receive. Bless His name! I trust this finds you in His most special care...

I wanted to tell you how much I enjoyed the printout you sent awhile back, "Our Own God" by G.D. Watson. That's probably the most important book I've encountered in my studies, and one that I'm going to find a way to keep with me. Reading it reminded me of the discussions you and I used to have. In the end, our union with God is what matters to Him. He's done so much to make it possible. I just want to cooperate with Him. He's forming His Son in us. There is such a landscape when it comes to an eternal Being.

Dr. Watson's book confirmed so many things for me, including why so much spiritual progress was blocked in my life by demonic concepts of God and a denial of the Trinity. But he balances the correct approach and doctrine with having the actual experience of God (abiding). Very powerful, but also a lesson in how the Holy Spirit already shows me the essential things, and so much good teaching is simply confirmation of what He's given, and good teaching also gives me a way to express what He's already said is true in Scripture and in my heart. That's one way He gets glory, is when I can express what He does in me.

The Lord has me in a very confident place with Him. I trust Him. His will is always best, and reigns supreme. There is nothing that He'll allow that isn't a master stroke of the Potter. I just need to stay still and centered on the wheel with Jesus.

At this point in the letter he begins speaking about a precious missionary who spent many years in both Guatemala and Bolivia and who we connected with him in correspondence since he loves to converse and write in the Spanish language which he learned fluently in his three years as a Mormon missionary to Colombia. This missionary is now up in years and very feeble, yet continues to shine for Jesus and correspond with him.

> Two times in the past two months I've received letters from our Sister ——. I write to her every week. She has such a wonderful attitude, and a love for Jesus. Her every thought is to serve Him and please Him. She's teaching me a great deal during this part of her journey. She's a pilgrim and has pilgrim faith.
>
> Sister —— has had an influence that will be with me even after she's with the Lord. She seems quite content in her surroundings, and is being a missionary and a blessing in every way possible.
>
> As this part of my journey winds to a close, [he has only a few more months in this state and then does not know whether another state will require more time from him or not] I'm finding out many ways the Lord has used me in my time here that I never knew about. He's blessed me with having people come and talk to me about Him. He's so merciful and generous with us.
>
> You are in my prayers, as well as Sister Cindy and Sister Debbie. I know you are all in the Lord's heart and so precious to Him. In His love, ——

The old song says: "From far-off places it brings us nigh, to precious blessings that never die; it will never lose its power!" Yes, the same good old-fashioned grace of our Lord works beautifully no matter what or where that far-off place was.

Thank you again each one for your prayers,

William Cawman

November 1, 2017

IT'S TIME AGAIN FOR you to visit the chaplain on a day of visitations. The day was October 19, 2017. So please make yourself feel welcome and come along.

9:00 a.m.: A man I had not met before has turned in a

request for a visit from the chaplain stating for the reason, "needing guidance—feeling overwhelmed." He is there promptly on time and is not long in getting to the point. He is thirty-four years old and is serving at least his third sentence. He just keeps falling back into drug abuse and this time he says he has hurt a lot of people; meaning, from what I can gather, his family. He says he is at the end of the road and can't go on this way.

I ask if he had any church background and he says that for a while he was going to a church, but he fell away and got into drugs again.

I told him that there are programs that are available that many say will help, but that there is a very slim margin of any real result out of them; but that if he would really begin to seek God there would be a positive cure for all of his sin problems. He said that whenever he has tried going to church, he did feel a lot better. I then told him about Charlie Wireman and how, as he sought God at the altar, he began to feel better, but Charlie said, "Feelin' better ain't religion!" As I tried to point him to what it means to really let Jesus come into one's heart, he got tears in his eyes and said he really wants that. I urged him to earnestly seek the Lord and confess his sins to whoever he has wronged and believe that God will meet him. I had prayer with him and told him I would follow up the visit shortly.

9:30 a.m.: The next visitor is on time as well. This is the second time I have visited with him. What or who he was before prison life, who would know if they had not known him then. At first glance he appears pretty well out of touch. At about the age of nineteen he was roughed up by an officer in prison and his head was battered in and so now he has a metal plate for a skull and wears a hard helmet to protect it. He distorts his mouth constantly as he talks. He is a product of prison, having been most of his life locked up. I try to feel out of his confusion just what he really does comprehend, but arrive at no certainty regarding it. I try my best to guide him to read God's Word and to pray to Him, and ask Him to come into his heart and change his whole life. He seems to comprehend that, but we will see. A pathetic wreck he is of what might have been.

10:00 a.m.: I have arranged a threesome meeting. Two shining examples of God's holiness, who work together helping mental cases on one of the units, come in and greet each other and myself with glowing faces and fountains of brotherly love. We sit for forty minutes and the atmosphere is much like a holiness camp meeting where in Scriptural language we "sit together in heavenly places." These two men are living a spotless life of biblical holiness. They are not sinning and have no intentions of it. They know they are cleansed from all inward pollution and they are growing in grace like July corn after a thundershower.

One of these precious men is about as white as a white man can be and the other is about as black as a black man can be, and they are blood brothers in Jesus Christ. The black man with tremors of excitement in his voice and face tells me that any approach of any sin whatsoever finds absolutely no entrance into his thoughts or heart. He declares his love to Jesus in no hesitant language at all.

Then he points to the white brother and says, "What a breath of fresh air stands there!"

I said, "Yes, I see another one over there, too," pointing right back at him.

I asked which of them was older and the white man pointed to the black man and said, "He is." (The black man is 57 and the white man is 53) Then with a mischievous burst of laughter the white man said, "And I'm really hurt that you had to ask!" I'm not sure that it would be possible to offend one of these men. They are living so far out in the heavenly love realm that they are proving absolutely what the Scripture promises: "Great peace have they which love thy law: and nothing shall offend them."

I must take leave of absence from them at 10:40 as they

must return to their cells for the count and noon meal.

1:00 p.m.: A few months ago I told you of a young Hispanic man who came in and as I tried to point him to the Blood as the answer to his obviously hungry heart, he said, "Can we do that right now?" As I prayed he opened his heart and came up a new creature in Christ. Here we are visiting again, and he has some questions but says that his questions are not stopping his love for this new life. And so, question number one is that he has been praying that if God would work out for him something he really wants to see happen, he will in turn obey God in everything He asks of him. He wants to know if that is the right way he should be praying. You and I know it is not, and so I tried to explain to him that many times God may withhold something from us because he sees it is not good for us. I told him that God loves him too much to allow him to be boss. I asked him if life had gone well when he was trying to run it.

"It sure didn't."

"Well then, now it is time to let God take over completely."

I told him some stories of those, including my own life, who had tried to put some of our own way into God's way and never found peace and real joy until God had it all. He listened intently and kept brightening up with each account. When it was time for him to leave, he hugged me with love and said, "Thank you for having me down today. I needed every word that you spoke to me." What a patient, loving, Jesus Who takes such a babe in Christ and so tenderly leads him into truth. Isaiah, you were so unequivocally right: "He shall feed his flock like a shepherd: he shall gather the lambs with his arm, and carry them in his bosom, and shall gently lead those that are with young."

1:30 p.m.: This man is here for his second visit also, and the reason for the second visit is that in the first one he expressed what seemed to be a genuine desire to find God. This time he seems to feel that life is going all right for now, and even though he is friendly and open, I don't sense the desire he expressed at the first visit. This is one of the things that so often troubles my heart. So many men come with an open desire and then it seems to evaporate so quickly. My hopes are raised for them and then so quickly disappointed. "And as he reasoned of righteousness, temperance, and judgment to come, Felix trembled, and answered, Go thy way for this time; when I have a convenient season, I will call for thee." Did he have a more convenient season? It seems so: "...wherefore he sent for him the oftener, and communed with him." But—sadly enough, there is no record that he ever trembled again.

2:00 p.m.: I wait, but this man (one I really wanted to visit with as he, too, is living a sanctified life) does not appear. One never knows the reason in the department of corrections. He may have had a double appointment, etc. I will have to reschedule that one.

Will you come back with me some other day soon? I hope so.

But let's move on to the following evening in Bible studies. Our lesson was about Paul before Festus making his appeal to go before Caesar. After briefly covering the subject that Paul did not consider it wrong to use civil law to protect the truth of a matter concerning him, we went to a topic that I knew many of them needed to hear. I followed Paul into this scene where, having done his best for years to serve the Lord and lovingly obey Him, he was surrounded by enemies who wanted him removed from the face of the earth. Paul, a Roman citizen, appealed to the highest court in the government to hear his case. But now follow him:

He makes his way by sea to Rome, and on the way is shipwrecked and has to swim or float to shore on a broken piece of ship. Cold and wet and weary he gathers a few sticks to throw on the fire so that he could recover himself. A poisonous snake comes out of the wood and strikes him a direct hit on the hand. He shakes it off into the fire and no harm is done. Paul could easily have looked up and said, "Lord, why are You allowing this to happen to me. I am doing all I can to obey and do Your will, and everything is going wrong. God, don't You care about Your servant?"

On they go to Rome where he has appealed his case to Caesar, and instead of being cleared and sent back to the churches to minister to them, he is put in prison for two years. Again, Paul could have said, "God, I don't understand this. The churches need me. I long to be preaching Your Word. Why am I shut up here in prison when I appealed to the highest earthly tribunal and am entirely clear of any wrong?"

Instead, he wrote thirteen epistles and possibly the Book of Hebrews, and thus has been a blessing to the entire world since.

Then I began to apply the lesson to their situation. I told them that probably none of them were in prison for preaching God's Word, but regardless of why they were there it would only make them sour and bitter to whine and complain and blame God for any of their discomfort. I told them that they should be praying earnestly, "God, now that I'm here I will by Your grace find the promise You have made: 'I will give thee the treasures of darkness, and hidden riches of secret places, that thou mayest know that I, the Lord, which call thee by thy name, am the God of Israel.'"

I could sense that the application was really sinking home and I told them that the reason I was bearing down on it was that nearly several times a week I hear men fretting or questioning God as to why things are going the way they are for them. I said that as long as they were going to do that, they would entirely lose the riches of rare grace that only flow from a fully yielded and trusting heart. I gave them my personal experience on both sides of such a yielded heart and told them that I was so happy since turning everything over to God that I was not even tempted to take things back into my own hands, or question Him when trials come that I would not have chosen. I mean that, too!

My wife is now officially a volunteer at the prison and she accompanied me last Sunday night. The men were so delighted to see her there and it helps so much in the singing to have a pianist.

There have been many interpretations— some good, some not so good— going through the prison about what Chaplain Cawman teaches and preaches. Men who have listened and opened their hearts to the truth of salvation from all sin are told that they are just followers of Chaplain Cawman. Sinning religion is still far in the ascendancy among the 350 or so regular attendees at the services and classes. Sunday night I made no effort to redeem my reputation. I preached to them from 1 John 3:9 and entitled the message, *The Supreme Cannot*— "...he cannot sin..."

Now did you notice that there are three dots before and after this Scriptural statement? Without letting the Bible fill in the three dots on each end of those three words, logical and justifiable objection could be forthcoming indeed. But the Bible clearly states that to a soul "born of God," there is an abiding of "His seed" (which the Bible says is "I come to do Thy will, Oh God!") in us which is the enabling to "cannot sin." And do you know that even those who do not come to my classes because of what I teach were nodding in assent. God's truth, when left to explain itself, is unarguable! It rings a bell way down deep in the inner conscience of men that they cannot deny, even if they are still loving their sin and wanting to continue living in it.

I haven't told you something for a while and I need to repeat it. I thank you, each praying brother and sister, for holding us up before the Throne. God is not finished yet and there are new awakenings.

Thank you!

William Cawman

December 1, 2017

ANOTHER YEAR IS ALMOST history, isn't it? Have I done my best for

Jesus? He did His best for me! He really has, too, and I have seen more of His loving guidance in my life than in any year in the past. "Oh, for grace to trust Him more!"

On the last day of October our dear Colombian brother—who had been gloriously saved and sanctified after forty years a violent, murderous Catholic, and then five years a Muslim—was transferred to one of the northern prisons. Whenever this happens, my first reaction is one of disappointment, but then I quickly realize that these precious souls belong to God, not me, and perhaps He has work for them to do somewhere else. This has been proven before, as in several cases I have heard a trail of reports for years of God working through men who were one time a part of our classes and Bible studies here. Do continue to pray for him that God will keep his face shining and his heart hot!

One morning in class this past month we had come to a part of our study where different views of how the work of holiness is accomplished, and since there were several new men in the class, I felt it best to step back and explain in detail what the work of holiness actually is, and what it accomplishes. As I went forward with this for maybe an hour, I noticed two men to my left deeply listening. Now, let me give you a description of the one: he is a black man of sixty years and stands six feet six inches tall. He has dreadlocks which hang well below his shoulders and a gray beard about five inches long. He has a very kind-looking face and is always very polite and respectful towards me. He has often had contributions to the discussion, yet has always seemed ready to learn.

He suddenly raised his hand and said, "Chaplain, I've always had no doubt that I was filled with the Spirit and I've preached the gospel for years, but as I listen to you, I am becoming aware that I still have a need down inside of me. Just the other night I was lying in bed and something rose up inside of me that I didn't like at all. I cried out to God to take it away, but I see I still need a cleansing." He said more than that and I let him have free rein to get his confession out. And then

I said, "Dear Brother, you are giving me a severe case of heartburn. I am excited about what God is showing you, for it is proof that He wants to and will deliver you completely from all sin if you will stay with Him.

I then went to Malachi's question as to who would abide the day of His coming or stand when He appears, because He would come as a Refining Fire. The man next to him spoke up: "I see I need a deeper cleansing, too. I have things in my heart that are not Christ-like and I do want a pure heart. I was planning to leave the class at ten o'clock and make some phone calls to my family as some of them are sick, but God asked me right here if my family was more important than the truth we are hearing."

I felt like shouting and I hope you will feel like praying that God will help them to go through the Refining Fire and come out completely cleansed. It is high time we have some more genuinely sanctified men in the prison. One has recently been released and is now a part of our church and another one has been shipped to another prison as I told you, and now we need some more sanctified soldiers to stand in the gap they have left.

When man wants to make a trophy for some achievement, he scours the woodland for a rare walnut burl out of which to make a base, and then searches for the finest of rare materials to adorn it above. When God wants to make a trophy of grace, He finds a dirty, wretched, miserable sinner and washes him so clean in the precious Blood of His Son that He is then not ashamed to call him a brother and take him at last into His throne with Him for all eternity. So now—

He came to see me after a few weeks in this prison. He is sixty-four years old and looks the part of a gentleman, indeed. He has lived a successful life as the owner of a small construction company. He has a wife and children who love him very much. But he abused drugs, drink, and women, and it finally caught up with him and he is in prison for the first time in his life. He sits before me and tells me that with this bombshell dropped on him, he is now awake. He said he knows he was headed straight for hell, and God now has his attention and has turned him around completely. He was in another prison for a few years and now has moved here. The parole officer asked him the other day if he felt that his sentence was excessive. He said, "Let me tell you the truth: I thank God for this prison sentence. It has completely changed me and I'm headed one hundred and eighty degrees the other direction."

He said his wife is a praying woman and that for years he belittled her for every mistake she made and was just miserable toward her. Now that he has landed in prison, she has not said one thing belittling to him, but is standing by him and encouraging him to go with God. As he spoke to me I could sense that all he has ever encountered are the teachings of sinning religion, but he says he is on a quest for more of God, and so I tried to point him to the "better way," and then loaned him a book I had in my bag— *Love Enthroned* by Daniel Steele. Please pray for him and I will visit with him again very soon.

Do you remember me telling you some time back of a doctor of internal medicine from Dominican Republic who is here in the prison? He has also been really growing spiritually and he told me the other day that he wants so badly to tell others about how good He is. His cellmate left and he prayed that God would give him an open door into some heart. Into his cell came a young gangster. Within a few hours of being there he opened up and said, "Could you help me to find God?" Our brother's heart leaped up with joy and he immediately began to point out the Scriptural pathway to God. The gangster finally asked, "Can I be a Christian and still continue to belong to the gang?"

"Oh no!" our brother said. "You must give up one to have the other; you cannot be both."

"Then," said the gangster, "I think I had better find God."

By the way, I have now had the privilege to meet and be counseled by one of Job's "comforters," so I have! Let me tell you about it. I have mentioned before a man who started coming to the classes and Bible studies with a strong Calvinistic background. I have met a few of his kind before. They are not only Calvinistic, but determined that the one in whose classes they have chosen to sit be persuaded of their error as well. This man has mellowed somewhat over the last couple of years as far as open opposition and argument in the classes, but he continues to wear that look on his face that I have come to associate with one deeply indoctrinated in the errors of Calvin. He continues to ask to sit with me in one-on-one interviews. And so, reluctantly, I called him in again the other day.

I tried to set the stage by opening with the suggestion that it would be far more profitable for him if he would lay aside his ardent pursuit of theological positions and concentrate on his own inner conformity to the Spirit of Christ. "Oh," he insisted, "I've been doing that diligently for twenty-one years! I know what God has done for me and I know my position in Christ. My prayer and desire is that you and I could come together in harmony."

I replied, "Well, obviously you are aware of the fact that we are not in harmony. I am aware of that also. There is only one bond of harmony, and that is the indwelling Spirit of Christ. I can tell you that I know men who are of the same theological persuasion as myself, but we do not sense that bond of harmony that you are talking about. It can only be achieved as two persons are fully filled with the Spirit of God."

"So you don't think I am? I know I am! I know what progress I've made in twenty-one years, and am I supposed to throw all that away?"

By this time, I realized that nothing could be gained by tact or dodging the issue, so I replied, "Paul had to throw away all of his years of training when he really met Jesus, didn't he? Nicodemus and the Rich Young Ruler both found after a lifetime of training that they had an inner lack, didn't they? And Jesus went right to the heart of the issue with Nicodemus and told him, 'Verily, verily, I say unto thee, Except a man be born again, he cannot see the kingdom of God.' Perhaps you too are lacking something."

There was no more harmony at the close of the interview than at the beginning, and I felt like I had been in an atmosphere totally opposite to the harmony of the Spirit. It was obvious that the harmony he is seeking is that I endorse him without any change on his part, as he is already "blood washed and spirit filled" (his words). There have been two or three others during my time working among these men that have after an interview left me feeling like I had been in the presence of Satan, not God. Unless I feel clearly that God wants me to, I will refrain from further interviews. He is too much a parallel of Job's "comforters;" dead right—it's Job that is wrong. Isn't it sad what the "doctrines of devils" can do to seal a man against truth?

This man feels that I am being totally un-Christian to name out the errors of Calvinism; I should be seeking to harmonize them with Arminians. Calvinism has done more to deceive its thousands than can be imagined, and it is harder to win a man away from this error than it is from Roman Catholicism.

Since I wrote in the first of this letter about our Colombian brother, I received a letter from him. Here it is:

Dear Reverend Cawman,

I am saddened that I could not say good bye to you before I departed to —— prison. Surprisingly, a process that usually takes 6 to 9 months took only ten days. I received approval for transfer when I was already here. Alas, I missed seeing you on my last appointment. Three weeks before I left South Woods I applied to Rutgers University through the STEP Program. The academic adviser's suggestion was that I should come to —— since they are already teaching the bachelor classes here. The process was too fast and I ended up here much sooner than expected; I was planning for a summer 2018 transfer.

Although I am attending church services, I feel lost. It is devastating that a Christian has to feel himself an alien at a church service. There is power and energy in their services, but this is world power; mere emotional outburst; there is an overt denial of Christ's power to conquer sin. On the one hand, I will have to be very careful as I walk in an environment that denies the second work of grace; on the other hand, it is an opportunity to witness to the power of Christ to save to the uttermost. I am most fortunate that it is God Himself who walks with me. In that sense, I feel like Enoch.

A great responsibility lies before me. I am praying right now that my initial perception of the church be just that, a perception and not a reality. I would hate to become too judgmental without reason. May God spare me from placing pride before good judgment. I, too, must take heed to remain obedient and in love with God, otherwise I may also fall.

I will keep this letter short since I just want to make my initial report to you. I am most thankful for your loving mentoring in my Christian life. If I had been presented with the message of a powerless Christ I would have remained a Catholic or a Muslim. Please pray for me, I will for you.

Yours, in Christ's perfect love, ———.

Please pray that God will use him as a light in a dark place. We have no right to ask God to keep all of our good sanctified men here in this prison when others are so needy.

In Christian love,

William Cawman

5
VICTORIES AND DISAPPOINTMENTS

January 1, 2018

THERE IS SO MUCH at the close of this past year that I want to tell you, so I will try and squeeze as much of it as I can into this letter. The year has held its victories as well as its disappointments, and I feel constrained to give you a cross section of each.

A young man from Haiti has been very faithful for a number of years at the classes and Bible studies. For the longest time he seemed baffled by even the rudiments of spiritual things and would ask questions with such a perplexed look on his face. But for the last several months I have noticed a real change come over him in his attitudes and comprehension. Then the reason for it suddenly came to the foreground.

In a class discussion regarding the reality of divine grace, he burst forth with this: "Men, I need to tell you something. For seven years I have been a fan of Jesus. I was troubled because I could not stop sinning. Then a few months ago I did something evil and was sent to lockup. I sat there reflecting over my spiritual state and why I was struggling so much. Then it dawned on me; I was only a fan of Jesus, not a follower. I opened my heart and let Jesus take over in me and I became a follower instead of a fan. I soon noticed that my TV watching was hindering me in being with Jesus and that it was opening the door to temptations, so I got rid of it. I suggest if you are struggling, start following Jesus instead of just being a fan."

In that same class time, God really settled down and I felt an unusual degree of anointing in teaching clearly the way of holiness. Toward the end of the class time, a tall black man with long dreads and a short beard spoke up. I've noticed for some time how intently he has been following the teaching. He said, "Chaplain, I was an ordained preacher for years outside of the prison, but I've been listening as you teach us and I'm hearing things I never heard in my life. I want what I'm hearing too. But I'm wondering what I should do about the years that I taught a false doctrine out there. I didn't know it was false then, but I do now."

I said to him, "Well, brother, Paul taught a false doctrine for years, too, before he came to the Light, but when he embraced the whole truth he just put everything there was of him into preaching Jesus crucified. If God wants you to do anything about the past, He will show it to you, but you just need to run after Him with all your heart."

I want to request prayer for my supervisor in the prison. He and I have worked together for almost nineteen years without a single scuffle, notwithstanding the difference in our doctrinal positions. Such increased pressures are being thrown at us from the state government that he has been tempted to just retire and get away from it. The other day he told me that he was awakened at 3:30 in the morning and could not go back to sleep. He wrestled with God for a long time with his desire to retire but could get no peace until he surrendered and told God he would stay on. Then he told me that if anything happened to me, he would be out of there the next day. God has certainly used him to keep this door open and so please pray for him that God will, not only continue to use him, but lead him into all the fullness of God.

I have been sensing all month long the hand of God upon me to relate a sad story to you not merely for the story's sake, but as a warning to all.

About eight or nine years ago a man who had been doing very well in prison was released on parole. His time under parole lasted only about two years and during that time he was coming down to our church from about two and a half hours north as often as he could. After he was finished with that he moved down and became a real part of our church family. He prayed through to wonderful victory again and again, but it is doubtful that he ever went far enough to find complete freedom from inward sin as is promised in God's Word. If so, he didn't keep everything on the altar and over the past several years his times of living in good victory grew shorter and farther between and his periods of defeat grew longer and more conspicuous.

Some time ago I wrote him a letter and warned him in no uncertainties that I was very troubled over this state of spiritual poverty which was getting worse instead of better. Everyone else in the church was burdened for him also. He had become a real part of our church, even becoming a board member. Other men who had been released from prison were looking up to him as an example, and he was good with them, too. But now we could see that he was drifting further and further into a very substandard state of Christian living.

We came into a revival in the church and we were burdened that there was so little move on his part. One night he did come to the altar but it seemed there was little real progress and worse yet, it seemed he was somewhat content that it be that way.

Then one night he confessed that he had become way too involved with a woman at his place of employment. We gathered around him and did all we knew to do to convince him that he was playing with fire and would lose his soul. He agreed and we had hope for a very short while, but then we realized he was not breaking off with her, and finally began spending his nights with her. He told our pastor that he knew he was dangling his soul over hell, but that when he was with her, he forgot about it. And so in the full light of how serious a thing he was doing he made the choice to go on gratifying his selfish desires no matter that hell could be his at any moment. He told the pastor that he needed to hurry and make out his will so that his daughter would get what he had, because he was living under the fear that God might strike him dead at any moment.

He sent a text message to various ones in the church, which said in essence that he had made a deliberate choice in spite of an eternity in hell and would not be responding to calls or texts. For all the time he had been struggling spiritually, he battled with his state. He had been married years before and had been divorced before going into prison. His wife lives only a few miles from him, but there is no reconciliation between them. This fact and the fact that he, in order to be true to God's Word, could not have another wife, would agitate him until he would allow bitterness toward her and even God. Toward the end of this he even allowed downright hatred toward her to possess him.

He has been warned by God and man. He has chosen to gratify a selfish desire that will undoubtedly soon turn into a tragedy. By then, Satan will be laughing soundly that he has him trapped out there, too far to return. He gave up the smile of God, a good Christian family, friends that loved and cared for him, and worst of all, heaven. He knows that; he is well aware of it. Why, why, then did he do it?

This is exactly why God wants me to write this sad story, which has been like a death in the family to our church. Friends, God is not one bit too demanding when He gives the commandment, "Be ye holy, for I am holy! ...Be filled with the Spirit!" We have seen played out in living drama that to leave one little closet within our heart which is not filled with the Spirit is to leave a key for Satan to enter. This dear man a few years ago would drive miles and miles in his employment listening to sermons from the good old firebrands of a few years ago. When he saw something that would tempt him, he would literally yell out loud in his truck, "Hell fire!" He declared, and meant it, that it was settled to go God's way forever. But he did not get rid of some "little" seed of inward sin.

He has disappointed his church and church family; he has disappointed the other men who have looked to him as an example; he has disappointed God! Our church family is shaking their heads in disbelief. They cannot fathom the utter insanity of such a choice, but such is the capability of the uncrucified human heart! There is only one safeguard against the backsliding capability of the carnal heart, and that is, "Be filled with the Spirit!" And that is not a one-time filling, but a continual flow of divine grace through a clean vessel. Have we not been told for years by faithful witnesses that it is holiness or hell? Please help us pray that this dear soul will yet turn from his folly and come back. He has come to church a few times since, but his countenance is dark, and how could it be otherwise when he still wants to have God, but is clinging to what God hates?

I feel I must take this a step farther. The Scripture warns us that "When the unclean spirit is gone out of a man, he walketh through dry places, seeking rest, and findeth none. Then he saith, I will return into my house from whence I came out; and when he is come, he findeth it empty, swept, and garnished. Then goeth he, and taketh with himself seven other spirits more wicked than himself, and they enter in and dwell there: and the last state of that man is worse than the first."

It is wonderful when the unclean spirit is gone out of a man, but what a tragedy when, after walking through a dry place, he returns to the house from whence he came. This is what happens to one after another of men who have lived an outwardly sinful life. Many of them get gloriously delivered from their awful lifestyles, but if they cool off in their love for Jesus, they go back to their old house. But what about the multitudes who sit in our holiness churches Sunday after Sunday and simply live and flow with the holiness culture; then one day are gloriously awakened and press through to wonderful victory, but then cool off and go back to simply living the holiness culture? Is there really a difference as far as God sees them from the man who goes back to the house he came from?

I have not easily written about a brother we have loved so much. Oh, how our hearts long that he will yet catch himself and renounce the choice he has made. But we are commanded in Scripture, "Them that sin rebuke before all, that others also may fear." If he does truly come back in Blood-honoring repentance, he will not find fault with this open story of how easily Satan can get his key into a lock not fully surrendered to God. It will simply be a part of that "yea, what indignation... yea, what revenge" marks of a truly repentant heart. Please help us pray for him, but please take warning. Not one of us are in heaven yet, and Satan is looking fervently for any back closet in you or me that does not stay "filled with the Spirit!"

As we enter another year of such over-extended mercy, we are reminded by Peter that "The Lord is not slack concerning his promise, as some men count slackness; but is longsuffering to us-ward, not willing that any should perish, but that all should come to repentance." To look around at the condition of this sin-rotted world is to wonder beyond measure why God delays judgment; but Peter answers that— He is "not willing that any should perish!" Indeed, what *longsuffering!* Now, if God, of whom it is said, "Thou art of purer eyes than to behold evil, and canst not look on iniquity," can be of such *longsuffering* as to delay His coming and His judgment, then what shall you and I do about that during this year of His extended mercy? Is there anything in this entire present world more important that being utterly in harmony with Him; than being laborers together in the yoke with Him? Oh, God, we hear the words of the old missionary hymn, "Master, forgive, and inspire us anew; Banish our worldliness; help us to ever live with eternity's values in view!"

Now, one more request: Will you please pray that the chaplain will live closer to the heart of Jesus this year than ever before? I am praying for that in all sincerity.

With love to each of you,

William Cawman

✝✝✝

February 1, 2018

THE VERY NEXT BEST thing to a clear relationship with God is watching another soul taking the path that leads to Him. The Scripture clearly says that "if we walk in the light, as he is in the light, we have fellowship one with another, and the blood of Jesus Christ his Son cleanseth us from all sin." Did you notice the very first effect of walking in the Light? "We have fellowship one with another." The moment a soul begins walking in the Light, there is a bond of fellowship with the redeemed that does not even remotely exist between professors of the highest standing who have ceased walking in the Light.

And so, several months ago I told you of a young Hispanic man who had come to my office with such a burden and hunger that he could not leave the way he was. Right there as I prayed a prayer he did not know how to pray, Jesus came into him so powerfully that when I asked him if He had come in, he said, "He came all over me!"

Ever since then, he has been walking in the Light. He came in at ground zero. The Bible was all new to him. The Christian walk was all new to him, and he would come in and ask about the things he was learning or going through and, just like a little bird with mouth wide open, take every bit of advice with a great big smile.

He is leaving in another week and so wanted to have a visit again before leaving. As I talked with him and prayed with him he said, "Chaplain, whenever I sit and listen to you I feel so clean!" We spoke of his finding a body of believers that would help him to live a clean, pure life, and that is what he wants, but northern New Jersey is a dry and barren land as far as anything I know about it. Please do pray for him. I told him he could write to me at the prison and then I could give him a contact address to keep in touch and he just beamed. That is what he wants and I trust nothing will derail him.

Later the following week he felt he should give his testimony in class. I invited him to do so and with great fear and trembling he stood before the class for the first time in his life to ever do such a thing. He began to tell his life's story and then how he had finally been won through the warm invitations of the Bible to let Jesus come into his heart. God anointed his testimony remarkably, and when he finished the whole classroom was on their feet waiting their turn to hug him. It created an atmosphere that lingered with a divine aroma throughout the whole class time that followed.

Won't it be wonderfully blessed when at last all sin has been purged from God's universe and every being that you meet will be filled with the anointing and presence of God? You do realize, don't you, that Jesus' promise is that the Holy Spirit will abide with us forever!? Forever includes all of eternity! How could we ever bear the thought of being one moment without Him? "Unto you therefore which believe, He is precious!"

Please continue to pray for the oversight from our state capital when it comes to religious affairs in prison. The new governor has already dismissed one figure that was giving us many devious orders. Now the one directly under them needs to go also, but we are not sure if that will happen just as we are not sure who will replace the one dismissed. Whenever I am tempted toward anxiety in this area, I have to remind myself that God opened this door, and as long as He sees fit it will stay open, regardless of antichrist orders from government officials. Notwithstanding this, please do pray.

Numbers of times I have told you of a man who for several years has been such a blessing to everyone around him. He lives a genuine life of holiness and literally beams the love of

Jesus everywhere he goes. He is the one who came into my office one day and said, "Chaplain, I've got a problem." I said, "Well, you sure look like it!" "Oh yes," he said, "my face hurts from smiling so much." I have his written testimony and I think I should share it with you. I am going to type it just as written, with no corrections.

> My name is M—— and I am fifty-eight years old. I am serving a Twenty-five year sentence for Aggravated Manslaughter. Jesus Christ is the Savior, and Lord of my Life, let me tell you how I got here.
> As a child growing up I had to be and act older then I was. I never had a childhood, I was always around my father. Who was not a very nice man. He taught me what he knew about being a man, a work ethic, stand on your own two feet, you don't take no mess from anyone. He never taught me about love though and I could not give something I did not have my self. I joined the Military to get away from home. That is where I was introduced to drugs. After the Military I got married to a beautiful Christian woman. She believed more in me then I did myself. We had a good marriage, we had two kids, I started my own Trucking Company, and a beautiful home and all the toys you could think of, but through it all I still had a drug problem. Trucking brought money, money brought better drugs, drugs brought the women and that started my down fall. Because I had no self-control, very low self-esteem and because I lied to myself, I lost everything. My company, my wife and family, my home, my self-respect, and my drug addiction caused me to murder two men. I murdered one man in February and one in March. I was on the run for three months. When the police caught up with me in North Carolina I was arrested. After arresting me they put me in a room all by my self. While in the room planning my lie, I heard a voice that said, "Tell the truth and the truth will set you free." I never in my life served God so I knew nothing about Him. I knew there was a God and I wanted nothing really to do with Him. I would go to Church with my

wife, I knew she believed but it was not for me. So I confessed to my crimes, I told them everything. After my confession, I heard that voice again and it said, "Life as you know it will never be the same." Man was He right. Waiting for extradition to New Jersey from county jail in North Carolina, a little old man came on the tier and was talking to someone else about Christ. That voice once again said, "That is what you need."

June 28, 1998 I accepted Jesus Christ into my life as my personal Savior and Lord. I was filled with the Holy Spirit in September of that same year. One day I told God that if You are real I need to know for sure. If You are truly God answer these four prayers for me and I will serve You for the rest of my life. He answered all of them. Some I just knew would be impossible, but He did them. No one can tell me that God is not real. I need no more proof. God has kept me every since that day and all He requires of me is to be obedient, to love Him and my neighbor as myself. To spread the good news of His Kingdom. To believe in His son, Jesus Christ and accept what He says about Himself and me. Who I am in Him. God has been good to me and I know I am blessed. My only regret is that I did not come to this saving knowledge sooner. God has a plan for us all and I am now on the road He predestine for me. There is not a day that goes by were I don't thank God for all He has done and going to do in the future. God is still in the blessing and miracle working business. May every one who reads this be always bless by God. God truly is Great. To God be the Praise.!!! For a day in your courts is better than a thousand. I would rather be a doorkeeper in the house of my God, Than dwell in the tents of the wicked. Psalm 84:10

I've been walking with the Lord for 12 years in Trenton State Prison and two years in county jail. In 2012 I was transferred to Southwoods State Prison and Chaplain Cawman taught me the doctrine of Holiness. I went on to experience the second work of grace and my heart has been cleansed from all anger, malice, hatred, lust and the works of the devil. Now Jesus has preeminence in my life. He sits on the throne of my heart. Daily

I'm lead by the Holy Spirit. I now have the power to choose life. Sin no longer has dominion or power over me. My Christian walk is my life.

I walk circumspectly, in the Spirit, making the most of every opportunity the Lord gives me to Worship, Praise and serve Him. To serve others in the beauty of Holiness. I walk in the light as He is in the light. I walk in love because God is love. When Jesus saved me, He placed a responsibility on me. I now have an obligation, a duty to God, my family, the lost, the church, and to myself to live and walk a life of Holiness. There is not a day that goes by that I don't thank the Lord for all He has done and is doing in my life. I am so thankful. This is from a man who's heart has truly been changed. In Jesus precious name. Amen. Bless your heart.

The other day I had invited both he and another man with the same Blood-bought victory to come together into my office. After a few moments together I felt much like I was in a glorious camp meeting service. Never will anyone convince me that there is a circumstance of life too great for holiness to work. I have seen the living proof of the keeping power of the Blood of Jesus, and never can I doubt it.

Now, just this morning I had just about the opposite experience. Of course, as you can well imagine, we have one of everybody here. And so while I was visiting with several men, I saw an email pop up from my supervisor asking that I visit with a certain inmate who had been turning in requests saying that he couldn't get to see a chaplain. I called him down between visits and asked him what it was that he needed to see the chaplain about. He complained that every time he sends a request to enter a Christian service they classify him as a Protestant. He said that he is a Christian, but not a specific one and he doesn't want to be classified as Protestant. I explained to him that the term was not a classification but just a distinguishing from Roman Catholicism, which he declared he positively, was not. But he still didn't want to be called a

Protestant, so I suggested that he was protesting Protestantism. Profitable visit, indeed!

In love,

William Cawman

March 1, 2018

DID YOU KNOW THAT the Precious Blood of Jesus that was shed to take away all sin is still doing just that every single day? Somewhere, among the seven billion-plus souls that He died to save, there are still those responding to the wooing of the Holy Spirit and the Blood is being applied. If that were not so, Jesus would return for His Bride.

Every little bit I find someone locked down in prison who is joining that number. It makes me realize with joy and gratitude over and over that the Holy Spirit is still preparing a Bride for Christ. Just two or three days ago I had received a request for a visit from a man who had just arrived in the prison. He is a native of Colombia, but grew up in this country and is very well spoken in his English. He immediately told me with a charming smile on his face that prison had saved his life. He was spiraling downward out of control in gambling and drink, but he is now thanking God for rescuing him by allowing him to be sent to prison. He feels definitely that God has forgiven him and lives within him.

We had a good visit together after which I enrolled him in several classes and services and then gave him two very good books to read. I will visit with him again soon, for I do believe he is genuinely changed.

Then the same day I visited for the first time with another man who is from Puerto Rico. He, too, seems to give good evidence that he has been recently saved and is enjoying his walk with God. Will you help us pray that many more will stop resisting the Holy Spirit and let Him do what the Father sent Him into the world to accomplish?

The dear brother who was a third-generation Mormon has written another precious letter just before his release from the NJ prison system. He still doesn't know whether he will have to serve time in another state, but what a changed man he is from when I first met him however many years ago. He is living proof that a hungry soul will find God to be just as hungry for them. His letters are so genuine and precious that I must share some of the latest one with you.

My Dear Brother in Christ, William Cawman,

Thank you for your encouraging letter of January 20, 2018... Thank you for your inspired encouragement in the Lord. One Scripture the Lord has allowed me to claim and declare is Joshua 1:9, "Have I not commanded thee? Be strong and of good courage; be not afraid, neither be thou dismayed: for the LORD thy God is with thee withersoever thou goest."

I have been, and will be, going to some "withersoever" places that most people wouldn't think about. The Lord has shown me that the withersoever in Joshua carries weight. Psalm 139 declares the extent of it. It has similar power to the "whosoever" in John 3:16. Both words declare the Lord's power and faithfulness. I know He is not capable of forsaking me, because He cannot lie. I am beyond doubt now that God is with me, not of myself, but because God has declared it so to me, in His love and mercy.

Thank you for the words to the hymn; and for including me in the sing-a-long of that moment when Mrs. Cawman was playing it at the piano. That's a family moment we share now. What a precious hymn.

Lately, I find myself humming or whispering "All the Way My Savior Leads Me." It includes: "...for I know what ere befall me, Jesus doeth all things well!" I know He will use what He does for me as a testimony to His power and goodness.

He has full power over my life. He's added an apostrophe that I won't take back: I am God's. [note: if you remember several years ago, he wrote to me and said that behind my back he calls me an "apostrophetic." He says that I added an apostrophe to his life and changed it from what he was taught as a Mormon, viz. "We are gods," versus "We are God's."] He can get glory from my life, death, and/or anything He chooses to do with me. And I'll worship Him in the beauty of holiness while He's at work doing it. I know that He's fully done a work in me, and is doing something amazing continually. I can't wait to see what it is. The full extent of it isn't even for this life (this life pales by comparison with what He's up to). We hear people talk about the Lord being the center of their lives, but not so much about who gets displaced by that—we do. If He's on the throne, I'm not. The selfishness of me at the center is destroyed by Him. His plan is unfolding and I'm cooperating. He aligns me with Him .

The Lord hasn't told me my earthly end, but He prophesied to Peter that the death by which he would glorify God would be crucifixion, then He said, "Come and follow me." No matter what God does, my life is His, and He will be glorified by it. This life will be full of tribulation, whether bond or free. But I'm of good cheer; He's overcome the world...

Thank you for your precious admonition to "keep my eyes on Jesus and my knees upon the ground." That is the prayer that I most request of you and Mrs. Cawman, that the Lord blesses me to do just that, and that He gives me the grace to do exactly that, at **all** times and in **all** places. Thank you so much for your loving care, your Christ-likeness, and for pointing me constantly to Him.

In Faithful Christian Love, —— Ps 73:23-24

I'm so happy to tell you that the volunteers who fill in so faithfully when I am gone in meetings get such a good report when I return. The men dearly love every one of them and they do not hesitate to tell me how much they appreciate them. While I know it sometimes places a heavy load on the volunteers, it does the men so much good. Hearing the wonderful way of holiness taught from more than one source is very effective.

I look back now as a twenty-year anniversary comes up for my start in laboring here in this prison and see more clearly than ever before the wisdom and definite leading hand of God in how He ordained it all. Let me share a bit of it with you. After volunteering for a year and a half I thought surely it would be God's opportunity when a position for chaplain supervisor came up. I applied, but another man was taken. He made a racial remark after three months in his position and was walked out on the spot. The position was posted again, and again I applied. Another man was taken.

Now that man is still my supervisor and for eighteen years we have worked together without a single conflict. He and I are both aware of our differences in theology, but we do not let the inmates play on it, nor do we argue with each other. He loves me very dearly and would do nothing to hinder the work that I and our church volunteers are doing. But I could never do all that he does with a clear conscience. I could not plan and make provision for false cults and religions to have a voice, but of course a State institution cannot deny them their rights. Had I been chosen for that position by now I would, just as he is, be totally swamped with legal and nonsensical concerns from all the forms of religion that have descended upon us. He is tempted often to resign or to retire, but he tells me that our church is the only reason he stays there and bucks the downward current.

When first I started ministering in the prison we had Muslim, Catholic, and Protestant services. Now we have those plus Rastafarianism, Buddhism, Native American, Santaria, Wiccan, Jehovah's Witness, Seventh Day Adventist, Odin, Heathenism, Jewish, and I may have missed one or two. My supervisor is responsible to see that each has a slot and the necessary equipment to practice their "faith."

And then there are constantly new faiths being invented by those dwelling within our barriers. One man declared himself to be a "Christian Hebrew." He wanted to get kosher trays for his meals. When my supervisor asked him what a Christian

Hebrew was, he said he was one like Paul. My supervisor told him that Paul ate meat. "Well no, see, I'm a Christian Hebrew."

And then there was the fine-looking specimen of humanity that entered my office with the handsome prefix of "Prophet..." Asking what I could do for him, he wasn't sure there was anything, for he was already a prophet. I asked him who ordained him a prophet and he said that a clergyman in Philadelphia had so done but that he could not remember his name. I asked how long he had been in prison and he had been in and out for twenty-some years. His gift, so he recalled, had been discovered several years back. I asked if he wanted to join any Bible study groups or classes, but he did not as he did not want to butt heads with any other Bible teacher, as he was already a prophet himself. I recommended that perhaps he lay his gift to rest for the time he was in prison and then see where it would fit after he was released. He concurred. At that point I felt clear to terminate the visit and suggested we do so. As he left he shook my hand, "In prison records my name is ―― ――, but my real name is Prophet Adoniah."

Now I thank God that I have these encounters but once in a while; my supervisor has them on a daily basis. So do you see why I thank God after twenty years that He opened a door whereby the State of New Jersey pays for my time spent there, but they have no strings on me? That is why I am free to be gone whenever in meetings wherever. I find it a definite blessing to have a split ministry, but I also feel obligated, since God opened this door, to make the ministry in the prison a priority over all others, except for my family.

Now, that was an awful lot about me, wasn't it? I apologize and will try to let that suffice for the sake of a twenty-year anniversary speech.

My wife loves to go in with me on Friday nights for Bible study and for any Sunday night services. She has been teaching the men some new choruses and they love it. This past Friday night we sang for them the old simple song, "The Old Ship Zion," and then asked them to stand and sing it with us and shake hands with someone and invite them on board. My, did they ever have a good time so doing. It appeared that one man wanted to invite them all.

Then we opened the study on "Psalms of Thanksgiving," and began to try to incite them to rise above the thanklessness of our present society. We discussed the glorious repercussions of praising and giving thanks instead of grumbling and finding fault, and suggested that if we could see our national news media do so, we could see a revival overnight! Shall we pray that it will happen?

Thank you, each praying one of you. With love,

William Cawman

6
EXTRA BLESSINGS

April 1, 2018

THIS PAST MONTH HELD for my wife and me a lifetime treasure. We had the privilege of touring the Holy Land. And we did not consider it a vacation, but rather a spiritual journey, and it was just that. We will never read the accounts of the Sacred Word of God the same again. We visited Caesarea by the Sea; Mt. Carmel where Elijah's God sent down fire from heaven; Nazareth; the Mount of Beatitudes; Capernaum; Bethlehem; the site of Jesus casting a legion of demons out into the swine; the Golan Heights—looking over into Syria and Lebanon; journeyed on down the Jordan River into the Judean wilderness; the Wilderness of Engedi where David and his men hid from Saul; Masada where the last remnant of Jews killed themselves in AD 73 rather than fall victims to Titus and the Romans; Qumran where the Dead Sea Scrolls were found; Jericho and the Mount of Temptation; and then spent several days in Jerusalem and the Mount of Olives and Gethsemane.

We were baptized in the Jordan River and ate our fill of olives and dates. But after all of that precious territory, the highlight of the trip was the last day, when we visited Golgotha and the tomb.

Now there is something we learned from that last day that you need to know, just in case you do not as yet. As we stood beholding the place where our Savior was crucified, our guide explained just where and how it took place, and then he said, "Now we are going a short way away to see the tomb where He was laid." Then raising his voice and his excitement level he said, "*But He is not there! He is risen! He is alive!* Have you talked to Him this morning? Are your sins washed away in His blood?" Our hearts were thrilled as we listened to the pure Gospel message being proclaimed right in front of the empty tomb. And thank God, this Easter He is still alive! Have you talked to Him this morning?

When we got back to the prison, we took the men for a picture tour and told them where we had been and what all we had seen. They were thrilled with the report and enjoyed it all immensely. They were so happy to hear that someone they know had been there and seen those things.

Today I was responding to a written request from a man I had not seen before. It went somewhat like this: "Well, Chaplain, when I wrote the request I was going through some real trials of my faith with my cellmate and the men around me, but I'm doing better now."

I asked a few questions and he told me that he has never been married at the age of fifty-one, but that he has a fiancé he wants to marry and she lives in Missouri. He wanted to move there but cannot until he is married to her as he is under the Megan Law. He has a brother that he has lost track of and a sister who he has little contact with, so he is almost alone in the world.

I then asked him if he had ever had a time in his life when he really repented of his sins and obtained conscious knowledge that God had forgiven him and made him a new creature. He dubiously replied that he thought so, and that he reads about three chapters in the New Testament each morning and then about five Psalms at noon and then in the evening about three chapters from the Old Testament. I told him that was good, but asked if he really has a living relationship with God. He replied, "I'm working on that part of it now."

I tried to clarify what I was saying to him and asked him again if he knew what I was talking about. He again looked anything but certain as he said he believed so and was working on it. I tried to tell him that such a relationship was not worked into by our own efforts but received by real repentance and praying to God to impart it to us. "Yes, I am working on that part of it now."

Oh, the blindness of the sinful heart! It is appalling beyond description! And so many are caught in it and are so cheated out of what Jesus died to give to them. What pain the heart of Jesus must feel as He looks upon a world of such lost souls! "When the living well is so nearby; oh, why will ye die?"

My supervisor continues to hold the fort amid increasing opposition from every angle. Certainly the devil does not like what God is doing here in the prison. It takes little more than complete blindness to see that the Muslim tide and strength is growing every day, while Christianity is being pushed into more and more of a corner. It is absolutely unbelievable the way the popularity and support of the Muslim chaplain is growing while he continues to act more like the devil all the time. One cannot look for very long at the surrounding circumstances without losing heart. But again and again I look up and remind God that this was His idea, and that there are too many good Christian men for God to forsake the work of His own hands or turn things over to the Muslims.

I am happy to report to you that whatever the level of my supervisor's relationship to and walk with God, he admirably steers his course according to the teaching of God's Word and the example of Jesus. The worse our Muslim chaplain gets, the more he treats him with tenderness and love. Not one ounce of it is given back in return.

I am going to do something that I have mostly refrained

from doing, and that is to report on men after they are released from prison; but we have one who is really in need of your prayers. He was released several months ago, and immediately began attending and enjoying our church. He is a blessing indeed to us all. He loves us and we love him. But during his sinful years he lifted a lot of weights and now his body is really suffering the consequences. He waited until he was out of prison to have his worn-out knees replaced, and now a couple of months later the right knee is still giving him intense pain and suffering. It seems that everything that could go wrong has gone wrong, and he still has the other one to have taken care of. Then he knew for a long time before his release that he had something wrong in his lung, but waited until he got out and now they find a large mass on his lung. As yet it is not clear just what it is, but naturally, all this is not easy for him.

Thank God, he is keeping the victory spiritually, and for that we all feel blessed, but he does need prayer and would be so thankful for it. We remind him that no doubt he would have had the same trials without God, but what a difference! He knows that and is keeping it settled to be true.

We are so thankful for the several volunteers from our church who fill in for us when out in meetings. Every one of them are a great blessing to the men, and it thrills my heart to hear the men say how much they love them and how much they are getting from them. There have been a few men lately who have a lust to teach instead of learn. They are deeply immersed in a spurious religion and consequently the Spirit of Christ does not come forth from them. The volunteers have been confronted by them, and God has definitely anointed them with grace and wisdom. There is something obnoxiously aggressive about false doctrines—but listen to this:

While we were in Israel, the tour took us to Caesarea Philippi, north of the Sea of Galilee and almost up to Mt. Herman. Near to the town of Caesarea Philippi, there are ruins of an area called "Pan," a series of temples carved out of the mountain to the Greek gods. The main one of these is labeled "The Gates of Hell." Do you remember reading this? "When Jesus came into the coasts of Caesarea Philippi, he asked his disciples, saying, Whom do men say that I the Son of man am? And they said, Some say that thou art John the Baptist: some, Elias; and others, Jeremias, or one of the prophets. He saith unto them, But whom say ye that I am? And Simon Peter answered and said, Thou art the Christ, the Son of the living God. And Jesus answered and said unto him, Blessed art thou, Simon Barjona: for flesh and blood hath not revealed it unto thee, but my Father which is in heaven. And I say also unto thee, That thou art Peter, and upon this rock I will build my church; and the gates of hell shall not prevail against it."

Now we know that Peter was not that rock! Jesus was saying that He would build His church on divine revelation and that the gates of hell (that is, every false god and every false religion) shall not prevail against it. He was not mainly referring to the hell we know as the tragic abode of the wicked dead as well as the devil and his angels. Jesus was very near what they all knew was called the gates of hell, meaning the Greek gods, or for that matter any false god. I took a whole new realm of courage from that. God is working His genuine work through the Holy Spirit among men in the prison. They are surrounded by false religions, some of which go under the name of Christianity. But Jesus promised that those false religions will not prevail against divine revelation! Hallelujah! That gives me courage to boldly go on preaching and teaching the truth, right in the very presence of every enemy of that truth. I say with confident certainty that anything that slips the least bit short of true heart holiness— which destroys every last fiber of the carnal mind, leaving the soul pure and holy— is going to fall of its own accord sooner or later. It does not even make sense. "Truth, crushed to earth, will rise again; the eternal years of God are hers. But error, wounded, writhes in pain; and dies among its worshippers."

And so, dear praying friends, "His truth is marching on…"

and that even in the face of the gates of hell! We do not have to argue our point to defend truth, for truth is inherently saturated with its own defense.

Now the Scripture says that the path of the just is as the shining light, that shineth more and more unto the perfect day. I know it is not my imagination that a couple of men who have for some time been living without a reproach the beautiful life of holiness right in prison, are glowing more and more in their countenance. Is that to be wondered at when they are walking that pathway that is as the shining light? Oh God, keep them true and keep them shining!

I am writing this just the night before Good Friday, because I need to get it printed, but we are praying that as a group of us go into the prison on Good Friday evening for four services with four different groups, the Blood of Jesus that flowed from His pierced side on that Friday many years ago will be applied to some needy souls. Oh, that the Holy Spirit could return back to the side of Jesus after those Good Friday services and report, "I have given unto them the words which thou gavest me; and they have received them, and have known surely that I came out from thee, and they have believed that thou didst send me." Please help us pray for fresh outpourings of God's Holy Spirit in prison.

With love and appreciation,

W Cawman

May 1, 2018

EVERY ONCE IN A while, I say to the men in prison at the opening of a weekly class, "We are now one week closer to wherever we are going. Are you sure that you know where that is?" Do you? Do I? What could possibly be a more important question? Multitudes, right on the brink of eternity, are deceived as to where that is. Oh God, save us from such a fate!

The Holy Spirit has again been at work this month preparing all who will let Him to be a part of that glorious Bride of Christ. When man has in mind to produce a trophy for some earthly honor, he scours the woods for an exquisite walnut burl from which he can obtain a rare grain of polished beauty. He then searches for the finest of gold and precious stones and fits it all together into a masterpiece of eye-catching splendor. When God looks for another gem to add to the crown of His own Precious Son, He picks up a filthy, wretched, deformed, and worthless lump of Satan-wrecked humanity and then washes the whole mess in the precious Blood of Jesus, and then is not ashamed to make him a part of that spotless Bride so soon to be presented. All hail! Blood of Jesus!

Just the other day a young Muslim officer from our prison committed suicide. To any of the staff who desired to attend the funeral, a message was sent out that they could only appear in very strict dress code. If a man, they were to have dress shirt and trousers, and if a woman, she was to have either a pantsuit or a floor length dress, which was not to be transparent. She was to have long sleeves and a high neckline and covered feet. Was this the funeral of a holiness saint? No, it was for the funeral of a Muslim who had committed suicide!

The above shows ever so dramatically that there is no reproach to any brand of religion at all, save to the Cross of Jesus Christ, the Savior of the world. How many who profess to be His are at least in a measure ashamed of any modesty of dress that His Word requires. Even those who truly are His will feel at times the reproach of being such. Why?

Because we are surrounded by the spirit of anti-Christ; not anti any other at all.

So be it for now! Our day is coming and that very soon, when in glorious triumph over all the reproach and all the unpopularity and all the persecutions of every other god, the Church of Jesus Christ will rise to be forever with her Lord! Are you one of His? Rejoice! As we see and feel the advance of pressures never felt before from every source imaginable and unimaginable, remember that our Jesus told us ahead of time this would come, and He said that when these things begin to come to pass, then look up, and lift up your heads, for your redemption draweth nigh.

But now let me turn from this side of things to those things that God is doing in spite of these tidal waves of evil. This month we had a week of revival services in our local church and our evangelist went in with us for the weekly classes and Bible study. It was rewarding to watch and feel the men (that is, those of them who are walking in the Light) responding to truth the same way my own heart does. I think it was every service, or at least all but one, that after arriving before the men, God redirected the evangelist to an area of truth he was not planning on giving. Every time it was just what they needed, too! Thank God for anointed truth.

This past Friday evening I did something I had never tried before and will think twice about doing it that way again, although it was somewhat amusing. A man who has been faithfully attending the Bible studies for several years came to me at the opening of the study and told me that he was suffering a lot from a herniated disk in his lower back. Actually, it is a wonder that all of them aren't, as you would understand if you could see the two-and-one-half-inch rubber covered mattress on a sheet of steel that comprises their "Posturepedic" for the night. I told him we would have special prayer for him.

After the study had opened, I told the men about him and that according to Scripture we should gather the elders together and anoint and pray for him. I told them about C. T. Studd, the missionary to Africa who was traveling through the heart of Africa with his future son-in-law, Norman Grubb. Studd became very ill, so ill that he thought he would die. He called in Norman and quoted this same Scripture from James. Then he said, "Now the closest thing I can come up with for an elder is you, a man half my age; and the closest thing we can find for oil is that gallon of kerosene over there, but we cannot afford to be narrow minded just now, so let's get on with it." He arose the next day and went on his journey.

So then I told the men that it just so happened that my wife and I had been distributing communion elements to the chapels for Sunday following and that I had some of them there with me. I called the sufferer up to the front and several willing brethren (we did not examine their eldership credentials) came to pray with him. As I prayed I "anointed" him with the contents of the communion cup and instantly realized (I must confess with amusement) that I had chosen a poor substitute for anointing oil. The red juice trickled down over his face just like streaks of blood. My wife found a tissue to rectify the situation before the chance of an alarm being set off over a bloody face in a Bible study! Spur of the moment decisions as to a course of action are often viewed in better light by what has been labeled "hind sight!"

One of our good sanctified brethren who has been with us for years, recently maxed out and went to his family in North Carolina. I just received a very good letter from him expressing how thankful he was for the ones from our church and for having been shown the way of holiness. He is doing well and I believe by the way he so steadily walked with the Lord while here, he will continue to do so. Please pray for him that God can use him as a shining witness to heart holiness where he is. He is one who completed the whole four-year course that has been taught here for the past seven years. Just now there is only one student left and he will be finished before another class time comes, so we may skip this year as far as the in-house classes go. Please pray that if there are others who are ready for this, God will open our eyes to them.

In one of the classes this past week one of the other men, who has also finished the four-year course, was listening to our evangelist. Suddenly he opened up and told the class that just that day God had showed him something he did not know was still in his heart. He came to the breaking point with his cellmate and felt something arise within him that wanted to kill him. We could all see that he was visibly moved and shocked by what he found still remaining in him. I had always had questions as to whether he had gone far enough, but he was a firm supporter of the doctrine and experience and understood it well in his head.

As soon as I could get a one-on-one with him, I followed it up and told him that God only revealed such things in us in order that we would cry out to Him for deliverance from it. He readily assented and told me that he had gone from that class and laid himself out before God in heart-searching prayer the rest of the day until he felt assured that God had cleansed it out of his heart.

He then told me the particulars of it. His cellmate, a younger man than himself, was being very loud and disturbing, and on top of it, very dirty and unkempt. The day after God had dealt with him, his cellmate was coming in the door very noisily and God spoke to him and said, "Now you just talk to him nicely about it." His first thought was that it would open a confrontation, but he felt it was of the Lord, so he said, "We need to talk." He calmly addressed his grievances with the man and immediately the younger man said, "Oh, I'm sorry. I didn't know I was bothering you. Why didn't you talk to me sooner?" "Because it would not have come out right before now." And so, God laid His hand on the whole situation and calmed the storm, but not until after he had worked a cure in the first man. You see, Jesus was well able to stand in the little boat and rebuke the winds and the waves, but not until He had first rebuked His disciples for their little faith.

My wife and I have been teaching the men some new choruses in the Friday night Bible studies and they are really enjoying them. We take a small keyboard in so that they can get the tunes faster and we are being very selective in our choice of them so as to get some spiritual food into them. We have not yet chosen the one that exalts apple red happiness and popcorn cheerfulness, although a touch of that would help at times. After getting into the lessons there is one man in particular that my wife feels could have less to say; however, it must be always remembered that a man who has nothing to say is seldom happy until he says it. Perhaps such persons are what the Scripture refers to in the admonition to be patient toward all men.

The other night I asked the men in two of the Bible studies if they really knew what it was to have communion with God in prayer. I said I wasn't talking about just saying words or a form or a list of prayer requests, but was asking if they know down deep inside that they are in contact with God when in prayer. Among the ones who raised their hands there were some shining expressions and facial certainties that spoke very loudly. Thank God for them. Please help us pray that there will be many more who will genuinely become partakers of the divine nature. Oh, the difference between a self-directed monologue and a Spirit-led dialogue. How well I remember the glorious change from one to the other!

Last Sunday night my wife and I were in the second of two services and an elderly man asked that we sing a certain song in the hymnal. Neither my wife or I knew it and while we were hesitating, he came up in his wheelchair and asked if he could play it for us. He did an excellent job and we learned a very good new song!

In Him,

William Cawman

June 1, 2018

WHAT A FULL AND different month this has been! But then, most of my months are different I guess, so what is new about that? On Friday evening, May 18, my wife and I had two Bible studies in the prison and one of the men gave the following testimony. He had been in the food line two days before, and a Muslim was just ahead of him with his meal on his tray, was trying to balance a cup of hot water besides to make some more food in his cell. There was not room on his tray and he was having trouble balancing it, so the Christian man offered to carry it on his tray and stop by his cell with it. The man looked at him and said, "Are you sure?"

"Of course!"

They started for the man's cell and he said, "Are you a Christian or something?"

"Yes, I am. I love Jesus and everything He created, so I love you too." The Muslim looked at him and said, "We need to talk some more about this."

The next day he came to him again and said, "Do you remember what you said to me yesterday?"

"I'm not sure, as I talk to a lot of people."

"About you being a Christian and loving me?"

"Oh yes, I do."

"Can we talk some more about that? I never heard that before and something's different about it."

Please pray for this man, that he will not only hear, but walk in the Light.

After the second study we bid the men farewell, asking for their special interest in prayer for the pastors' conference in Malawi from May 25 through 30. They are deeply a part of the mission in Africa in their prayers and interest. We then left early Monday morning to fly out of the DC airport for Addis Ababa, Ethiopia, and then on to Lilongwe, Malawi. Then after a five-hour drive from Lilongwe to the town of Mangochi we dropped wearily into bed and were soon asleep, even though it was rather different from New Jersey frogs to have a hippopotamus lullaby for the sendoff.

The following day we did errands and gathered supplies for the conference, as well as the great grand opening ceremony of the long-awaited clinic in Jahle. Many of you have followed the progress and sometimes the distressing lack of progress on the opening of a clinic out in the bush where our daughter had first opened a village church. While waiting for all of the government documents and inspections and so much other red tape and tape of every other color, the news was spreading about the newly coming clinic. On the morning of the grand opening, it appeared that the whole countryside turned out for the event. Several leaders of the Presbytery that are supplying the operation of it from now on were there. Fifty-three village chiefs were there (many of them are Muslims), including one who had at first opposed our daughter's mission there and had chased her out of his village. He was loudly and conspicuously supportive. A government official was there who in his speech told the huge crowd of hundreds that this new clinic would be looking after the physical needs of seventeen thousand people in the twenty some villages around there. Previously many were poorly looked after and many died for lack of medical aid.

Along with many speeches in the hot sun which lasted about three hours, they sang songs which they had composed for the occasion and which exonerated our daughter so lavishly that anyone who has ever heard the story by the Schmelzenbachs entitled *Praising the King* would have an idea of what it was like! At the close of it we presented them with a gift of a very expensive microscope and a centrifuge for testing blood for malaria and anemia. These had both been given to the mission by members of the Mennonite Church in Vineland, NJ. We certainly thank them from our hearts. The occasion and celebration may have well been one of the biggest and well-attended commemorations ever held in that part of the world.

And so now, with the opening of the clinic and medical personnel, our daughter will be able to turn her focus much more largely to the training of the many pastors who are coming for help. It has been the case for several years that groups of pastors under various churches have become dissatisfied with leadership and teaching that cannot deliver from out-broken sin, and they have pulled away and gone on their own, only to discover that they themselves need help to live the Christian life. What a wide-open door! We opened the conference on Friday night with forty-five of these pastors from various areas around the country, from as far as three or four hours away.

Our heart cry was that God would anoint the teaching and open hearts to understand and receive it. We were conscious the very first night that God was hearing and answering prayer. The interpreter is a very good, sanctified man who is full of wisdom and grace, but is not exceedingly proficient in the English language. We had prayed and asked the men in prison and others besides to pray specifically that God would give him clearness of understanding and anointing to get the truth across. After the very first session we were all amazed at how God helped him in such a marvelous way that he was able to pick right up and translate without a hesitation. Afterwards he told us that he still has trouble always understanding what is said to him in English except when translating a message of truth! Thank God that the true Biblical gift of tongues is still alive and well!

My wife and I just loved to hear these men sing. We have been in many a service in the States where it appeared from the platform that people were just singing from memory without even obviously paying attention to what they were singing, but not so with these men! They were singing from their hearts.

Now, dear friends, since this letter is somewhat different anyway from the usual prison report, let me share a delicious tidbit with you from my personal life. I have found it so precious that the helpmeet God has given me is so in love with the prison ministry and the men in there, and now after the third trip to a mission field outside of our good old USA, she has proved to be just as adaptable and helpful there. The many spiders in our humble dwelling beside the river in Malawi, and the many other critters such as lizards of all sizes in the house with us, evidenced very clearly that she would never turn back from any area of ministry God might call us to. I bless the Lord and thank Him for her! I must say with greater conviction than ever heretofore, "God gives His best to those that leave the choice with Him!" (Insertion: I did not test her far enough to offer her one of the deep-fried mice being sold for snacks along the roadside. Now tell me if I am not all heart!) One day she looked at me with tears welling up in her eyes and said, "I feel so unworthy and privileged to be here!" Aren't you glad that God does not bestow His blessings on the merit system? If so, where would we be, and that for all eternity?

And yes, my wife very much enjoyed meeting face to face a number of elephants and hippos and crocodiles only a few feet away from our boat. We also took a few hours and went to the old Baobab tree under which David Livingstone set up camp when first in that area.

What a privilege it was to teach and preach to men who gave not one evidence of rejecting a bit of it, even when it was directed at correction for them. One morning quite early they were meeting on their own in a time of worship. As they sang together, I was sitting on the veranda of our little cottage not far away and I could sense God's presence and blessing on it. Then they switched to a different "song" and soon began to repeat one word over and over and it became more rhythmic as they went. Soon, I looked over and they were dancing about to it. I felt the Spirit lift from it and got up and was on my way over to say something to my daughter when they ceased and went back to something more worshipful. So later that morning I told them exactly how it affected me and went on to describe how God is grieved when our focus turns from a pure worship of Him to a sensual excitement. They were nodding to each other in full agreement and I felt no resistance from them whatsoever.

Several times at the close of a service numbers of them would come to the front and stand in a row wanting to be prayed for. Many times it was a physical need, which they have plenty of, but several of them asked for prayer for God's direction and guidance as they turn from what they were formerly and join the new group they are finding to be what they have looked for. Those who lined up for physical needs made me think so much of when Jesus was on earth and they surrounded Him with just such needs and "...He healed them all." As I prayed for each one individually it was constantly on my heart that God would be glorified in granting healing to draw them closer to Him.

It is almost unbelievable how these men— some of them elderly, too— would sit for hours on the ground with their feet straight out in front of them and listen intently to the truth preached. Among them were two village chiefs, and one afternoon in question time they asked if it was all right for a preacher to be a chief as well. I told them I wished every chief was a preacher! Then I just warned them of the dangers of letting favoritism or anything else obstruct honest judgment in all things. One of them impressed my wife and me from the start with his intense interest and worshipful spirit.

Next door lives the main chief of the whole district. Several of his family members came into the tent and asked for prayer as well, notwithstanding their Muslim attire. We gladly prayed for them, asking Jesus to show them the true way, for after all, they had not gone to the mosque to ask for prayer, had they?

Of course while we were there the Muslims were celebrating Ramadan, and so late at night and early in the morning the call to prayer went out over loudspeakers and then we could hear the pathetic and doleful wail that they call prayer. It was the same I often listen to in the prison on a Friday afternoon, and the only way I can describe it is that it sounds like the wail of a lost soul. That is exactly what it is, too. I love the Muslims, but I passionately hate Islam, when I see the millions it is deluding and leading to hell.

At the close of the conference the preachers very zealously sent their love and greetings to the men in prison. I will gladly take it to them with some pictures of the conference, and I know they will pray for the continuation of the work. You might even pray that God will call some missionaries from among them! We already have one who left us and is now in

Sierra Leone, and calls me from there once in a while and seems to be doing well.

Thank you so much, each of you, for your prayers.

Yours for God's wonderful work, wherever that may be next,

William Cawman

7
IN SPITE OF POLITICS

July 1, 2018

I MUST START WITH one of God's micro-managing wonders. On Saturday, June 2, we had returned from Africa. I was planning to return to the prison with my classes on Tuesday, June 5. On Monday I received a call from my supervisor telling me that our new governor had suspended all part-time and special services employees of the state and so I was ordered to not go in. I asked him if I could go ahead and come without pay. He asked the local prison administration and they had no problem with it, so I just went on as usual except for recording my time. The following day I went in to see the administrator of the prison whom I have known for nearly twenty years. I told him that I wanted to thank him for keeping a door open there for me and that I was committed and was willing to continue to work without pay. He thanked me profusely and told me that the decision was from the governor and that everyone in the prison knew I was needed there.

Later that day I was walking down the compound when I met the administrator and the state commissioner (the man next in office to the governor) and as I passed by and waved, the administrator called me over. He gave me a real honor before the commissioner and told him I was just carrying on my work, dedicated enough to do so without pay. The commissioner thanked me graciously and also said he knew I was needed there. Two days later I received a call from my supervisor stating that he had received a call that we were to return to work on Monday with pay. I don't know, and don't need to know what all that was about, but I do know that God opened a window for it to be known to those and others that I was not there for money but for the good of the men. There have been negative vibes coming from the state office and maybe God was using it to back down the designs of Satan to remove us.

Before I had left for Africa an inmate came to me in distress over the fact that he was soon to be released and his wife from whom he has been separated had said she did not want to have anything to do with him. I told him to take it to God and be sure his own heart was right and then to trust the Lord and pray about it. When I returned, his countenance was bright and he told me that his wife had told his mother that she was willing to give it a try and see if they could be reconciled. Please pray for him, for certainly that would be God's will, wouldn't it?

We have started a very large book on Christian ethics in our Christian Living Class and since I cannot give each of them a full volume, I have been duplicating a chapter at a time. We are in the first chapter and the men are loving it. One of them asked if he could have the second chapter already as he has read the first one through twice. It is so good to have eager learners!

But, they are not all that way! One man attended classes for a while and was such an expert at discord and dissension and theological eccentricities that another volunteer and an officer requested his dismissal. I just received a request from him to be reinstated in the classes. I sat down with him first and told him I could not reinstate him until I had asked him some questions. I told him plainly that he had been trouble and had created friction and that the men were very uneasy with him in the classes. I asked him if he was willing to learn, or if he felt he had to teach his viewpoints. He said he was willing to learn, but that he did not agree with what I was teaching. We should be worshipping on Saturday instead of Sunday, and he was convinced that God revealed His truth to certain people and not to others (in other words, very clearly indicated, he was the one to whom truth was revealed, not me). At that point I told him that if he did not agree with what I was teaching there would be no profit whatsoever to him or anyone else for me to reinstate him into the classes. I did not even offer to pray with him, for there is such an evil spirit coming out of him every discerning man feels it.

Those of you who have received these letters for a number of years would be able to trace the beginnings of the following story way back, but for others and for the sake of giving an update, I will brief you in on his story once more and then bring it up to date.

I first met this man nearly twenty years ago. He had just returned to prison with a new violation. He had been locked up for seven years over drug charges and when released on parole, went straight to the streets with a demon inside and within thirty days committed a fresh crime. As he reentered the prison he was very broken over what he had done. His dear wife and two small daughters had wanted him to come home, but he had not even set foot inside their door before the demon took over and caused him to commit a fresh crime.

For perhaps a couple of years he was so broken and angry at himself that I could not get anywhere with him. Finally he began to settle down a bit and then for the next several years he would come to my classes and then listen to all the preachers on TV and read all the new age books that came into the prison and would get very confused. One day he came to me and said, "Chaplain, I'm tired of playing around. I know what the truth is and I'm going after it." He prayed through to forgiveness and then for a time earnestly sought and without a doubt was fully sanctified.

When he was released from prison again on parole, he came to our church and for three and a half months was a blessing to us all. His heart was fully in tune and he loved us and we loved him. It is part of the requirement of parole that the offender try to get a job. He finally landed a job at a recycling plant. It was long hours in the dead of winter outside, and he began to wear down physically. He started to neglect his early morning devotions and began to lose the keen edge from his experience. Early one week Satan suggested to him that he didn't have anything in his heart because he didn't feel like he did. All week long the devil pounded him with it and on Friday night when he finished work he was so tired and cold and hungry the devil saw his chance. He had invaded him all week long with discouragement, and now he was ripe for the next step. Satan said, "It has been so long since you had a drink, you are no longer addicted, and just one drink would make you feel so much better."

He yielded. He took one drink. All the demons of the past came rushing in just as dramatically as is portrayed in Matthew's Gospel, chapter twelve, verses forty-three through forty-five. He drank some more and before the evening was over had broken into three stores and robbed them.

When he came to himself, he was trashed. He called the pastor and the pastor called several of the church men and we went to the church to pray with him. That night he wailed the wail of a lost soul, and finally after a long time in prayer felt the Lord speak pardon to his heart again. He said, "What do I do now?" I said to him, "There is only one thing you can do, for the Bible says that if we cover our sin there is no forgiveness." On Monday morning the pastor took him down to the parole office and he walked in with his Thompson Chain Reference Bible under his arm and did not come back out.

It was just like a death in the church. We wept together and prayed that God would minimize the damage. God answered and he was given only two or three more years to serve. Again he got out and did well for a while, but then in a period of soul leanness he committed another robbery. Again he was sent to prison, but this time in another state. We receive letters from him every little bit, but he has been up and down spiritually ever since.

But God never gives up; does He? Bless His merciful heart! Now this letter just came from him:

> Dear Bro. Cawman,
> You're loved and missed very much...
> I really had hoped that I would have been rooted and grounded in the love of God by now. Instead, I've struggled and I'm in the bondage to sin. Up and down; that has been my experience.
>
> I've made numerous vows to God only to be broken. I'm seeking to be wonderfully saved from all sin as I won't settle for anything less than <u>His Victory!</u> I've had some good times of reading His word, but oh how I need complete victory and more time in the prayer closet.
>
> I've given up all plans and want to do His good and perfect will. Too much time has been lost serving self, sin and the devil. I owe all to Him!
>
> I just finished reading Isaiah, Jeremiah, and I'm almost finished with Ezekiel. What an excellent time I had this past weekend reading these Major Prophets.
>
> Bro. Cawman please send me 2 or 3 good holiness books. I do need to get really saved and then go on into entire sanctification.
>
> I can't settle for religion, but want Jesus reigning in my heart; having the smile of God! Doing what is pleasing to Him; being a witness to full salvation; holding Bible studies; telling others that Jesus can set them free from <u>all sin!</u>
>
> How I miss church services at my home church in Vineland with the saints of God. I have many precious memories of our times in church. Please do pray that I get settled in the Lord <u>for good!</u>

How is married life, Bro. Cawman? How is everyone? You're loved and missed. Hope to see you in church a couple of years from now.

In need of Him. ———

I do have some good books laid out to send him and let's pray that this long, long wilderness will be ended in complete victory in Jesus!

This morning I had a visit with a man I had almost forgotten about. He was in my classes and I had numbers of visits with him years ago, and then like others, he slipped into a pigeonhole somewhere until the other day. He came in hardly able to choke back the tears. "Chaplain, I've just lived in sin. I've made such a mess that now everybody has my number and I can't turn anywhere to get away from it. If I've committed the sin of ——— can God forgive that?" I assured him that there is only one sin that God cannot forgive and that is the sin that I will not bring to Him. That seemed to give him some hope and comfort. I told him that he needs to seek God until he knows that he is really born again and then whenever and from whatever source he has to face the consequences of his past life, he can rest in the fact that he is now a new creature in Christ Jesus and not that old man anymore. I trust he will really take a hold of that and pray clear through. Surely the "…thief cometh not, but for to steal, and to kill, and to destroy: I am come that they might have life, and that they might have it more abundantly."

In His love to each of you,

William Cawman

┼┼┼

August 1, 2018

THE MONTH OF JULY slipped by almost faster than any month heretofore; at least, it surely seemed that way. Thank you for praying for us. God is definitely at work and I must start by sharing with you the precious day of Wednesday, July 25. On Wednesdays I have two classes, one at 8:30 to 10:30 and another from 12:30 to 2:30. These are two different groups, one in Facility 3 and the second one in Facility 1.

After we had prayed and sung a couple of choruses, I did something rather on the spur of the moment that perhaps I have never done quite that way before. I said, "All right, you may be seated unless God has been doing so much for you that you need to tell us about it." One man remained standing and another would have had he not seen him do it. The man gave a very good testimony of how God was working in his life and in his heart. Then another stood and gave thanks in testimony; then a third; and the atmosphere was definitely one that was glorifying God.

After several of these a young man who has been in class for a while now, but who is very quiet, had several fingers pointing at him and a brother from across the aisle bumping him on the arm. I said, "Do we have someone here who needs to testify?" They all shook their heads affirmatively and turned to look at him. He smiled shyly and then stood to his feet. From his heart he began to give thanks to God for what He was doing in his heart and it was ever so precious. When he sat down I said, "Now, dear brother, do you feel better for doing that?"

"I sure do!"

I said, "Men, God is being lifted up this morning and I feel His smile on what we are doing."

About that time another young man stood in the back and said, "My testimony is a little different from the ones we have had. I'm struggling in my life right now. My life has been a struggle. I've been in a lot of trouble. I've been shot four times and spent three months in a coma. Now just two months ago my grandmother died and I'm struggling with guilt because I feel it's my fault she died because I wasn't there for her. I want you brothers to pray for me."

I got up and closed the partially open door to the room and

then said, "Now, brothers, we will stop for a while. We have heard some precious testimonies and praises to God. Now we have listened to a heart cry from this young brother. Even though we have a course of study that we are doing, that is not more important than us helping one another to get ready for heaven. I want you to know that this class is always a place where you can share your hearts and seek for help. We are here to help each other and to bear each other's burdens. Now we are going to pray for this dear brother who has asked us for help."

I took some time then to talk to him about the fact that when we ask God to forgive any sin that we have committed, part of the acceptance of that forgiveness is to forgive ourselves, and that is not always easy, just like we had heard him say. We then had a time of prayer for the man and God's presence was there among us. When we finished the prayer, one after another of the men rose to relate similar struggles and to encourage him to look to Jesus for forgiveness and help.

We finally had a bit less than a half hour for our subject material, but it was a time well spent.

That afternoon the very same thing happened in the other class. I had asked if any wanted to give a testimony or give thanks to God for fresh victory, and after a few good testimonies a middle-aged man said, "My testimony is going to be different. I need help. I have been trying for a long time to life to live a Christian life, but I keep falling back into sin. I don't want it to be this way, but I don't know what to do."

I exhorted them for a while and then we went to prayer for that man. I would ask you to please pray for these two men that they will not stop short or become misled before God can satisfy their inward cry. And while praying for them, also remember before the ear of God the many, many all around us who also are less than fully satisfied with their lives the way they are living.

The following Sunday night in preaching to them I told them that while my wife and I were in Ireland, July 8-19, we had met a number of people that I would call "silent, suffering seekers." They are not satisfied the way they are, but for whatever reason or lie of Satan, they are afraid to come out and honestly confess their lack and seek for something that will satisfy. I said, "They are not all in Ireland, but some of you are also in the same state. You know you do not have complete victory over sin in your life. You know there are others you meet who have something more than you do. I beg you to listen to me and quit going on that way when God has a perfect remedy for whatever is your problem."

Oh, the tragedy of the multitudes who are deceiving themselves into thinking that all will be well in the end when it is not all right now. How we should pray for them and ask God to so fill our lives with Himself that they will see an attractiveness in the Spirit-filled life.

The Calvinistic man I have mentioned at times has pretty well hung himself. He spent over a year— I'm pretty sure it has been that long— studying very intricately a book on Arminianism written by a Calvinist. He has been possessed of a passion to prove that he is right while refusing to get right. He came to me with piles of notes that he had written from the book and told me he had finally finished his study of Arminianism. I said, "Now if you would spend that much time getting right with God, you would be getting somewhere."

"Oh, I am right with God!"

Then he began again in the class to openly argue and defend his erroneous views. I told him to stop and he kept right on. I pointed to him and said, "I told you to stop, and I mean it. You have said enough and you are not to try anymore to promote Calvinism in this class for it is a false teaching." He reluctantly stopped, but the next week when one of the volunteers was there, he started it again. They also told him to stop and he got up and stormed out of the classroom saying he would not be back. Pray for him too, if God will lay him on your heart.

Then let me follow up a note about another one that I wrote

about a short while back, that I had refused to re-enroll in my classes because he was such a disturber of the class with his rank errors. A new teacher who came in wanted to teach a Bible study. The supervisor gave him a slot and he immediately began to teach the men that we could not live without sin, and that anyone who claimed they could was living under a false halo of super righteousness instead of the truth. Click! Our Calvinist was immediately pleased to hear such and is fast becoming his adherent. However, of the dozen or so men the chaplain had enrolled in his Bible study, several are so appalled at his false teaching that they are asking to be removed from enrollment in his class.

Wouldn't you think that even the least of human intelligence— not to even bring in grace— would sense a red flag of discrepancy over a teaching that we cannot ever live as Jesus came to enable us to live? This proclaims Him the most colossal failure ever known to man on earth. It is, in short, antichrist! But such is being taught in the largest portion of what is called Christendom today. Satan loves it; it is his doctrine.

I have recently received such wonderful letters from two inmates who are now in other prisons. Both of them report that the work of holiness is keeping them from sin and giving them victory even in an atmosphere where there is an appalling dearth of spiritual help. One of them writes that all they hear is that we must continue in sin, but God is helping him to keep sweet while letting his light shine in such a dark place.

I do try my best— I hope I do— to instruct the men that when they hear such abominable and antichrist teaching they need to remember that some of those who teach that we cannot live without sin may be doing so out of a non-scriptural definition of sin, and that before they judge them or argue with them they need to find out what it is that they are referring to as "sin." The very same chapter that tells us clearly that "Whosoever is born of God doth not commit sin," gives the Biblical definition of sin: "Sin is the transgression of the law." Sin is not being tempted to sin; it is not human infirmity or mistakes; it is not evil thoughts coming into the mind, but it is a willful transgressing of the known will of God.

Sadly enough, many are not thus ignorant of a definition. They are deeply in love with their sin and resent the teaching that one can be free from it as the Bible so clearly teaches. Such are nothing short of antichrist, for they completely annul the very Scripturally stated purpose for which Christ came: "...to destroy the works of the devil." Oh, the fiery judgment that awaits the willful teaching wherein "Christ is become of no effect."

I thank God for the precious backing of these men in prison. Returning from the meeting in Northern Ireland, I was greeted by several "Welcome back, chaplain. We had you and your wife covered with prayer the whole time." You see, I am not in prison just for the benefit of others, but I receive a priceless benefit, too. One night I was preaching in Ireland on living a life of complete freedom from sin and living up to God's standard for us: "Be ye holy, for I am holy." A young girl wrote to us afterwards and said, "It was good to hear you preach again, and as I said on Sunday, it was a message I needed to hear!! I have to admit, a few times, I caught myself thinking, this 'be ye holy, as I am holy' is impossible... and as you told about one of those men in prison, who shines with the Joy of the Lord... Even when he was in the awful sticky and smelly dumpster, I was thinking... it's easier to be holy in a prison, away from the temptations of the world... If you are thinking right now, this gal has no idea about prison life, you are totally right, I don't!! It is impossible, right?! Without God!!"

But thank God, that with God, not one standard raised in the Word of God is beyond our lives here on earth. And we are praying that this precious girl will open her heart to the whole will of God and be filled with that Power that makes the holy life a glorious reality here on earth, and that whether in prison or out of prison.

I must tell you a little something that really pleased me while in Ireland. We were in the town of Londonderry up on the waterway leading in from the North Atlantic, and were visiting the huge cathedral built in 1633 into which John Newton walked from the slave ship after being saved from a wicked life at sea. The curator asked my wife if she would like to play the pipe organ and of course I readily responded that she did. What did she play? Why, of course, "Amazing Grace, how sweet the sound that saved a wretch like me!" Thank you, John Newton, for that precious hymn!

We may soon be switching the two Friday night Bible studies to Tuesday and Wednesday evenings, which would be before prayer meeting time in our church, but would then place all of the scheduled services on those two days. It would be easier for the volunteers when I am gone. Thank you again for your prayers.

In love,

William Cawman

September 1, 2018

DO YOU REMEMBER THE man from Colombia who, after being raised a Catholic and then trying Islam for five years, came to me in distress, saying that he was not happy? God marvelously saved him and sanctified him completely and he was a shining example of holiness. He completed the four-year holiness Bible school course in a year and a half, then was moved to a northern prison. Would you like an update from him?

> Dearest and respected Pastor Cawman,
> Eight months into this journey to enemy territory, I miss more and more my fellowship with you, your volunteers and friends, and our small community of sanctified souls at South Woods. I call this place "enemy territory," because the devil has so great a power over this prison that the church, with some notable exceptions, does his bidding. Most Christians in the world do not have any problem in understanding that salvation is by faith alone, and not works. Disappointingly, however, most

Christians do not see sanctification in the same way; they want to live a life of continuous working to eradicate the roots of sin.

To me, it is inconsistent with both fallen human nature and Scripture that we pretend to have what it takes to become a sanctified soul. At best, and for the worst, those souls realize that they cannot do it on their own, and resort to explaining their condition as imputed holiness. They hide behind the righteousness of Christ to explain their failure to live a victorious Christian life.

I long for a spiritual awakening in this place; a realization that God has freely offered the Holy Spirit, and that His baptism completes the plan of God for those who accept Christ. The soul is cleansed by God, not by works. Unfortunately, most do not want to hear it. Alone, in my experience of sanctification, I only receive odd looks and derision at my suggestion that we can enjoy freedom from sin by appropriating the work that Christ did at the Cross, and the aid of the Spirit.

But you already know that. I am sure this is not a surprise to you, as you have been preaching the gospel all your life in enemy occupied territory. You too, have been working behind enemy lines. (I remember an illustration you once gave).

What I came here for has not materialized in any way. The college program has me at a stand-still and in a couple months, at the latest, I will know if it is over for me. I do not know yet why I am here, aside from my own desire to obtain the degree I wanted. What I do know is that I turned my head to look upon a shiny thing in the world, and I dove head first into this harsh place. I do not take for granted what God has given me, and the cost at which my salvation was bought. I acknowledge fear. Some because my faith might not be as strong as I would like it; some because the devil roams these corridors, and some more because I feel alone. I know I am part of the universal church, but I miss my interaction with the local church. I am going to put my trust in the Lord to place me at His will in a community like the one you opened for me.

In the meantime, I will continue testifying about God's power to save to the utmost. The more unpopular I become for that reason, the more I will continue doing it, in love, and with respect. I only pray that my life does not contradict in any way what I say. Please extend my love to Pastor ———, and your wife. I remember your daughter's mission frequently in my prayers. Until we see each other again, you are in my heart and in my prayers. ———.

Please pray that God will be able to use him to the fullest extent to radiate true holiness as long as he is there. I would hope fervently for his return to this prison, but he belongs to God, not to us, and wherever God chooses to use him is totally up to Him. Right now, he is our missionary to that dark prison.

God has been helping us in the services, and Satan has been hard at work with his cohorts trying to stop it. It is absolutely unbelievable what unethical and demonic efforts the Muslim chaplain and the man in charge in Trenton are carrying out to remove my supervisor and myself. Downright lies have been told in Trenton as to what we are doing. My supervisor and I have met and laid it out before the Lord and then committed it to Him. Please help us pray that God will circumvent the evil designs and keep the doors open for His work to go on. I cannot believe that God will abandon the men in prison who are earnestly seeking Him and living for Him, but neither will we take this for granted and fail to pray for the covering of the Blood.

It was only about one year after I had started ministering here in the prison that I had to have a kidney removed due to a cancerous tumor on it. Two weeks after the surgery I went back into the prison on a Good Friday night and had a Bible study in the Minimum Unit. It was a good time of God's help even though I went home tired out from incomplete recovery. About 10:30 I turned the bedroom light off and laid down in bed. No sooner was the light off than something happened that I only tell with some degree of trembling even yet. I saw Satan standing against the bedroom wall glaring at me and threatening with these words: "You're on my territory in that prison and you have only one kidney left." I got out of bed and walked the living room floor in hand-to-hand combat with Satan himself. No one can ever persuade me that it was an apparition. It was a desperate battle with Satan. After some time in utter exhaustion I went back and laid down on the bed and continued to fight. It was too intense. I rose again and renewed the battle walking in the living room. Back and forth until every once of strength was exhausted, I finally laid down on the bed once more after four hours of this intense conflict. About two o'clock in the morning there suddenly shone a ray of the brightest light from the upper right-hand corner of the room with the words: "Oh the Blood of Jesus!" Satan fled!

But I have never forgotten the lesson learned that night almost nineteen years ago. Satan is anything but passive toward us invading His territory, and he will use any means possible to stop us and take the territory back. The battle is the Lord's and we will obey Him.

It is so thrilling to literally watch men grow in grace and to see them walking in the Light. We know the end result of walking in the Light, don't we? "...the Blood of Jesus Christ His Son cleanseth us from all sin." We have some shining examples of that very thing among us right here in prison. Oh, may God add to the number!

I have made a few schedule changes starting in September. For years we have had two Bible studies each Friday night— one in Facility 3 and then another in Facility 1. Facility 2 we have only been in for Christian Living Class which has been a small attendance, and then once in a while on a Sunday night. By the new arrangement we will still have the four Christian Living Classes each week and then a Bible study in Facility 3 on Tuesday evenings at 5:30 and another in Facility 2 on Wednesday evenings at 5:30. This groups all of our scheduled services, except for Sundays, on Tuesdays and Wednesdays so that when we are out of town a volunteer can do everything on those two days. So often a meeting outside the prison starts on a Friday night, requiring them to be held by a volunteer. Even though we hated in a sense to leave the large group in Facility 1 Bible study, we feel it good that we can start one up in Facility 2 and there are already thirty-six names enrolled for the start of it. Please help us pray that these changes will be all for the best.

There are men in Facility 2 who, years ago when we were having Bible studies there, were bright and clear with a shine upon them. Over the years of almost solid Calvinistic teachings, some of their countenances look dark and troubled. They have been duly warned against the "false doctrines" that we teach, and so please pray that God will draw many of them back to the way of truth. I find it ever so inconsistent with any degree of sensible theology that the very thing Jesus came to do is termed "false doctrine." Oh, the deadly disease of sin! It is far more lethal than the worst cancer known to man. Oh, that men could wake up to the warning of Jesus that the "thief cometh not, but for to steal, and to kill, and to destroy!" And he works the most deceitfully when clothed in priestly robes.

There has been a definite and noticeable slipping of any form of godliness in many of the volunteers from other churches who come into the prison in just the twenty years I have ministered here. When I first began, nearly every man entering the prison as a minister of the gospel would be dressed in a modest business suit— fitting attire for their profession. Rarely do you see that anymore. They come slouching in with hanging out jersey shirts and jeans looking more like they were prepared for eighteen holes than for the pulpit. In fact, when I was but a boy, I recall seeing men coming to and from churches all over town in suits and ties and white shirts. The god that the present age is going to church for demands no more respect in his presence than does an auctioneer. This is the decline we are battling up against in holding before them a God who is indeed loving to the infinite degree, but who is also intolerant of the least iota of sin.

While we ardently desire to see many more men catch the

gleam of truth and take the narrow way, I confess a motive for prison ministry deeper yet than that. It is simply that I may stand before God now and then with His clear and complete smile upon me. "It is worth all it costs to be holy!"

Lovingly and gratefully,

William Cawman

8
WHY SO MANY DULL EARS?

October 1, 2018

Could I start right out this month with a prayer request that has been growing heavier on my heart? I would ask you to pray for me that I could have more of the Holy Spirit's discernment in knowing how to help men who seem to be impenetrable to the light of the gospel. So many times, I sit with a man for a half hour (the normal length of an individual interview) and afterwards feel as though not one thing registered with him. I try to explain to him what it really means to have real connection with God in prayer until he can know His will and be rightly related to Him, but it seems he cannot— just like Nicodemus— grasp the spiritual because they are so focused on the mechanics. To them, getting closer to God means to study more. to witness more, to go to church more, to do good to others, etc. The concept of a spiritual union with God seems to just slide off of them like water off of a duck's back. It would appear from the Bible record that Nicodemus finally did grasp what Jesus was telling him, for he appears twice more to Jesus— the last time at His death with ointments for His embalmment.

I can only hope that some of these go away to ponder what has been told them and allow the Light to break through to them. The number of these is way too great. Please pray for them and for me. Thank you!

You might remember some time back my telling of a man who was about to leave the prison and go back to his family on parole in northern NJ. I sat with him and tried to impress upon him how he must have God dwelling in his heart if he was going to be different than before. To everything I said, he replied in glaring self-confidence, "Oh yes, of course!" I tried to wave a red flag in front of his "Oh yes, of course," but to the red flags his response was, "O yes, of course!" Well, he is back again. He violated parole by getting drunk. He somewhat sheepishly appeared at the door of the Bible study and asked to come back. I enrolled him and then he said he wanted to visit. I put him on the appointment sheet and when he came in I could sense that a little reality at least was finally breaking in on him. He began to lament to me that it just seemed he couldn't free himself from slipping back and away from God. He said he had started out by going to church, but that he got busy and drifted back again. I could sense that at least there was a crack in his self-confident façade, and so I tried again to urge upon him that he really needed to be born again and then he would have the power to go on with God instead of slipping back. For one moment, it seemed he caught a glimpse of this and said, "I'll do that." Then self rose to its feet again and "Oh yes, of course" returned to his aid. Such is the dark abyss of the carnal mind.

Oh, I must share something with you from our formerly-Mormon brother again. Believe this or not, they have recently installed in the prison systems kiosks that allow email connections to the outside. The inmate can purchase a tablet from commissary and communicate with his family or friends that way. Our brother thought that perhaps this would be advantageous in communicating with me as it saves him a postage stamp and would be faster than land mail. He proposed it and sent me the logistics of it. I examined it and then replied to him that had it been simply email I would be happy to communicate that way, but that the way the prison set it up required access to the internet, and that I didn't have such in my home. I gave him some reasons why I don't have internet connection in my home. I told him that if occasion arose where I really needed to use an internet connection I could go to a library, but that I didn't want to bring everything that was in the library into my home.

I was holding a meeting somewhere— where, I do not remember— and a dear sister got up and testified that she had weighed the issue of having internet connection in their home and finally decided it might be all right. She had ordered it installed and soon a big white truck pulled into her driveway with huge letters on the side of it saying, "We Bring the World into Your Home!" It shot an arrow through her heart and she went out to meet the truck and canceled the order. Bless her heart! I must of necessity go out into the world, but I don't need to bring the world into my home! That is my privilege as the keeper of my home, and I live under God's smile in so doing.

These are in short some of the reasons I gave him for my choice. Here is his answer:

> I received your letter with true joy! Your words and spirit have a special resonance with me. Your approach to the internet rings true. Although I have almost no personal experience with it, having been incarcerated since 2000, what I hear men lament about here is that their families don't (or stopped) spending time together because of it. Fathers talk about how they used to shoot hoops or go on activities with their children, but such time kept falling more and more by the wayside due to on-line friends and games. But what really gets to me is men in their 20's who say that they lost their fathers (and sometimes mothers) to internet time, increasingly, in the last 15 years, and that that played a role in the activities they got into that eventually resulted in prison time.

I wouldn't want the internet to steal time from good, classical reading, <u>let alone</u> steal time from my family, Christian fellowship, or especially from the Lord and His Word. Jesus is in union with my soul. There's not a thing from the world that could fit between that. But my experience is that the enemy is continually trying to do so anyway, looking for ways to infect, distract, weaken, and steal, like the "weeds" in the soil parable. The Spirit will warn about weeds. The internet seems pretty much like a weed to me.

Then he writes of something else very interesting:

We've been without a chaplain here since May, and have been praying for the Lord to send us someone He's prepared. Volunteers have been coming in and running the Sunday services, but other programs have been on the hold. The Lord answered our prayers by calling one of the guards here as the new chaplain. (He was a guard on my unit until 2 weeks ago) He's no longer "officer Thorne," He's "Chaplain Thorne," and you can tell he loves the Lord. No one I know has ever had a chaplain before who knows completely what day to day life on the living unit of a prison is like in <u>all</u> its detail. I believe this will be a real blessing and I'm praying fervently for him.

At the close of his sixth page of ever so interesting reflections he writes:

Well, just try fitting all this in an email! Good thing we're both "old school" and prefer letters. Thank you so much for your guidance in my life. Much love to you, and my prayers. Your spiritual son, ————.

In the last letter I told you about some schedule changes I had made. Just as we got them all in place and were ready to start with the new schedule, I entered the prison one morning and my supervisor was just coming out of the front administration area. He came to me and said, "Well, guess what? Our prayers of seven years now are going to be answered; we are getting our chapels back!" Some of you would remember that we had requested prayer for this right after they took the officer out of them, closing them down except for Sunday nights. Thank God, He still answers prayer! Very soon the officers will be posted there again, but the plan is that in order to limit the officer post to one shift and yet to cover evening services and Bible studies, the chapel will be open from one in the afternoon until nine at night. So just as we get started on our new schedule, we will have to make some more adjustments soon. One wonders if DOC means "Department of Corrections," or "Department of Change." Whatever, we are so thankful that we are getting them back. Now all religious activities will be held there and we can reopen our religious libraries and so much more that we have been unable to do for the last seven years. Thank you for praying, even if you have forgotten that you did!

My supervisor has on his desk a stack of requests for Buddhist services. Just at the same time as all these requests are coming in, the only Buddhist volunteer, not only for our prison, but for all of the ones in NJ, if I understand it correctly, has suddenly been banned from entering any state institution for some reason. So be it!

Along with this, increasing requests are coming in for Odinist services. For these we do have a volunteer who comes in to teach "heathenism." (That label is his own.) He comes under the resounding title of "Distilfink" with a very impressive looking document of his credentials. He not only teaches the Odinists but the Arians, Rastafarians, and perhaps a few other stripes of similar colors.

And then we are also experiencing a present reviving of the use of the sweat lodge for the American Indians. Some years ago, a high-paid executive from Trenton came down to the prison here and then a van was sent to all the NJ prisons to gather up the American Indians as well as the "would-be" ones and they spent a day erecting a sweat lodge out of special willow poles and then procured a supply of white trunks for them to wear. They had a pile of rocks which were heated over a fire and then water poured over them to produce the sweat which was to cleanse them of their evil spirits. This has not been used for several years and we have watched the lodge deteriorate until it was just a pile of sticks. Another is now being constructed and orders have been given to fetch forty rocks to be used in the ceremony this month.

Our present America is lost in heathen darkness!

But over top of all of that mess, the most damning religion by far is the viciously aggressive insistence that we cannot lose our salvation. Sometimes I wonder if these teachers have anything else to teach except that! And so, over and over we encounter the question in our classes as to whether one can or cannot lose his salvation. I have learned better than to spend a lot of time arguing this point. I simply point to a few basic discrepancies such as the fact that if one cannot, then Lucifer will be forever saved in heaven and that if "once a son, always a son," then there is hope for none of us as we were all the children of Satan. Then I conclude with the observation that such an argument is either true or false; either we can lose it or we can't. If we can't, what is the point of spending so much fervor in teaching it. No one feels it necessary to teach over and over that we cannot fall off of the earth into space. But if it is possible to lose our salvation, let's live so that we don't. That usually quiets the question, but only until the next session of pounding their minds with the Scriptures that prove we cannot lose it. The Bible itself calls these "doctrines of devils," and such they certainly are! And they are opposed to any other teaching with a very un-Christlike antagonism.

But amid all the heathen darkness, God is still answering your prayers! Thank you for them!

William Cawman

November 1, 2018

COULD I SUGGEST ONE more blessing that we should thank God for this Thanksgiving month, just in case you haven't thought of it? Please thank God sincerely for saving you from what might have been! Any of us who have been forgiven and cleansed and are keeping clear with God are certainly thankful for all that we have been saved from, but none of us know what we have been saved from, that might have been.

As I listen to one man after another tell his life's story, I am still staggered— even after twenty years of listening— at the realms of sin's bondage that I have never known, nor would I want to know. Sin is not a toy! Little wonder that God in His infinite love and goodness instructed Adam to stay away from the knowledge of sin.

A man in mid-life and who would appear to be an average American citizen joined my classes a few weeks or months ago and has been a very intent listener. The other day he told me he would like a one-on-one visit. When he came in he began to tell me what was troubling him. A Cuban man came up to him in the courtyard and said, "Could I speak with you for a minute?" Then he told him that he had been involved in a lot of black magic and such things in Cuba and that he had an ability to see things in people that others cannot see. He told him he could see a big black square over his head and he knew he had some trouble in his life. He then began to tell him things about his past (deaths in his family, failures in business, etc.) that he would have had no way of knowing. He then told him that a female had stolen a shirt of his and had used it to cast a spell on him that was causing all this trouble.

The man telling me this called his father and asked him about such a possibility and his father told him that a woman had entered the house without even unlocking the doors and stolen his clothes. Then the man told me that when he tries to pray or read the Bible, his mind just darts off somewhere else without his being able to control it. He said, "Chaplain, I don't want you to think I'm crazy. I'm not letting this totally traumatize me, but I am bothered by it and don't know what to do. Is there anything I can do about it?"

I looked squarely at him and said, "I do not think you are crazy. These things are real." (He had also told me that he had played some with the occult.) "There is only one deliverance from all of this, but it will work. You must come to God in prayer, rebuking through the Blood of Jesus the distracting thoughts that would keep you from praying, and then begin to clean up your past as God shows it to you and repent of it all. Then you can plead the Blood of Jesus to seal the doors that Satan has opened in your life. Don't think of the Blood of Jesus as just another charm or amulet that can be used the same way witchcraft is used. The Blood of Jesus will only cure the disease of sin and the works of the devil as you enter into a covenant with God to obey Him no matter what He requires of you, but if you will do that, the cure is absolutely sure."

I asked him if he understood what I was telling him and he said he did. He told me that he had a niece that he didn't get along with and that they hadn't spoken for five years. He asked if he should reach out to her. I told him that of course he should, because God's Word says that if we don't forgive others, God will not forgive us. Then I told him I would not leave him alone but that I would call him down again soon and see how he was getting along. And so, he is struggling with broken family relationships; he is divorced from his wife; his son and his sister and his mother all died (just as the medium told him); he is locked up for beating up a man and leaving him tied up which caused his death; he is haunted by evil spirits… Do you see what I mean? Please stop right now and thank God for what you have been saved from— that which might have been!

The other morning, we had such a wonderful class time discussing, of all things— the law. At the beginning of the class a man who has been there for a long time and is very teachable and loving confessed that he had really had a struggle that morning with his cellmate, who is a Muslim. He said he had to really hold himself in check with an urge to lay a blow on him, but that God had seen him through it. Of course, I did not let him by with that without pointing out that through the incident God had revealed to him that there was something in him that needed to be cleansed out. Then we proceeded with the subject at hand.

As we got into the subject of the "law of life in Christ Jesus" making us free from the "law of sin and death," the atmosphere became more and more charged with Divine help. I was pointing out to them how the prevalent teaching of today is the New Age "here's how to be a Christian." I told them that it completely ignores the Blood of Jesus and takes on the "doctrines of devils," which is, simply stated, "I don't need God; I can do it myself— I will be God!" We then saw how that when the Blood of Jesus is imparted into our nature we have a power to love, even when the object is unlovable.

All of the sudden the man who had told of his encounter with his cellmate lit up! "I got it! I got it! I am convicted! I've got some work to do!"

Then as the discussion went on about the power in Jesus' Blood, God just settled down on the group with a weight of His divine presence. It felt as though the whole class was "in one accord."

That afternoon, of course I desired to see the same truth go through to the much larger class in Facility 1. No sooner had we approached the subject there than a man— who always has nothing to say but has to say it, and who has no grace at all, but a belly full of east wind like Elihu— rose to the occasion. "Wait a minute! We have to remember that this takes time. There is a lot we have to unlearn and so we don't reach that state all at once..." And it would have taken the rest of this page to continue the period marks to fill in all the rest he had to say. I interrupted him very soundly and told him that there is a maturing in grace that often does require unlearning old habits and response mechanisms, but that we dare not make grace of no effect. The Bible states clearly that "...as many as received him, to them gave he power to become the sons of God, even to them that believe on his name." And that "...if any man be in Christ, he is a new creature: old things are passed away; behold, all things are become new." And that change is brought about by the instantaneous application of the Blood of Jesus, not by time.

It took some time (speaking of taking time) to get the atmosphere cleared of his devilish doctrine but once again God came and helped in the latter part of that class, too. Spirits like his make so evident the Scripture that says "...one sinner destroyeth much good." And with all of that, he would feel himself out and above and beyond everyone in the class, including the teacher.

Now about a week later: I felt as shepherd of the little flock here I owed it to the rest of the class to address this dear soul who was endangering himself of rejection by many in the class for his much talk and little content. So I placed him on the visit list and when he came in he appeared a bit apprehensive and said, "What's this for?"

"Let's have a visit, Brother. Have a chair. Now let me ask you a question. If I saw a developing object on your forehead that I recognized as a very harmful growth, would I be your friend to not tell you about how serious it is?"

"No, you wouldn't."

"Well, please let me tell you that I really want to see you living in the fullness of all that God has for you, but you are not there. Sometimes you have good things to say in class, but most of the time it is just coming from you. Jesus said to Nicodemus, 'That which is born of the flesh is flesh; and that which is born of the Spirit is spirit,' and so much of what you say in class is just coming from the flesh. God has something better for you and I don't want to see you missing that better part."

He dropped his head a bit with a faint smile and said, "Chaplain, this is the second witness. L—— N—— (another inmate in the class) said the same thing to me this very morning. I think God is trying to tell me something. I need to humble myself and get more of Him."

I went on and tried to instruct him in what it really means to be filled with the Spirit and emptied of self. He listened and agreed. When he went to leave after we had prayed, he turned back and said very thoughtfully, "Chaplain, I love you, man. I can tell when somebody really cares about me, and I know you do." Please pray for him that he will truly humble himself and surrender and be filled with the Spirit of Christ. A one-time inmate who is now our Sunday School superintendent said the other day, "Anybody would make a good Christian!" Amen!

I heard something very touching today, but not from the man it is about. Numbers of times over the past seventeen or eighteen years I have told things about a very dear man who is about to finish a thirty-year sentence for the murder of his wife and mother-in-law. He has been walking in the beauty of holiness for over fifteen years now without a break. A man he has helped greatly was visiting with me today and told me that when this dear brother gets out, he wants to be baptized in his prison clothes and immediately change into new ones. I haven't had a chance to speak to him directly about it, but I was so very touched by the thought. I don't know just how it will all work, but I doubt if he will be able to stay under long enough to come up with the new ones!

I told you of our excitement in that the executives in Trenton told us that our chapel areas would definitely be opened back up and officers posted there. Then in the midst of preparations the administrator of our prison was replaced by one who had been the administrator for a year or so several years ago. We were not disappointed at all in who they chose as the replacement, but they said that the process of getting approval for the opening of the chapels would have to start all over with him initiating it! So now we don't know just what the outcome will be. We don't feel he would be at all opposed to opening them, but government loves red tape, you know. Please pray that God's will be done in all of this.

Today I had several interviews in the morning and then stopped in at my supervisor's office and he pointed to his desk and said, "Look at this; I'm swamped. I'm so far behind I don't know when I'll get it all done." I told him to give me the stack of new enrollments and I would go find a vacant computer and help him out by getting them done for him. He was most grateful and I did get them finished. Among them were several more requests for enrollment in my various classes and Bible studies; in fact, enough that I will need to reprint the rosters in order to take the roll call. This is one more reason we really need the chapel areas open during the day hours. At least two of my classes or Bible studies are over the fire code limit for persons in the rooms we use.

Would you be interested in a statistic from the prison complex? I've developed quite a friendly relationship with the locksmiths, of which I believe there are three. One of them told me they are having a hard time keeping up with the needs as there are almost two thousand locks in this one prison. Their shop is very fascinating to me and I think it would be to most men.

Please help us pray for revival power through the coming winter months.

Gladly in Him,

William Cawman

December 1, 2018

WE WISH EACH OF you a very blessed Christmas! And thank you each and every one for all the prayers and support you have sent our way this past year. Eternity alone will reveal just what measures of grace this year has meted out to men in prison.

Your prayers are so vital in this happening; so thank you!

This month has been very full and very traumatic as well. Let me tell you about it as up to date as I can at this point. I have mentioned briefly in past letters as to the shift in vision and viewpoint from the state capital. It is getting more and more distressing and that very rapidly. Our governor is no friend to conservative values at all, let alone Christian values.

Both he and the assistant commissioner above him are very ecumenical and want to push that to the limit. They do not want chaplains who are loyal to their faith— that is, unless that "faith" is anything other than Christianity. In other words, it is acceptable to be Muslim, or Jewish, or Rastafarian, or Buddhist, or Heathen, or Odinist, or Native American; just anything except Protestant Christianity.

And so about two weeks ago he passed a new ruling that no part-time chaplain could any longer schedule one-on-one interviews with the inmates. He said he would follow it with a prohibition against a chaplain having his own classes or groups for his faith. In other words, my job would be to provide coverage for all the doctrines of devils that have no chaplain to cover them and that's it. He scheduled a meeting with us all and then did not come himself. Then he scheduled a meeting in Trenton that was mandatory for all part-time chaplains. There he promised to tell us what we could and could not do.

Now let me stop and explain something here. The one-on-one interviews with the inmates have been the one avenue of ministry that has proven the most effective in spiritual growth over the past twenty years. It is there that a man can feel safe to unload his heart; to seek greater light; to express his hunger; or to actually pray through to an encounter with God. The classes and Bible studies would be next in value; the Sunday night worship services would be perhaps the least fruitful of all this.

For days after the edict that I could no longer schedule visits with the men. I felt as though this heartless man had thrust a dagger through the very heart of what God has so graciously opened the door to here in this prison. And then when we heard that he was even going to stop us from having classes or groups, I was prepared to attend the meeting in Trenton and come away having surrendered my resignation. At that point I would just become a volunteer again like I started out twenty years ago and operated for a year and a half.

Several churches engaged in fervent prayer for this pending shutdown of God's great work here.

I drove my supervisor and another part-time chaplain up to Trenton and we enrolled our attendance at the meeting. After all of the due recognitions and a few speeches, the man we so much dreaded took the table and began to outline our responsibilities. He did not prohibit us having classes and then stated that we could conduct interviews but to keep them to about fifteen minutes each. Then he said he would be coming to each prison in the near future and sitting with each chaplain to be sure their schedule was in conformity with his new program.

We left the meeting in a pelting snowstorm and headed home, all three of us astounded. We all knew that God had answered prayer! Nothing else could have made this man change his direction like that. We had a prayer of thanksgiving together and I immediately began calling those who had prayed for us to let them know that God still answers prayer!

And so, while the door to labor here is still being held open by the same God who opened it to start with, it leaves us with a sense that just as God had mercy on America in the last two elections and gave us a little longer to work, so it is here. The night is coming, and coming fast, but thank God that He is still in control and is giving us a little longer to bring the light to a few more souls.

Now, I want to make something clear to you who have labored with us so long in this harvest field. I am not called of God to pull a paycheck. I am called to minister to men in prison. The paycheck has helped us over the years to be able to spend more time than we would have as a volunteer. But if the choice comes down to playing the game the powers to be want us to, I will not hesitate for a minute to turn in my resignation as a state chaplain and then re-enter the ministry as a volunteer.

I would ask that you help us pray for this situation. I belong to Jesus and that will not change. I do not belong to the State of New Jersey, and I do not, as those over me in the government, belong to a paycheck. But through it all my only concern is to remain in perfect obedience to God and of service to men in prison as long as God allows it to be.

You might be interested in how my supervisor feels about all of this. He has seen it coming and has tried to shelter me personally, even while giving me warnings of its approach. When it came to this point, he announced his plans to retire next July. The man in Trenton, upon taking his office, would call my supervisor nearly every day asking him how to do things as he knew he had the reputation of being the best chaplain in the state. Once seated on his self-appointed throne and obsessed with hallucinations of his importance, he launched his program as somewhat described above. He then told my supervisor that he was the only chaplain who had not conformed to his new order. My supervisor told him that he had no plans of conforming to it. Now he has told me privately that if things somehow change in Trenton in a further answer to prayer, he will continue and not go through with his retirement, but if not, he too will retire and come back in part-time as a volunteer. Please pray for him also.

Now — I would like to make an observation here that comes from my heart. In the last two national elections many Christians prayed fervently, and without a doubt God heard and answered and gave America a reprieve from what could have been had evil been turned loose. Have we simply thanked God and then returned to our various pursuits of happiness and personal gratifications? I was holding a meeting in a small church during the last mid-term election. We gathered around the front and prayed for the upcoming election. A dear grandma then said, "Let's all place our hands on our Bibles and plead the Blood over the coming election." As we did, I felt God draw near and honor our united prayer. My prayer was, "Oh God, please let the evil tide in this great country receive a clear message that America is not going in the direction of those God-forsaken would-be-leaders who hate Him." Perhaps the outcome was not as strong on the side of right principles as we hoped for, but it could have been far, far worse. Now, don't we have an obligation to pray just as fervently that God would send a humbling spirit of the fear of God into our government officials as we prayed that they would get there?

I see a parallel in what just took place at the meeting in Trenton. Numbers of churches and people of God were praying that God would stop the actions of that man who hates God while professing Him. God definitely answered the prayers sent up to Him and the door remains open for a little longer to work with these precious souls in prison. Thank you for praying; thank God for answering; now— will you please join us in prayer that God will further work out His great purpose concerning the men in prison? We dare not fail to thank Him for answered prayers to date, but He has invited us to ask largely, hasn't He?

We are again planning a Christmas Eve service in each of the facilities. Several people have expressed a desire to help in it and we are in the process of getting them cleared for it. Christmas is such a vital time to share a message of hope with men in prison, and that Hope is Jesus! Please pray for these services that God's presence will anoint all that is done to soul-saving effect. There is not one ray of hope of any kind whatsoever in the multitude of "religions" that the officials in our government are so ardently pushing recognition for. The one and only Source of hope is the One the world is rapidly becoming anti— not anti-religion, but anti-Christ. Don't you think, those of us unto whom He is precious, that we ought to give ourselves more fully, more lovingly to Him than ever before? "O come, let us adore Him!"

There is another thing that I must tell you as it has changed along with all that is above. We thought and were promised that we were getting our chapels back, but now this same man is telling us that in our request for them we failed to make a strong enough case to merit them being given back. There must be a reason in God's Word for us being admonished to not grow weary in well doing. Satan surely doesn't care if we grow weary and just give up the battle, but we will continue to rely on God and trust His great heart and hand.

It was a blessing again on the 13th and 14th of November to take our evangelist from our church revival into the prison. One service, he very effectively brought a thought I had never heard emphasized like he did, that when Jesus said in several places, "If any man have ears to hear, let him hear," He was saying that if we would open our ears when He speaks to us, He would have more to say. I could feel that message getting through to numbers of the men. He brought out that multitudes heard the parable of the sower and the seed, but only the disciples with ears to hear more, did hear more of the meaning of what Jesus was teaching.

As we look back from this month it was nineteen years ago that the first of these letters was sent out, December 1999. Many prayer requests have been printed in them. Many answers to those prayers have been recorded. I want to stop for a moment now and thank God for all the answers to your prayers that neither you or I know about. It is not infrequent at all that in visiting with a man I find that God has been working in him in greater measures than I would ever have known had I not visited with him. As I travel here and there, I am often asked the question, "Are you the one who has the prison ministry?" To be honest, that is not a comfortable question to be asked. I don't have or own or perform a ministry. God chose my unworthy person to simply pull together a ministry that He Himself is doing and that you are a vital part of. We are laborers together with Him. Isn't that a glorious privilege?

Now, one more request to you. As the month of December lies just before us, and if Jesus tarries, I want to spend more than my usual time in the prison calling in the men one by one to see how they are doing and to encourage the work in them. How much longer this privilege will be open God only knows and that is one reason I want to work while the day lasts. Please pray with us that it will be a fruitful month in Him.

Blessed Christmas to all,

William Cawman

9
AND STILL HE TARRIES

January 1, 2019

ANOTHER YEAR! AND YET He tarries! Why? They are not all in yet, and so with a renewed commitment to God and lost souls we will enter this new year with our hand in God's and our times in His keeping. God has certainly seen us through the past year with all the unexpected turns in the road and the many snares the enemy had laid for us. Oh, how faithful He has been, and will be. And so, as of now, the door to minister in the prison here remains open as a definite answer to many of your prayers. Thank you for every prayer sent up in our behalf. We will work while the day is.

I have spent much extra time this past month visiting one-on-one with the inmates who are enrolled in my classes and Bible studies. Some visits are so heartwarmingly precious; others are just the opposite. And then others— well! Let me tell you a few on both fronts.

I have several Spanish inmates in classes— some from Mexico, some from Guatemala, and some from Honduras and on down the isthmus and into South America. One dear man came in for a visit and let me know that he couldn't speak much English. I love that! I am very limited in Spanish but enjoy the challenge. As I asked him of his spiritual life, he enthusiastically told me that he really loves Jesus. With tears in his eyes he said ever so feelingly, "I love Jesus too much! Oh, I love Jesus too much!" Pray that he will love Him still more, will you? This man is from Guatemala and was very excited when I told him that I have been there twenty-eight times and am planning to go again in January.

Then another from Guatemala also expressed a real relationship with the Lord. It is so rewarding to visit with a man that I have known nothing about previously and find that he is of a truth walking in the Light and finding real peace with God. This again shows that God is answering many of your prayers. One after another, as I have been visiting with them, have expressed very deeply how much they appreciate my wife and me and the other volunteers from our church. One or two of them told me, "You are different than others. When you come in we see Jesus all over you, and you and your wife are such a blessing to us. We believe you when you tell us that God gives His best."

And then there are others who are not inspirational at all. They seem so hopelessly buried in human and fleshy performances with absolutely none of the power of God. I have tried many times to get through to them that there is a real change that God can bring into the heart that gives power over sin, and the response is, "Yeah, that's what I'm doing." They are so grounded in the belief that works will save them. No wonder Paul warned strongly against such a false hope in his Epistle to the Romans.

One man told me the other day, "This is my fourth time in prison, but I'm done with it now. I'm not coming back!" Many say that they know now where they went wrong and they can get it right this time. I feel like screaming at them, "No, you won't get it right!" But they seem to know something that I don't???

For maybe a year or two a very nice-looking young man

has been coming to the classes and enters the discussion with interest. I have learned that he has his own Bible study on the tier. He is about to leave this Spring and go back home and so I was visiting with him. I asked where he was going and tried to find a church near him that he could safely go to. I told him of a good pastor just over the river into Pennsylvania from where his home is in New Jersey and I said to him, "I know he would really take an interest in you and follow you up." He replied, "Well, I don't really need that. I am now able to help others, so I won't really need help like that." Again, I wanted to wave the red lantern in front of him, but I have learned that self-confidence in a man does not crumble by warnings; only by catastrophes. I fear for him. He is way too sure of himself.

We just received another shipment of about twenty boxes of New Age books for the men. They are loaded with Satan's lies that one can be a Christian if one just practices it. The changing Blood of Jesus is totally bypassed as well as the power of the Holy Spirit. I groaned when I saw the pile just outside my office door. I said to my supervisor, "What can we do to stop this stuff from coming in? The last shipment is still sitting where we left it and no one seems to want it. We have lived to see a non-reading generation. Books are almost obsolete anymore. If a person can't get it on their tablet or phone or laptop, forget it." He agreed and said he would tell the senders to send no more unless we asked for them. To begin with, I have not the heart to pass them out, for they will help no one to heaven, and it is not likely they will even help them to stay out of prison. "That which is born of the flesh is flesh," Jesus said, and flesh is helpless to help flesh.

I do not have exact figures to give to you, but I can tell you that our numbers in Christian services and classes are shrinking. For one thing, Rutgers University and another school as well have started offering classes in-house to the inmates and it is taking men away from Christian activities. But also, there is a rising number of false cults springing up, as well as increasing numbers of Muslims. Just in the last year, Odinists have multiplied. There has been only one volunteer throughout the state who was coming in to hold Odinist services, and that person was banned for some reason, so now there is no one. Notwithstanding, requests keep coming in for enrollment in the Odin "religion."

December 21 was the yearly feast for them (the High Feast of Yule) at which they eat pork chops and drink apple juice. The powers that be in our state government are very tuned in to give them all that is necessary so that they can practice their faith. In the middle facility there were sixteen enrolled in such and so that many pork chops and some to spare were sent down to the assembly room for them to hold their feast to Odin and Thor and whatever other gods accompany such nonsense. Five inmates showed up for it but the pork chop pan was pretty well emptied. I didn't follow it up to see if there were any nurse calls that night or not.

All of the reasons given why Christians need not be provided for to practice their religion goes out the window for these false cults. And of course, Christians who have not an indwelling Christ are rising up more and more with wrong attitudes about it. I continually tell the men that no matter what rights are taken from us, we have no right to be other than Christ-like about it. His rights were completely removed, and that without a word from Him.

The other day one man brought it up in class and asked why Christians don't fight back against such wrongs. I told him that God committed to His Church one weapon, and a mighty one at that— the weapon of prayer. The churches of today have long since lost all power, if not all pretense of prayer, and so that leaves us wondering, "Where are the Christians?" Christianity without Christ is the weakest, most foolish entity in the whole world. He agreed.

A week or two before that I sat in with the Jews for two evenings as they celebrated Hanukah. A cheap Chinese Menorah was provided along with just enough candles (much the same as birthday cake candles, except made especially for

Hanukah) for the eight days. One more candle is lit each day for eight days. The main Jewish inmate, who causes quite a ruckus if he is deprived of any rights, was there in all of his glory to superintend the ceremony. On the last of the eight days they found they were two candles short. Before going in I looked about and found two candles in a Christmas decoration about twice the diameter of the others, so took them along to complete the episode. The Jews are not to blow the candles out, but let them burn all the way down. As soon as they were gone back to their cells for count, however, I blew them out and went to clean up. The two fat candles had made a lot of extra wax and I picked the Menorah up too quickly and spilled melted candle wax down my trouser leg. I was to go right from there to our church, but had to detour past the house and change my trousers as they bore an appearance that would lead one to 4think I had unloaded a bad stomach on them.

The day after Hanukah the above-mentioned inmate was saying his prayers in the chapel and his allotted time was up and they needed the chapel for classification overflow. The officer went in and told him his time was up. He ignored him. He went in again and he told the officer he would come out when he was finished. The officer called in the sergeant and he was sent to lockup. From there he must have created enough disturbance that he was sent to the hospital on PHD watch. The officer in the hospital called me to know what he was supposed to do as the inmate was calling for his phylacteries in order to say his prayers. I knew from experience that to do anything other than provide them for him would be to hear from the powers in Trenton. You see, New Jersey runs on a good quantity of Hebrew money and this inmate's father is pretty influential in it all.

And so, Judaism without Christ is just as much of a mess as any other false religion.

I received a beautiful hand-made Christmas card from our formerly Mormon inmate. Written on the inside were the words:

Dear Dad and Mother Cawman, Merry Christmas!! May your home be filled with His love at Christmas and always! Your son and brother in Jesus, ——.

Then he wrote:

I've been transformed by the love of Jesus, and by your love as well, which is His love… You have from me the love of a son to his parents, as well as the love of a brother in Christ, and for eternity it will be so.

My heart ached for him, that he by God's grace could write such a wish of tender love for us while he has not known the love of a home for over twenty years and may never again. A few more lines from him:

I'm so grateful to God for His Holy Son. I'll be forever grateful to you for leading me to Him, and for helping me find ground where my spirit could hear the Holy Spirit. There are no words or thanks sufficient for that. Maybe it's okay that there are no words, in fact, one of the authors (whose works you introduced me to) said, "It's not what we say about our blessings, but how we use them that is the true measure of our thanksgiving." My gratitude to you, and to the Lord, will have to be shown by what I do with having Jesus and His salvation. He's faithful to live in me and do His work in me and through me. I'll be faithful to let Him! To let Him have His way; that is my gratitude and my thanks. I can't really "Do" anything, just offer myself a "living sacrifice," and let Him do well. He always does.

The Christmas Eve services went very well this year and I do believe numbers of men heard from heaven during them. One man told me on the way out that it was the best Christmas service he was ever in, and yet there was nothing that would have been related to the world's order of service. God speaks like no other! Pray now that the Holy Spirit will find access to their hearts to follow it up with definite victories.

We are looking to Jesus for souls in prison this coming year, if Jesus tarries. We covet and need your prayers as never before. I am personally seeking God for a fresh anointing for this ministry. Whatever the cost of that, I am not willing to face the cost of being without it. Thank you for all your prayers.

In Him,

William Cawman

February 1, 2019

IT WAS SUNDAY AFTERNOON, January 27. My wife and I were to have two services in the prison that night, so we decided to go in early and do some bedside visiting in the prison hospital. We usually find the officers there very helpful and not at all reluctant to accompany us to unlock the doors of the cells so that we can go in and visit and pray with the men. After we had visited several of them, we went into a cell where there was a middle-aged man with a trachea in his throat and so was unable to talk. We introduced ourselves and he immediately brightened up and tried to say something which we could not get as there was no noise and with several teeth missing it was hard to even read his lips.

We asked him if he would like us to sing a hymn for him and he beamed an assent. We asked if he had one he would like and we managed to make out his lip movements that they were all good. We began to sing, "What a Friend We Have In Jesus," and the nurse joined right in with us. Immediately tears filled his eyes and he was obviously feasting on the song. We read some Scripture and then I asked my wife to pray for him. As she did, I saw him heaving with emotion and deep feeling. He began to cough and I was afraid his deep emotions might even prove dangerous to his fragile condition, but he was feeling so much that it was a joy to see his response. I asked him if he had a living relationship with Jesus and he positively shook his head "Yes." We encouraged him to look to Jesus and love and obey Him and he seemed delighted with the thought. It was in all a very rewarding visit that made our time and effort worth it all.

We then visited with several others and then had two services at two different locations in the prison. At the close of the first service a young man was passing out and shook my hand and with deep feeling said, "I really appreciated that tonight!" Such a response brings joy to my heart that a soul is responding to the call of God on him. Believe me, God is still working in prison and out of prison.

I want to thank all of you who prayed for the political pressures that were mounting a few weeks ago. I had written as carefully and discreetly as I knew how, about the powers in Trenton that were threatening our removal or at least demanding subscription to their agenda. We went to a meeting in Trenton and came away saying to each other (my supervisor and the Catholic chaplain and myself) "God definitely answered prayer!" Since then things have quieted down from that front, and not only that, but they made a decision that part-time chaplains would be entitled to a day of sick leave for every thirty days they worked. Now I was somewhat amused at this provision because if I get sick for a day, who is to decide whether that was a work day or a day off anyway?! However, it just showed how wonderfully God answered your prayers in our behalf and has once again kept the door from closing on His work here in the prison. Thank you, thank you! God still answers prayer!

This past week God has definitely been answering some of your prayers for us. There has been an unusual sense of His manifest presence and help in the studies and classes. Ever since we have had the chapels closed except for Sunday services, we have had to use the old original chapels, which are crowded and without equipment. We have had hymnals in the larger chapels, but none in the small ones, so we have pretty much relied on choruses at the beginning of each service. A few weeks ago, our supervisor put out a plea for some hymnals to be donated so that we could have them in the smaller chapels as well. God was so wonderfully gracious as to have a church donate almost three hundred used hymnals, just like the ones we were using. They are a good edition with many good old songs in them. So now that we have them in the Bible studies and classes, my wife and I have been trying to teach them some new songs, and it has been such a blessing.

In one Bible study this week one of the men asked if we could sing the song, "Saved, Saved!" They did not know it, but very soon were lustily singing it and the tide was rising. I stopped them and told them that if they were at a ball game it would be very acceptable to shout out their feelings, so it was even more in order to let the shouts ring out if they knew they were saved. I never heard them sing like that before. They were reaching for the highest note that fit the harmony at the end of the song with their hands held high in the air. Perhaps indeed some were singing it that way to go along with the tide, but some of them were genuinely giving vent to the joy of knowing they were saved, and God surely did honor it!

The lesson that evening was on "Putting Our Trust in God," and the singing before it and the atmosphere it created made the lesson alive and vibrant to them. There are in that class two men who are cellmates and who both evidence a humble yet vibrant joy in their Christian testimony. One of them asked me a while back for some reading material and one of the books I loaned him was Dale Yocum's *The Holy Way*. He came back raving over it and telling me it was dynamic. That is a good sign, isn't it? Well, at the close of that Bible study and just before the closing prayer, he asked if he could give a prayer request. I assured him he could and he said, "Could we pray that God will give us more hunger for Him?" I told the class that such a request would be honored by God and that we would join with him in it. Then his cellmate said, "Could we also pray that He will increase and that we will decrease?" We prayed— we will continue to pray— will you help us? How could we ask for anything greater than those two requests?

Now, the following morning in class one of the men who has been with us for a long while, asked if he could say something. This man has a humble and teachable spirit and I believe he really does love the Lord, but I have seen evidence a number of times that he is not yet filled with the Spirit. He said that one of his jobs is to post the schedules on the bulletin board in the day room on his tier. He said that so often men do not pay attention to the proper times for their barbershop appointments and so go down when they are not scheduled. So, he made up very artistic and colorful signs of the times when they were to go and asked the officer if he thought that would work. The officer told him he didn't think so. He told him they were just too stupid to read them even as outstanding as they were. Well, he posted them neatly on the bulletin board and went down to Bible study.

When he returned, someone had already unpinned one end of the sign and put his name there, and it so upset him that he just ripped the sign down and took it to his room. After his rage calmed down the Lord began to speak to him and tell him to go put it back up and ask the officer to forgive him for his action. He said he didn't want to but the conviction just got so heavy that he had to obey. Then he went to his cell to ask the Lord to forgive him for what came out of him.

As soon as he finished, I said, "All right, men, the case is now before the jury, so let's examine it. Let me draw a parallel from the life of Jesus. For three years Jesus had been with his disciples, teaching them and helping them to grow in knowledge of His Father, and now they were in the Upper Room on His last night. He was pouring out His heart's desire before them that they would receive and be filled with the Holy Spirit whom the Father was to send upon them. While He was pouring out His heart to them, they were sitting there arguing over which of them would be the greatest! So did Jesus come unglued and lash out at them and throw a fit of rage at them?"

They all readily responded with a resounding *"No!"*

"Well, then," I continued, "it sounds like there is still some work to be done, isn't there?" Our dear confessor readily agreed that he needed to dig deeper.

Then (and it seems so often humanity works like this) another man began to confess an uprising that caused him trouble within and without. And so, I then began to explain to them that when Jesus comes into our hearts, He brings light where once was all darkness. But just because the Light has come in, it doesn't mean that the "whole body is full of light," as Jesus said it should be. I told them that until the light comes on in a room, dark areas do not appear. I pointed to the filing cabinet in the corner of the room where it could be seen through the cracks between the drawers that there was darkness inside. I said that they should not be at all surprised if just after a precious time of enlightenment from God's presence, they find it showing up a dark area in the background of their soul, but that to leave it that way was a very dangerous thing to do and was not at all God's will for them. I went on to instruct them to do more than just ask for forgiveness and then walk away. They needed to seek to be filled with the Spirit until no dark areas remained that could open up and give them trouble. God used the whole episode to really speak to them.

Please help us pray that the full light will dawn on many of these men and lead them into the fullness of God. It is the only way they will continue in the path that leads to heaven.

You might ask just what the response is to the teaching of heart holiness among these men, many of whom have never heard anything like it before. Well, if you will turn to Luke chapter twenty-three, you will find an exact parallel in the responses around the Cross of Jesus. Verse 27: some "bewailed and lamented Him." Verse 35: some "stood beholding." Verse 35: some "derided Him." Verse 36: some "mocked Him." Verse 39: one of them "railed on Him." Verse 42: one said, "Lord, remember me when Thou comest into Thy kingdom." Verse 47: the centurion "glorified God." Verse 48: some "smote their breasts and returned." Verse 49: some "stood afar off, beholding..."

There you have it. Every single one of those responses is very evident to the preaching of holiness among them. Did you notice that it was only one who asked to be remembered? Did you notice that it was only one who glorified God? It is that one here and one there that we are thanking God for and continuing to be faithful to the message of full salvation from all sin. To all the rest, please help us pray that we will be as free from their blood on that great day as Jesus was from those about Him.

At present we have only a few men in the class out in the minimum-security camp, but we continue to go there each week and there is very good interest among the few. For the next quarter, we also have a Sunday night each month out there. This past Sunday night my wife and I had gone out and after some songs and prayer and an exhortation and a few testimonies, the call came for count, and so I didn't really have time to preach to them. The next Tuesday afternoon in class one of the men began to tell the class that he had had a dream that I was preaching to them and then began to tell them what I had preached. He was giving such good truth that I forgot he was relating a dream and began to think he must have me mixed up with someone else as I had not preached that to them. Then it dawned on me again that he was relating a dream in which I was preaching to them. With that I thought, "Well, well, God, that just shows how much You really need me to do the preaching, doesn't it?" I don't now remember all that the man was saying, but it was certainly God Who was talking to him, as all of the men were getting help from it. Isn't God interesting? I find Him so!

For some time there has been a very large and rather formidable looking black man who passes by our Bible study door on his way to the library. He is a Muslim, but for "some reason" I have just been attracted to him. I invite him with humor into the Bible study and actually get him to sit down for a minute. He has a very put-on gruff front to him that causes me to play around with him, while actually trying to get through to him. Yesterday afternoon my wife went with me to the study and he came in and sat down. He pointed to her and said, "Is that your wife?" I assured him with joy that she was. She went over and began to talk to him and he told her that he was a Muslim. She wasn't deterred by that and told him he could come and stay. He looked at her and said, "Pray for me!" We are. Will you?

William Cawman

March 1, 2019

WE HAVE WATCHED ANOTHER month of God answering your prayers in very real ways. Thank you, and please continue. The very real threat from the powers in the state capital has at least for the present died almost completely, while we are enabled to continue to carry on the work God has opened up just as before. The classes and Bible studies are going well and God is helping in them. The one-on-one interviews continue without interference. This, Dear Praying Friends, is definitely an answer to prayer. Full well are we aware of the growing invasion of evil forces in our country. The antichrist agenda is pressing hard to silence the voice of God. But God is not finished yet, and He has made this known afresh in the last month or so. How it reminds us, however, that we dare not take our gospel privileges for granted. And so, we will not take this lull in the inroads of sin for granted, or take it lightly. God is not finished yet in the prison here. There are too many precious men who have heard, have walked in the light, and are leaning hard on a continuing ministry among them. There are others who, even though they are struggling, do desire to find the "Better Way." We are thanking God also for a donation of hymnals from which we are learning new songs each week. The men love my wife to come in and play them for them to learn, and she loves to do it too. Her mother heart reaches out to them and they very obviously feel it. I think I told you, perhaps in the last letter, how she had spoken to a very large and very gruff-looking Muslim man. Last night as he passed by the door of the Bible study on his way to the library, he poked his head in the door and said, "Tell your wife I said 'Hi!'" I had met him in the hallway earlier in the day and when I stop and speak to him like that, all that gruff exterior melts away and there is a tender longing in his eyes that I wish so much I could get into.

I want to leave a prayer request with you. One of the volunteers who helps out when we are away in meetings comes all the way down from four hours away in Pennsylvania. He loves to be with the men and they feel it, too. He has recently been trying to find an open door to minister in one of the state prisons up in Pennsylvania close to where he is. Please do pray that God will touch the heart of the chaplain there and allow him to carry the message those men so need to hear in to them. Of course, don't pray that he will find such an open door that he can no longer come down here as well!

This morning I visited with a man who is just about to turn sixty years of age. He is serving his third time in prison and has ten years yet to go on this one. He told me that when he finally gets out, he will be almost seventy years of age and will have spent forty years of it in prison, not counting time done in county jails. He has completed the entire four-year theological course that God so blessed the men in prison with. He understands at least in a large measure the doctrine of holiness, and he is living a good life, but I have never felt I could say that I would have no questions about whether he has really gone all the way into a likeness of His death. He told me that when he gets down to pray at night there are times when he feels he must ask God to forgive him for something; other times he doesn't feel that way. I asked him what it is that makes him feel the need of forgiveness. He said it is three things that bother him: his anger, his lust and neglect of study. He said he doesn't know whether those things are still lurking in his heart or whether they are the result of his long-time association with them. He sees things that are not right around him and then dwells on it too long, thus allowing feelings of anger to arise over them.

Please pray for this man that he will come out into clear Scriptural victory over all sin. I told him that wherever he finds something unlike Christ coming to him, he needs to plead the Blood of Jesus to fill that spot where sin has been, rather than try to cleanse the sin out himself. I tell men like this over and over that the literature and sermons they hear so much of today focus on making ourselves better instead of being filled with the Spirit, which alone can cleanse the heart.

Basically, they are struggling with the same stumbling block that I struggled with so many years; viz. trying to get rid of sin so that God could dwell within, instead of opening the door and letting Him, the only sin-cleansing agent, come in. I liken it to light and darkness. There is no way of getting rid of darkness except to turn on the light. And there is no power within or without us to rid us of inward sin except to let in the full Light of God's promised Spirit. This man also told me that it is not even his focus anymore whether he ever gets out of prison or not. He just wants to live for God and please Him wherever he has to be.

Another man I visited this morning came to prison at the age of nineteen, has been in for nineteen years, and also has ten years ahead of him yet. He fathered three children while still in high school. The youngest two (by two different mothers) were both born after he was in prison. His youngest and only daughter has a very good relationship with him and calls him for advice, but he has not seen her for several years as she lives a good way away. He is also taking theological studies from one of the Bible colleges, and does seem to be walking in all the light he has had up to this point. He is a full believer in the way of holiness, but again, I don't know if that work has been perfected in him.

We heard a disappointing thing just this week. A man who had gotten out of prison several months or even a couple of years ago had come to our church for some time. Then he began to drift away and was just arrested again and is on his way back to prison. Isn't the devil's pathway just adorable? And yet he has so many blinded into thinking that God's pathway is one without interest and without pleasure. What a liar he is indeed!

The group out in the minimum-security camp is small, but very vibrant right now. There are several men who are very intent and interactive in our discussions. They use the men in the camp to go out along roadsides and into parks, etc., and clean up trash and mow grass. This keeps many of them from attending a daytime class who otherwise would. In a previous letter recently, I told you that our supervisor of religious services has turned in his intent to retire this coming July. I believe I asked you to pray about this, for his leaving would open a door that Satan would love to fill with the wrong person. The supervisor and I have worked together nearly the whole twenty-one years I have been here and he has never tried to hinder God's cause in any way. Now he tells me that it might not be the best for him to retire quite yet, and that it might be an advantage for him to wait at least another year. He is planning to attend a work session on retirement to see for sure what would work the best for him. Would you please pray that God would keep him here as long as He sees fit? He has definitely been God's agent to keep a door of ministry open here for all this time.

I've had a growing population of Hispanic men enrolling in my classes and Bible studies. Some of them understand pathetically little English and speak even less. Just what they are getting only God knows, but several of them really seem to be feeling the presence of God. We do have Spanish services in each facility, but perhaps what is offered there is not meeting their needs. Once in a while I will call on one or the other of them to pray, for I want to encourage them to feel a part of it, and God understands their prayer as well as others of that language. I guess if they want to keep coming with as little as they understand, I can at least give them an opportunity to express themselves to God. There are enough of them that at least that way they get something in their language.

Every so often we have a communion service for the men. We leave it up to their conscience as to whether they are worthy to partake of it or not. We order little sealed cups of grape juice with a wafer attached to the top of it. Recently, I realized it had been some time since we had given it out in the minimum camp, and for this quarter our church has had a service there each month. I checked into the locked cabinet where we keep the keyboard and noticed that there were enough of the cups to serve the Sunday night group. When I picked them up, I noticed that every one of them were sunken in on the side. I thought it might not be wise to send the men out of service staggering, so I took them downstairs to the lieutenant, whom I have known for years. He looked at them and grinned understandingly and took them to their destiny. We will try again later.

Thank you again for all your valuable prayers.

William Cawman

10
WILL IT WORK WHEN THEY GET OUT?

April 1, 2019

GREETINGS TO YOU ONCE again at the opening of another month. There is a very precious Scripture in Jeremiah the Prophet which reads: "The LORD hath appeared of old unto me, saying, Yea, I have loved thee with an everlasting love: therefore with lovingkindness have I drawn thee" (Jer. 31:3). How very conscious of this one becomes when hearing the stories of men from all walks of life. That "everlasting love" is still loving. That "lovingkindness" is still drawing. Thank God for it. But I want to take some space in this letter to open my inner heart to you as to men's response to this, God's part, that I see in ever-repeating drama.

Thank God for every victory in lives from prison that is holding still today. One of them is now our Sunday School Superintendent in our church. Some are now moved on to other prisons where God is using them to tell others. But for the few who have kept their choice made, many walk with God for a while and then turn back. This part of prison ministry gives many a heavy heart and profound disappointment. I want to share some deep feelings with you over this.

We have seen a number of men now who seem to do so well in prison, and we would have no reason to doubt the genuineness and reality of their experience with God. They then get out and some of them come to our church for a while, some for quite a while, and then turn away and go out from us. This is almost worse than a death within the congregation. Some of them have been such a blessing for a while. They are needy; they have nothing to start with. Our faithful pastor has spent hours and days looking after them and taking them places to try to help them get on their feet again. He has given up family time and personal time to look after them. Others in the church have helped also, although anyone who is a volunteer in the prison must observe state guidelines in being associated with them.

And then after all of that investment in them, they turn back into the paths of sin. This has been the case more often than not, until sometimes Satan lays blow after blow against my heart, telling me that this ministry is only causing pain and grief to the pastor and the flock. I lay it out before the Lord, but can never question His calling and leading into this area of ministry. Then God begins to speak to me in the following ways.

First, Jesus Himself suffered such a track record of disappointments. The Scripture gives this scenario of Jesus' ministry at one point. "From that time many of his disciples went back, and walked no more with him. Then said Jesus unto the twelve, Will ye also go away? Then Simon Peter answered him, Lord, to whom shall we go? thou hast the words of eternal life. And we believe and are sure that thou art that Christ, the Son of the living God. Jesus answered them, Have not I chosen you twelve, and one of you is a devil?"

Jesus told His disciples, "The disciple is not above his master, nor the servant above his lord." Jesus has let me know that He felt the disappointment even more keenly than I feel it. And He continues to feel it when one of these men who seemed so promising turns back.

10: WILL IT WORK WHEN THEY GET OUT? 167

We see this disappointment not only in prison, but on mission fields as well. The battle for souls is laced with heart-breaking disappointments.

But then God has brought another reason for this before my attention, in Matthew 12:23-25—

> "When the unclean spirit is gone out of a man, he walketh through dry places, seeking rest, and findeth none. Then he saith, I will return into my house from whence I came out; and when he is come, he findeth it empty, swept, and garnished. Then goeth he, and taketh with himself seven other spirits more wicked than himself, and they enter in and dwell there: and the last state of that man is worse than the first. Even so shall it be also unto this wicked generation."

As long as a man is alive, God will never cross his free moral agency, neither will He remove all temptation by coaxing a man to heaven with a sucker in his mouth. And so, there are times in the Christian's walk when he walks through dry places. His feelings are not at white pitch such as they were right after a crisis experience with God. When that happens, many do just what the Scripture says: they go back to the house they came out of. Now, let me draw two life scenes in parallel.

Scene one: A person is raised in a good holiness home with everything in his favor to make him want to be a genuine Christian. He has been planted in good soil in a goodly vineyard. He becomes a "cumberer of the ground." God in mercy walks about and sees him taking up vineyard space and vineyard privileges and says to the keeper of the vineyard, "Cut him down!" The keeper of the vineyard pleads with the Owner of the vineyard to let him alone one more year and let him dig around it and fertilize it and give it one more chance. (I must stop and place myself, yes, the one writing these reflections, exactly here) The once-dead vine now begins to blossom forth and bear fruit. All around rejoice, and the keeper of the vineyard has high expectations. But alas, after a season a dry spell comes and the fruit bearing slows down and finally stops, and the soul being described goes back to the house he came out of— a benchwarmer among the righteous. He continues to take up vineyard space. He continues to partake of vineyard privileges. And in doing so, he arouses no particular attention from those about him.

Scene two: A man grows to adulthood having never known anything except the whirlpool and trauma of sin. He is deprived of parenthood; he is surrounded by evil influences; he is a victim of evil habits and vices. He is a trashcan for drugs and alcohol and all the lusts of the flesh. The glamorous drama he is addicted to comes to a screeching halt with red flashing lights and handcuffs, and that night he is rudely awakened on the cold floor of a county jail cell by the realization that this is not what Satan had promised him. He has had just enough exposure in his life to the idea of church that he begins to pray to a God he knows nothing of as yet. God hears his cry. Suddenly his inner being and his eyeballs turn into floods of tears and a peace comes over him that he has never known before. A miracle has begun.

He feels the need of help and so he goes to the prison chapel and begins to listen to the call of the Gospel. The God who loves him with an everlasting love is now drawing him with lovingkindness. He listens as truth is presented to him that he can be delivered from the evil strivings within him that led him into his previous life of sin and shame. He responds to that call also and prays and seeks until his heart is fully cleansed from all sin. What a blessing he becomes to all around him. His zeal and love for God puts many a benchwarmer in a holiness church to shame. He spends the remainder of his prison time a blessing in the prison.

Then he is released on parole and he wants to continue this good life. He begins to attend the best church he knows of or can find and brings with him a refreshing new voice and spirit into that church. He blesses everyone and is blessed himself. His new church family love him and have great hopes for him.

He is now a part of the family of God and the past is forgotten in his newfound joy of living.

Then reality begins to set in as to his existence outside of prison. Little by little his focus shifts from loving God with all his heart to the demands of life about him. He fails to stay filled with the Spirit every passing hour, just like the man in scene one, and before long self and its desires begins to assert itself once again. The brightness in his testimony begins to dim. The dynamics begin to fade from his love for Jesus and his new family. Then, suddenly in a dry spell, he remembers and goes back to the house he came out of. He is in church on Sunday, but by Friday night he has found the pleasure once more of an adulterous relationship and is now ashamed to come the next Sunday.

The church family he just left is staggering with disappointment and unbelief. How could he? Why would he?

Scene one and scene two are identical in the sight of God; it is simply in the realm of social impact that there is a difference. If the condition continues, they will spend eternity together in hell— the dirty, rotten sot and the benchwarmer.

We have been literally traumatized by the man in scene two; we are almost immune to the tragedy of scene one. God isn't!

Now— can you understand why at times Satan levels an arrow at the ones involved in this ministry and makes them almost shrink back from any more tragedies? Shall we give place to him? The answer is a definitive, yet trembling *"No!"* But at the same time, we feel such an ever-recurring sense of utter bankruptcy that can only be relieved by fresh anointings from the God who called into this work to start with.

I trust I have not done wrong in being so open-hearted, but I think you who are praying have a right to hear this. It was not written to call attention to the laborer, but to the crying need of the Scriptural cure for it all: "But be filled with the Spirit." And that cure is not only applicable to men who have come out of prison, or to new converts on a mission field, but it is the desperate essential if benchwarmers are ever to make heaven.

For a few weeks now I have noticed a younger looking man in the Bible study in the middle facility. One evening we were discussing the very verse I quoted at the beginning of this letter. I was telling them that not one of them would be in that Bible study had it not been for the everlasting love of God that drew them with lovingkindness.

Suddenly this young man lit up and said, "I need to testify about that!" He then told us that he was thirty years of age and that the whole thirty years had been nothing but trauma. He said, "I have never heard of any trauma worse than what I have been through. I had no knowledge of God, but once or twice I tried going to church and that just brought more trauma from my mother, who didn't want me to go. But now, since I have been turning to God, I feel that lovingkindness and I feel a peace coming into me."

As he spoke, my heart just went out to him and I asked the men to pray for him. The following Sunday night he was in the service and I stopped him on the way in and asked him for his name and number, saying that I would like to call him in for a visit. He really brightened up and readily wrote it down for me. I am eager to hear what God is doing for him, and oh, how I long for men like this to come to know the fullness of Jesus. Please pray for him. It is pitiful to see what Satan does to a man almost before he becomes a man.

I would also ask you to pray for the Muslim chaplain. I have mentioned some about him in previous letters, but we do not know what is happening with him at the present time. He refused to let a gay man attend Jumah service, and the man sued him. It could turn into a major episode but I don't know anything more about it as of yet.

It is more and more obvious that people are being awakened to a sense of need. We are receiving many requests for such things as Odinism or Buddhism or Judaism. Isn't it a tragedy that Satan stands between the call of God and the ear of man? What a thief and robber he is. I honestly believe that all of these requests that we are receiving (and I can never remember in twenty years of the such like) are a misdirection of understanding as to Who is calling them. I well remember a man I was working with several years ago who stopped what we were doing one day and said to me, "I know God is knocking at my heart's door. I ought to yield." Then he turned to a highly charismatic Pentecostal church, where a woman told him that she had a vision that when he received the gift of the Holy Ghost he would be wearing purple pants and a yellow shirt, or some such thing. What a deceiver is that angel of light.

Thank you again for your faithful prayers for us.
With love to all,
William Cawman

✝✝✝

May 1, 2019

WE HAVE HAD SOME encouraging and refreshing times in the Lord this month in the prison services and classes. God is still sending the Holy Spirit among men in prison to prepare a Bride for the soon-coming King of Kings. Aren't you glad He sees beyond where we often do, and beholds, instead of a wreck of humanity that Satan thought was his, a gem in the rough for the crown of Jesus?

We had to be gone in a meeting over Good Friday and Easter Sunday, but volunteers from the church did a wonderful job of which I heard much appreciation when I returned the Tuesday afterwards. I certainly want to thank each of them for all they did to bring Easter hope to the men in prison.

Last month I told you about a young man who burst out in class that he needed to testify and then said that he had never heard of any trauma happening to anyone beyond what all had happened to him in his thirty years on earth. But then he said that now that he is opening up his heart to God, he is finding a peace he never knew existed. I scheduled him for a visit and he was eagerly awaiting it. He told me in brief of his thorny life in a battle-torn home where sin was open and unashamed. In the trauma of it all he tried a few times to go to a church, but when his mother found out about it, she inflicted all the more trauma on him for going. It was a rough thirty years prior to now, to be sure.

I talked to him very deeply about a living relationship with Jesus and he was so open and hungry for it. I do not know just how far that relationship has gone, but he is definitely on the path that leads back to Father's house. Then I was gone for a couple of weeks in meetings and when I went to schedule him for another visit, I found he had been moved to a northern prison. Please do pray for him. The Holy Spirit can do what none of us can, thank God!

One afternoon we were opening the class in Facility 1 with a time of worship, and my wife started the song, "His Name is Wonderful." I wish you could have felt the sacred atmosphere that settled down deeper and deeper as they sang. A few "Hallelujahs" began to ring out in the middle of it, and heaven bent low. God comes like that when there is true worship of Him and when He sees hungry hearts searching for Him.

For a number of months, we have been studying some foundational material preparatory to a study of the Ten Commandments and how they apply to our present age and culture (and by the way— they do!). We studied the subject of love as it being the motivating force behind all we do. Then we studied the subject of law, and how impossible it is to live without being subject to one law or another. Then we studied quite extensively the subject of sin and all of its aspects and where they came from. Now we have taken up a look at how society today, as well as great sectors of what is called "Christianity," has rebelled against the commandments of God and gravitated into situational ethicists.

We briefly looked at the profound change, and not for the better, in our nation and in the world, since we decided, like

Lucifer, that we didn't need God or the Bible or His commandments. We looked at what the world itself has labeled the "New Morality," which came because they rejected God and the Bible, but of necessity needed some code of ethics. So the new ethic is "love." But it is love shorn of law, which is as hollow as a penny balloon. We looked at both the secular mindset and the church mindset relative to this new ethic. We discovered that the secular mindset has for its center, the love of myself. Whatever is good for me is what I'll expect of you. After all, if love is the fulfilling of the law, must not love begin at home with me? Abandoning the law of God, it is perfectly consistent with this code of ethics if I divorce my wife because she isn't bringing me the happiness that I need.

The church version of this law of love is love of another. So without law, if grandma is suffering and her quality of life is gone, wouldn't it be the most loving thing for her to be artificially sent on out of life? If a member of my congregation is suffering from singleness, wouldn't it be ever so loving to provide them with that type of love, even if I have a living spouse? If an ultrasound scan detects that my unborn baby has an abnormality, wouldn't it be the kindest, most loving act for me to abort it?

By the way, we are only preparing to land with all four feet on "Thus saith the Lord!" I am finding these men to be fully agreed that we have gotten ourselves into a demonic mess by finding our own ethical standard instead of the Written Word of God. When prayer and the Bible were taken out of our schools, Satan rushed into the void with fury. Drugs are being blamed; guns are being blamed; but the real problem is that God is no longer anywhere on the horizon. There is and always has been but one moral standard for God's created man— God's own Word.

Please continue to pray for the political atmosphere of our prison system. I realize that I need to exercise some degree of caution in how much I say in these letters as I never know into whose hands they will fall, but the past year or two has been about as predictable as a roller coaster missing its tracks. My supervisor has definitely made his decision to retire as of the first of July. As you have gathered from letters in the past, he has been used of God to hold the door open for us to minister without restrictions here. God only knows what will happen now, but then God is the One who opened this door to start with, isn't He?

I would love to ask you to pray for our Catholic chaplain. He is a joy to work with and a very sensible and capable man. For the sake alone of you gaining a perspective of our relationship, let me copy here a note he sent me two days ago.

> Dear Chaplain Cawman,
> I have the highest respect for you because you are a man of God and a complete gentleman. It is a pleasure to work with you. I am looking forward to many years of service in the Lord's vineyard. We are a team and coworkers in the Lord's vineyard. I truly appreciate you. Whatever I can do to help you, please do not hesitate to let me know and I will do the same. I know I can count on you. We work for the living God. You are my brother in the Lord.

But— almost unbelievably to the two of us and our present supervisor, the administration and custody of the prison are pushing relentlessly to make the Muslim chaplain supervisor. I am not sure whether there are a majority of Muslim officers or if it is a case that he makes them comfortable in sin, but the tide is strong. I could say a lot more, but perhaps it would not be prudent. Probably whatever you might read into this between my lines would not prove to be as serious as it really is. Please help us pray for this situation, as it could make the difference between light and darkness in our future work here.

A couple of weeks ago one of the men who has been in classes and Bible studies for several years, and who has been a diligent seeker after God, had a misfortune which removed him from us for a while at least. He is an elderly black gentleman with a tender and gracious heart. He awakens at 3:00

every morning and spends time sitting on his bunk praying and reading and singing softly.

One day he was sitting there softly singing a song of praise to the Lord and his cellmate came over to him and said, "I've had enough of this. I'm tired of your slavery mentality. Why do you always have to sing and worship that white Jesus? That's the mindset of slavery."

Our brother replied, "When you first came in the cell and I gave you a pair of shoes and things to eat, was that slave mentality?"

With that, the cellmate picked up our brother's wooden cane and cracked him over the head. Our brother whirled around and before he could hit him again, he threw him to the floor and began punching him and yelling for the officer. Of course, they both received a charge and were sent to detention. However, the blow to his head broke a blood vessel behind his eyeball and he had to be sent out to a hospital on the outside for surgery. I went to the hospital to visit him and his spirit was still sweet and he was refusing to allow any wrong attitudes about it. I really love the dear man and will miss him.

Please remember in prayer the men who have been moved from this prison to others in or out of the state. Some of them correspond with me and God is using them as shining lights for holiness where He has allowed them to go.

On the last Sunday night of April, my wife and I went into Facility 1 for two services. We were to leave after midnight Monday morning to drive out to Newton Falls, OH for the funeral of Sharon Palmer, who went to Malawi a few years ago and was a tremendous help to our daughter there. She had to return home with lung cancer and the men have been praying for her. I told them of her triumphant home-going and then told them we were going to sing the song for them that she had requested we sing at her funeral: "And the Devil Was Defeated Again." They had never heard a song like it and especially to be sung at a funeral, but that was Sharon's triumphant request.

That afternoon God had impressed upon me to take Jer. 17:9 and Mat. 5:8 and talk to the men about the journey between those two verses. After we had our song service and prayer and had sung that song for them, I told them to pick up their chairs and turn around and go to the other end of the chapel where there is a whiteboard. I then read the first verse to them, "The heart is deceitful above all things, and desperately wicked: who can know it." I asked them if they really believed that to be the truth, and there was an overwhelming "Yes; it was true." Then I had them turn to the verse in Matthew: "Blessed are the pure in heart: for they shall see God." I asked them if they really believed that the Blood of Jesus could produce in man a pure heart. They did. Then I proceeded to sketch six hearts, one after another on the whiteboard while explaining the stages of man's heart.

The first heart was the Created Heart, the heart God gave to Adam with nothing in it except the fullness of His own Spirit. The second heart was the Infant Heart, a heart like Cain came into the world with as well as all the rest of us. I explained to them that neither Adam and Eve, nor any parent since, could breathe into their child the breath of life— only Jesus can do that. And so I drew that heart with just a spot of sin in the center of where the nature of Jesus had been. They said they were following.

The third heart was the Child's Heart, and out of that sin spot roots were developing but they were not as yet willful sins, and so brought no guilt. I used some pretty raw and down-to-earth illustrations and they were getting it.

The fourth heart, the Sinner's Heart, now had a tree growing out of those roots, for conscience had awakened and the very first violation of that conscience made the person a sinner.

The fifth heart was the Saved Heart. The person who was a sinner was convicted by the Holy Spirit and came to God with that awful tree of sin and guilt weighing them down and asked God to forgive them. Through the Blood of Jesus, God wiped away that tree with all of its ugly branches and they were now saved! There was a ring of applause that rippled through the crowd. But in the picture, I not only showed the tree cut down, but the roots still remaining and Jesus enthroned above them. I began to explain the warfare that would soon be felt between the roots within and the love of Jesus over them. I told them that if they allowed the roots to gain the consent of their will, they would sprout again and then it would be no different from the heart before it— that is called "backsliding."

The sixth heart was a Sanctified Heart with all the roots and the stump having been removed by the Spirit of God filling the heart with Himself. Now Christ was crowned within and the fruits of righteousness were blossoming forth.

At the close of the service one man shook my hand with these words: "Chaplain, in all my sixty years on this earth, I never heard it explained so clearly." Pray that the Lord will use such simplicity to reach many of them with the reality of a complete work through Jesus Christ.

Thank you again for your prayers.

William Cawman

June 1, 2019

WAS IT JOHN WESLEY who said that there will be more people in hell over despair than over any other one cause? Let me share with you a case of deep despair. I received a request from a name I didn't recognize and when I went to schedule a visit, I found he had been sent to the prison hospital. I went over to the hospital and asked to see him. They let him out of his cell and we sat down together in the dayroom by ourselves.

With a look of deep dejection, he began, "Chaplain, are you familiar with Santaria?" I told him I knew what it was and some about it. He said, "I was raised in a Christian home, but that doesn't allow me to do the things that I want so I turned to Santaria. Now I'm here at thirty-one years old in the hospi-

tal with colitis and not doing well at all. Do you think all this has come on me because I turned to Santaria?"
I looked him in the eye and then said, "It might be!"

Then I tried to direct him back to what he really already knew to be the truth. "But Chaplain, you see, I'm gay, and God won't take me that way, will He?"

I never plunge into a scenario like that without first asking a few questions. I asked him at what age he became gay and why. He told me he grew up in a normal home and all of his siblings were straight, but that from an early age he just had no desire for women. He had tried a few and never wanted to be with one again. And so, he had been with men and still wanted that, but that he was miserable beyond words.

I asked him why he would not want to let Jesus come into his heart and give him power to stop sinning and then fill the void in him with something worth living for. He said, "I know I should, and I know what you are saying is right, but I'm not ready yet for that, because I still want some things that God doesn't want."

I said, "Let me ask you a question: How much worse does this have to get before you will be ready to let God straighten you out?"

"I don't know, but I hate the way I am and have tried over and over to change. I've never succeeded in anything except doing and selling drugs. And so, I finally just gave up and accepted myself the way I am."

I then quoted to him the observation regarding despair. I said, "You are in despair, and this is not going to get any better. Unless you turn your life over completely to Jesus, you are going to continue to spiral down and out until you end in hell."

He said, "I know you're right, but I'm not ready yet. When I get out of here I want to have a man in my life."

I said, "So you don't think you can live without that? Let me ask you, how long have you been in prison?" He said it had been almost three years already. I said, "So it's obviously a lie that you cannot live without a man, because you have been doing it here!"

"I know, but I'm not ready yet. I'm just the way I am."

I said, "Will you at least think over the things I have told you and ask to see me again? I really care about you and I don't want to see you continue to live in this miserable downward spiral."

He shook his head "yes" and promised to ask to see me again.

Despair! Oh, what a thief and a robber! Oh, what a deadly weapon of Satan's. Please pray for him.

But on a brighter note— and thank God there are some!— we have recently had a definite upswing in attendance and interest out in the minimum-security camp, outside of the main perimeter. The classes there have been very interactive and with good spirit and result. One of the men who has been very interactive for some time recently, just out of the blue said, "Chaplain, I want to keep things real. I am not finding from God what I was some time back. I have prayed about it, but I need something more than what I'm finding."

Thank God for honest hearts! Oh, how many times I long for such confessions from longstanding churchgoers. God has something far better for all of us than to look back on better days spiritually. At any rate, he has been digging and I believe finding some good spiritual growth.

In about two or three weeks our class out there more than doubled and among them a couple of men completely new to what it is all about. One of them spoke up and said, "I'm just a new Christian and I know that it's going to take time for me to quit sinning." Immediately, the man who had confessed his need said to him with genuine compassion, not judgmentalism, "Wait a minute. Christians don't sin. You need to ask Jesus to come into your heart and He will give you the ability to not sin."

That opened wide a door to the pure gospel, that Jesus came

to save His people *from*, not *in* their sins. It was a very good and profitable class time. And the man who was new to it all made no obvious objection to being faced with deeper truth. Once again, the truth of the words of Jesus became so vivid: "...the publicans and the harlots go into the kingdom of God before you." For so often we see those who have been around church all their lives and who are living such a substandard lack of victory, resent being cornered by truth just like this man was.

Every time I hear of fresh rumblings from the powers that be up in Trenton, I become more conscious of three things, and I want to ask you to join in prayer for them. Here they are:

1. The night is coming in which we can no longer work. This is clearly prophesied in Scripture, and in some measure is being fulfilled even now.
2. God is the One who opened this door into this prison twenty-one years ago. He didn't get permission to do so from Trenton, nor did He follow their prescription for getting it done.
3. I need to be in prayer as never before to the one and only true God who can hold back the night and keep the door open.

Granted, according to Scripture, "For the mystery of iniquity doth already work: only he who now letteth will let, until he be taken out of the way." What has up to date prevented His removal? Is it not the prayers of God's people? Then, this is no time to let up or even to just simply continue as before. The signs so conspicuously call for more fervent prayers. Oh God, help me in this! I don't want to be guilty of standing before His judgement throne and finding that had I been more faithful in prayer, a door for other souls could have stayed open a little longer. Will you pray for me and help me in prayer? I am not able, or at least it would not be prudent, to publish some details of what I am seeing and referring to; in fact, I just did type something in here and then felt checked over it and deleted it, not knowing where this letter might end up. But one thing is certain: things will not always continue as they are or have been.

So— we will work while the day is; tomorrow belongs to God.

I wish you could see the glow on the face of a little man from El Salvador (if I remember correctly where he is from). As he sits in the Bible studies there is a picture of peace over his countenance, even though I can see that he does not understand a lot of what is being said or sung. Then as he passes by me, I love to ask him if he still loves Jesus, and this is the answer I get from his beaming face: "I love Him too much! I love Him too much!" Isn't it precious as to where all Jesus has His jewels? He is soon going to call His waiting Bride away to be with Him forever, and He will not miss one of them, either.

Sometimes I like to remind the men that if they truly love Jesus and are washed in His blood, it matters not if they are on the first floor, bottom layer of cells, with four layers of reinforced concrete above them; He will take them right up through it all without an effort. Oh, help us pray that the number will increase of those who will be ready for that Great Day!

There are two men who were in my classes some time back who are now returned again. Both of them violated their parole specifications. They both seem very repentant and possibly awakened more than they were before by the setback. Please pray that they will go all the way with God until they do not fall again. Such tragedies so portray the truth of God's Word: "The thief cometh not, but for to steal, and to kill, and to destroy..." Oh, that they could turn from him and find Him who said, "I am come that they might have life, and that they might have it more abundantly."

Still reflecting on these pathetic cases, let me draw a parallel. We have in our country many people who have had the privilege of growing up in America. They have tasted all of its privileges and benefits, and known nothing but freedom and prosperity. Multitudes of them are rising up and wanting to destroy this wonderful country that has given them all of that.

If they only knew what it is like to live in a country that does not have all of that to offer, they would be ashamed of their ingratitude and insensitivity.

We have many people who have grown up in Christian homes with all of the benefits of a Christian community, such as church, school, family, etc. Many of them are finding fault with their upbringing to the extent that some have even sought out the help of physiatrists and counselors to help them to cope with their "wounded past." Shame on them! I do not take that back! I hear and see the stories of men who have had none of those privileges and what it has done to them. If some of those ungrateful hearts could only crawl inside of many lives that I have become acquainted with over the past twenty-one years, they would throw their ingratitude to the wind and thank God for the home they were given.

There will be no extra charge for that observation— it just came out that way! Working among the wreckage of our self-centered and Godforsaken today's society leaves little sympathy for complaints or even faultfinding about a Christian heritage. I thank God for every influence that helped me in whatever measure to come closer to Him.

Whenever my wife can go in with me, we are trying to teach the men a number of choruses we often hear in our camps and meetings. The men are enjoying it and those who really love the Lord are recognizing in those choruses something far deeper than most of the modern songs they generally are exposed to. We have only one keyboard, which we have to cart back and forth to the various facilities to help her teach them, so our supervisor has put in an order for three more new ones so that we will have one in each area. Ever since they closed down our larger chapel areas except for Sunday nights, we have had to use the original chapels, which are smaller and did not have a piano in them. The Catholic chaplain also uses the keyboard in some of his services and it is so easy to forget who needs it next and where.

Before I run out of space here, I want to give you an update from this afternoon on the group out in the minimum camp. Two weeks ago I had given each of them a copy of two books: *Pilgrim's Progress,* and John Wesley's *Plain Account of Christian Perfection.* Today the very man who felt the need of more of God as I related above, raised his hand and said, "Chaplain, I need to say something. I want to thank you for those two books you gave us. I started reading the one on perfection and it drove me to the Bible and then the Bible drove me back to the book. Back and forth I went and all the while I was understanding more about God and our relationship to Him."

The other men agreed with him, and then questions and testimonies took up the rest of the time. And everything this man said just rang a bell with the truth of God. It reminded me of the dear old grandma that some traveling Christians discovered out on the western plains, isolated from any other Christians or a church. They discovered in her such a love of God and His Word that they told some other Christians and they got their minds together and decided to buy Granny a set of commentaries. Later one of them stopped by and asked her how she liked them. "Oh, children," she said, "I love them, but sometimes I find things in them that are hard to understand. When that happens, I go to my Bible and it straightens them right out!" God bless Granny and God continue to bless these precious men!

With love and gratitude to you,

William Cawman

11
LIFE'S CHANGES CONTINUE — BUT GOD!

July 1, 2019

WHAT A GOD WE serve! Shortly after writing the letter for last month I was standing in front of one of the classes as we were singing these words: "I'm glad I know that my sins are forgiven. I'm glad I know that I'm cleansed by the blood. I'm glad I know it's settled; I will serve Him. I'm glad I know that I am clear with God." I suddenly noticed the fervent expressions of three men right in front of me, every one of them murderers! My heart was melted at what the grace of God can do. I absolutely have confidence that they were singing these words from honest and sincere hearts that God has redeemed from Satan's grip. They are now living lives above sin and show it all over their countenances. Surely it is Scripturally true: "For the LORD taketh pleasure in his people: he will beautify the meek with salvation." God not only has a way of removing the hardness from the heart, but the hardness from the countenance as well. Bless His name!

This season of the year I am usually away quite a bit in camp meetings, and God has blessed the ministry with a faithful servant from four hours away in PA who comes down with joy to minister to the men while we are away. The men love him and it is so good for them to have multiple witnesses to the truth of heart holiness in a place where so many other volunteers scoff at it and fight it. Please help us pray that more will truly enter into the experience. Endorsing the doctrine does not put the glow on the face and the victory in the life; only the experience does.

As of the date of this letter (to the day) we no longer have a supervisor for our department. Only God knows who next will fill that vacancy and just what their attitude toward God and His work here will be. This is a very critical prayer request for sure. The man we have referred to in previous letters who is in charge of all chaplains in the state has been coming down more frequently, and for the present seems to be non-confrontational as to what I am teaching and doing and to when I am there. I do not know if this will continue, now that my supervisor who has long stood in the gap for me is no longer there. God is the One who opened this door. He is able to do whatever He sees best, even with powers that do not have respect for Him and would even fight against Him.

Would you permit me to share a thought with you that would definitely constitute a departure from what is normally covered in these letters? I would not do it except for the comparison I have thought about. You see, the men in prison, along with my wife and I and the rest of our family, have recently had a very pleasant surprise come into our lives. My son and his wife had been happily married for almost twenty-six years when they broke the news to us that we were to be grandparents to a little girl. Her name is Clara Joyce Cawman, and we are welcoming her with wide open arms. Even though I have been called "Grandpa" by many young people across the country, and even though I inherited six grandchildren by marrying my precious wife, on the twentieth day of May I became a real grandpa. Now of course you will not be tempted at all, I am sure, to suspicion that I would be harboring any grandpa pride, would you?

Now, let me tell you that after waiting for almost twenty-six years, my son and his wife are hardly letting this little one out of their sight, and it is doing my heart good to see them. There is nothing that can possibly be done for little Clara that is not abundantly provided for. Every ounce she gains is carefully documented and treasured. Every new development is hailed with joy. She is surrounded by an environment of absolute tender loving care.

But I now think of the Apostle Paul's words to his little babes in Galatia. "My little children, of whom I travail in birth again until Christ be formed in you..." Clara's mommy did not labor just until she came into the world; she is still laboring for her little one. Daddy or Mommy or both will get up in the night whenever Clara is needing anything at all. In fact, my son says he will not be listing her on his next IRS form as a dependent, but rather as "Head of household."

Now is where I bring this back to the men in prison. We have some spiritual babies in the prison, and I love them. I have seen some of them come into the spiritual world. I have labored over some of them. Now, I know that these men need the same loving care that little Clara is getting as she is labored over with such loving care. And when they get out of prison they need oh so much laboring over so much of the time. Our precious pastor has been so extremely faithful in providing care for them. He has the same heart as Clara's daddy and mommy have for her.

But there is one factor that presents a vast difference between Clara and these babies in prison. Clara came into the world she is in with absolutely no baggage. These babies in prison are loaded to the point of overload with baggage from the past of their lives. Clara has nothing to unlearn. These men do. Clara has no false pseudo-parents to interfere with her care. These men have them coming from every angle. Clara has no one to come behind her mother and snatch away the nourishing food she gets and feed her poisonous substances.

These men have false teachers who are doing this very thing to them every week.

This is where your prayers can be such a vital part of caring for these little ones. You may wonder why? Do you remember the missionary song that says, "Throw out the lifeline to danger fraught men; sinking in danger where you've never been"? Every so often, one of these little ones I'm referring to has come from such a background and with so much baggage that it is impossible for me to crawl into their mind and look out of their windows. I sit with them and try to understand them and help them, but I have never been where they have been. This is where perhaps only prayer can reach to where they are.

Jesus Himself said of some, "This kind can come forth by nothing, but by prayer and fasting." I have felt almost helpless at times as I listen to the infant cry of a soul just coming into consciousness spiritually, while yet struggling with such a background of sin and dysfunction. Just as little Clara might cry with some inner distress that her daddy and mommy cannot discern, but would do anything to help her, so it is with these. They do not know themselves, nor can they tell me, what the real problem is. All I can do is pray for them. You can do just as much in this as I can. Thank you for minding God every time He lays one of these little ones on your heart, even if you do not know which one it is or what their name is.

There are actually four separate areas of the prison in which we hold the Bible studies and services. There are three identical facilities within the main compound, and then the minimum-security unit outside the secure area. I have noticed for all the time I have ministered here that the atmosphere changes from time to time within the different areas. At any time, one or two of the areas will be more responsive and interactive than the others. I may not know for sure what the cause of this is, but I think it is mostly due to one or more of the attendees bringing this with them.

It points out pretty clearly the influence that even one soul can have in a service or a church. The Bible says that "...one sinner destroyeth much good." I have seen this in living drama over and over. One self-righteous hypocrite can often depress or oppress the atmosphere of a whole Bible study or church service. But one hungry soul can bring light and liberty wherever they may be. So due to the fact that very often a man will be moved from one facility to another, he brings whatever atmosphere he creates along with him.

Not all are this way. There are many who, just as in every church on the outside, simply increase the attendance record by one digit. That is the sum and total of their contribution. Some time ago I had one of these as a regular attendee and it seemed he made no impact either for better or for worse. Then he was gone for a long time and then returned. He was there for a while again with the same level of zero influence. Then he was missing for a long time again. A third time he reappeared in class and resumed his position just as before. Each of these absences and attendances were perhaps two years in duration. Finally I scheduled him for an interview and he sat down across the desk from me. I asked him how he was getting along. As nearly as I can recall it, this was his extremely relaxed and drawn-out story:

"Oh, okay, I guess. I mean, I'm not in any hurry. God wasn't in any hurry for me, so I'm not in any hurry for Him. You see, it's sort of like when you're baking a cake, you know. You put the flour and the shortening and the milk in a bowl and mix it up and then put it in the oven to bake. God knew all this would happen to me anyway. See, I had a couple of two-year bids," (then I understood why "now you see him, and now you don't") "but God saw I wasn't finished yet so He gave me another ten. So now it's sort of like He has me in the oven and He turned the volume up."

Another who was here until about a year ago, would leave every Bible study or church service with a polite, "Thanks for the encouragement." It mattered not that the truth should have revealed to him his spiritual poverty; he was encouraged!

I am not wishing for more of this likeness, but neither am I eager for yet another self-made repository of infinite wisdom who is more ready to teach than be taught. I would love to have more of the men who bring into whatever area they are, a hunger for more of God and a teachable, humble spirit. It is a pleasure and delight to feed such hungry souls and to watch them grow more and more like Jesus.

There are two men in particular that I want to request prayer for. Both of them are returned to the prison on parole violations, and both are feeling the seriousness of their inability to walk straight more than they did before. I can sense a gravity in both of them that I sincerely hope will set them to really getting right with God this time. Both are in middle life and have had plenty of time to taste the fruit of their own way. "My way," never, never lasts very long until it is the devil's way, and that no matter whether it be in the high circles of society or the tent city behind Walmart or a little prison cell. Oh, that everyone could taste the utter joy and satisfaction of the life sold out to God and His sweet will!

Also, please continue to pray for the big Muslim man I wrote about recently who beneath his huge and formidable exterior gives evidence of a soft spot way down inside. I can't explain why it is that I feel a drawing toward him, but I do, and I will not ignore it. I am trying to strengthen the friendship we both feel to where I would sense a clearness to schedule him in for a visit. Have you ever known of a hunter who has his eye on a big buck, or a fisherman who sees a big catch waiting for him? That's exactly how I feel about this man. I can almost taste the joy of seeing him fall in love with Jesus; and by the way, I can't detect that he is all that excited about Muhammad, anyway. What is there about Allah or his prophet Muhammad that would excite anyone?

I do believe that God alone has kept this door of ministry open this long, but I also believe He has done it in answer to your prayers. Thank you, and please keep praying!

In His love,

William Cawman

✝✝✝

August 1, 2019

IT IS SURPRISING MANY times to find out just what lies behind a given countenance. A new man arrived in my classes and after the first class period he waited back to talk with me. "Chaplain, once I was saved, but I sinned again. My mother and my aunt are telling me that I will have to be baptized again to be saved again. Is that the truth?"

I said to him, "No, you do not need to be baptized again, but you need to confess your sin and ask Jesus to forgive you and come back into your heart."

"Will you pray with me now?"

"I surely will."

"Can I pray after you?"

"Yes, surely." I prayed with him, but in our limited time space after a class I encouraged him to keep seeking the Lord until he knew that Jesus was back in his heart.

And then a man just about forty years of age has landed himself in prison and requested to see me. I sat down with him and found another case of utter disappointment in Satan's failure to fulfill his promises. As I tried to talk and pray with him his eyes moistened and I could read way back behind them a desperately aching heart. Such grief pulls my heart out, not only in sympathy, but with such desire that a man like this find the Living Well that is so near by. I tried to direct him that way and he assured me that it is what he wants. I told him I would follow up the visit and not leave him alone. He really seemed to hang on that and I will call him down again soon. Please pray for him.

This has been a month of changes in the prison ministry. This is the first month in twenty years that we have no supervisory chaplain. In fact, we haven't heard a word from him since he left us. As a temporary arrangement until another is appointed, the man from Trenton who is in charge of it all comes down each Friday to help out and to oversee the needs as he can.

In case you have exhausted your items to be thankful for, let me give you one that we all need to be ever so thankful for, and that is, that we are, according to Scripture, and hopefully by experience, *not under the law, but under grace!* And I do not mean that in the sense in which it is being interpreted by much of the religious world today. If one should pull the cover off of the meaning most people attach to that it would sound like this— if you will excuse the NJ street language— "I ain't under nothin'; I'm good to go!" That is exactly the opposite of the true interpretation of that beautiful Scriptural provision. Under grace, there is desire and power to keep the law! Thank God for it!

So now, back to the reason for my bringing it up. For a number of years now we have had a Jewish inmate whose father— whatever else he might be— obviously has the State of New Jersey finances wrapped tightly about his finger. As a result, his son (in his fifties) is here, but necessitating everyone far and near to walk on pins and needles as to his needs. Notwithstanding his breaking of God's law as well as civil law that has him in prison for years, he is now so under law that he can hardly function in prison. He has become well known throughout the department of corrections statewide, not because of his father, but because of his special religious needs of living under law.

A while back, he was praying in the chapel and the officer in charge needed the space to hold a number of inmates waiting their turn for classification. The officer told him he needed to wind it up and leave, but he did not. The officer again told him and he said he would leave when he was finished. The officer called in the sergeant and they locked him up. From there he went from one area to another and they finally shipped him out to another prison. They would have nothing to do with him there, so he was sent to yet another. Finally he was sent back here, but the lieutenant in one facility warned them not to send him to his facility or he would kill him. In all of this moving, his tefillin came up missing.

Immediately the State of New Jersey was on high alert and was being held liable. My supervisor was contacted with orders to come up with it. He replied that he had nothing to do with it. Search was made but no results were forthcoming. Letters and emails were flying back and forth from the main offices in Trenton to the prison and finally the State purchased a new, genuine (that it must be) tefillin and had it ratified as being authentic by an influential scribe, as well as the Jewish rabbi chaplain (so they said).

At this point, I walked into the office and the supervisor from Trenton said, "Chaplain Cawman, I have a job for you."

"Yes, sir."

"Do you see this tefillin and this paper? I want you to wait a moment while the officer brings down inmate 'X' and I want you to meet with him and explain what we have provided and get his signature that he has received it. This is a very loaded assignment. Do you understand?"

"Yes, sir, I am very well acquainted with the gravity of the situation and have followed the sequence of it up to now."

The officer brought in "X" who has always respected me and bows to me upon meeting whenever I pass him. I presented to him the tefillin and its professed authentication and asked him to sign the paper. He said that he didn't think he could religiously sign the paper because it was not coming to him in the Kosher way. His tefillin had been given him by his father at his Bar Mitzvah and it should come from his family to be valid. He had talked to his father who said he had purchased him one and it was waiting for the chaplain rabbi to pick it up.

"So you are refusing to sign the paper?"

"Yes, I am refusing."

"Then you go to the waiting room while I report this to my supervisor." Upon hearing it, the supervisor got up with the same type and degree of emotion as Ahasuerus upon his finding Haman on Esther's bed, and took myself and another chaplain with him to meet "X" again. He explained to him that the State of NJ had lost his tefillin and even though they apologized, nothing could be done about it now. So in its place they had purchased with State money a new, genuine, tefillin at the cost of over one thousand dollars and had it ratified by Scribe ———. "Do you know him?"

"I know of him and he has a good reputation."

"Then I want you sign that you have received this as there is nothing else that we can do to provide for your religious rights and needs."

"X" was shaking visibly as he replied that he could not religiously sign the paper as requested. The supervisor returned to the office with a volcano about to erupt inside of him and sat down to write letters to heads throughout the State, proclaiming that he was done with him.

I left at that point to pursue better things, but not without deep reflections: "My dear man, don't you know that if you would just open your heart and let Jesus come in, you would enter such a glorious freedom from the 'bondage of the law'?" Surely Paul, you had it exactly right— "...until this day remaineth the same vail untaken away in the reading of the old testament; *which vail is done away in Christ.*" Maybe I took too much space to tell you that, but I want you to know that I am seriously and earnestly thanking God for Jesus Christ. There is much in the news today about anti-Semitism, and I hate it and want no part of it. But it cannot be denied that there are dire consequences to rejecting Jesus Christ!

Do you remember the dear man from Colombia who left here for a northern prison a few years ago with a burning heart full of holiness? I was disappointed that he had to leave, but God has a right to put His own where He needs them. Here are a few statements from an update letter from him.

> I continue seeing multitudes of thirsty people, living in a dry and thirsty land of their own making. It seems that many are determined to die of thirst when Jesus has promised "a well of water springing up into everlasting life."
>
> I have heard numerous messages disparaging holiness. Satan must surely hate the holiness movement; otherwise, why would he put so much effort to preach against it?
>
> I do not despair, even if we might be few. Twelve men transformed the world, and we are called to follow in His example and in their steps. God has preserved right doctrine, and it will continue spreading out through those who love each other and dwell in unity of purpose... We will prosper despite the world's allures; we will conquer despite Satan's campaigns, and the word will spread out because it is God's desire. Many have attempted to bury the doctrine and testimony of the holiness congregations, but to them I answer as Wesley would: "Let the Lord do as seemeth Him good."
>
> Once in a while I have been surprised by people living the blessing intuitively, not because they were taught about it. God continues separating people unto Himself. I met about a year ago a brother from Uganda. I immediately noticed something different about him, and after multiple conversations with him, and after observing his public testimony and walk, I am more convinced that he is saved to the uttermost. Something similar might be happening in the life of ——, a Korean brother. God will know the truth about the true state of their souls, but as of now I take every opportunity I can to explain to them the Second Blessing.
>
> Regarding ministry... I am holding back to some extent because I cannot compromise what I believe. I cannot teach any of the regular classes because their doctrinal foundation does not square with the Bible. For the same reason, I walked away from a ministry as translator at the services. I came to the conclu-

sion that if I am placed in the position of having to translate a doctrinally unsound sermon, I could not do it.

It is hard for me to do without the fellowship of more people saved to the utmost; but, without any doubt, I know my great responsibility to share with others the Word of God. I had been assigned a responsibility in the Christian counseling ministry, but I came to the realization that such ministry, without the right doctrinal foundations, is simply a palliative effort to bring comfort to people who do not desire a fundament change in their lives through the Spirit. I stepped away from most of the responsibilities in that ministry, not because I do not care about my brothers, but because I do not want to encourage methods of dealing with sin that rely on human effort. Only the Second Blessing can bring an end to the perpetual cycle of sinning and repentance that most Christians embrace as natural.

I must follow up as to the visit I had with the big Muslim man I requested prayer for. As he told me his life, I began to seriously wonder, "Why, Lord, did you lay him on my heart?" But then I realized it was for my benefit as much or more than his. I do hope he will think seriously about it, but he told me he had been a Christian and was ordained in the Methodist Church to serve in the food line, then was made an elder in the Baptist church, but when he encountered Islam in 1990, he loved it because it had all that Christianity had and even more. Christianity ends with Jesus, but Islam goes on with Muhammad and so he took up with that.

I saw as he spoke what a void modern "Christianity" leaves in a person, that can make them vulnerable to such deception. Obviously he had never even remotely been introduced to Jesus Christ in those churches. He told me that he has made his peace with God and has nothing against anyone and takes all the blame for his sin. He had a sweet-spirited friendliness that is not found most often in Islam. God only knows what he really is down on the inside, but woe be unto the false shepherds of today who are daubing the wall with untempered mortar and false christs. If God lays him on your heart, will you pray for him?

William Cawman

September 1, 2019

THE MONTH OF AUGUST was pretty well occupied with camp meetings and so I was not in the prison for most of it. Thank God for our volunteers who kept the good work going, however. If I were to share with you the prospects for the future of ministering here in the prison I would be at a loss. Since the retirement of our supervisor, who for over eighteen years kept the door open for myself and the volunteers from our church, the future looks anything but certain. From what I can gather, I think the supervisor from Trenton may install another chaplain in our prison and then continue to act as supervisor himself of all the state prisons. Right now, with all the extra work from our retiring supervisor, it would be almost impossible for him to get rid of me, but just what the future holds for that I do not know. God knows; that is enough!

I will leave the above paragraph as I typed it, but true to what it prophesied the very next day things began to happen that would demonstrate this uncertainty. I went in for the classes, and the week before my pastor had taken them. The men in the first class told me that very few of them got to class because they did not call it out and they would not open their doors. That evening my wife and I went in for a Bible study and only about half of the usual number were there. I began to enquire and found that only one of the housing units in that facility had come. I went out and told the officer that only one housing unit was there and he just shrugged his shoulders and said, "I called them." It seemed to bring an unusual sense of depression or something over the whole Bible study.

The next morning was the time for Christian Living Class in that same facility and the men began to ask me if there was a Bible study the night before. I told them that only House 6 had come and all of the ones from House 5 said it was not called out on their unit and so they would not open their doors. I began to have a strong feeling that with no chaplain supervisor they were beginning to push over on the Christian activities. Now I believe that Paul and Jesus both demonstrated that when their personal rights were attacked, they turned the cheek; but when the cause of God was at stake they stood up and fought— like cleansing the temple. As soon as that class was over, I went to a computer and sent an email to the director in Trenton, copying it to the superintendent in our prison. Within an hour I received a copy of a letter from Trenton to the administrator of our prison. Within fifteen minutes later I received a copy of a response from the administrator saying that he would handle the problem immediately.

Now let me make an observation that is too obvious to miss. I stated in my letter to Trenton that this negligence to properly call out the Christian classes was not only disruptive to the sequence of teaching to the men, but that it was a potential security issue because the men were fully aware that the Muslim services were highly announced and given top priority. Do you see? The anti-what is moving in rapidly— anti-not religion; not any false cult; but anti-*Christ!*

That afternoon I went to Facility 1 for the Christian Living Class and I told the men of these happenings and then told them that we are facing into a wonderful opportunity to be Christians. The class nearly exploded with joy and happy approval of the opportunity. All the depressed feelings of the evening before vanished before the rising sun of true Christlikeness in their expressions of delight to be like Jesus. I felt a new wave of love for these dear men.

The next morning I learned that we are getting a new supervisor of chaplaincy in our prison. And I know him. I will tell you a story of him from a number of years ago. He did his internship in our prison and then volunteered for a while before becoming the chaplain of the prison nearest ours. While he was volunteering, he was teaching a Bible study in the minimum-security unit outside of the secure boundary. The man who is now our Sunday School superintendent was incarcerated in that unit and had already prayed through and found the Pearl of Great Price. The volunteer was teaching them that after we are saved we still have an old nature that rises up and causes us trouble and sin. Our dear brother raised his hand exultingly and said, "I got rid of that!"

I had been away at a meeting and when I returned my supervisor said to me, "I think you need to talk with that volunteer who is also having Bible studies out in the minimum camp because there seems to be some conflict out there." As soon as I could I went to him and said, "I understand that there is some conflict going on out in the minimum camp?"

"Yes, there sure is!"

"What does it seem to be about?"

"Well, it seems to be about this issue of sinlessness."

I tried to keep a straight face as I refrained from saying what I wanted to: "Oh, do you enjoy sinning still?" I was good, wasn't I, to not say that?

This is the man who will now be my supervisor. Do you see why I leave the first paragraph of this letter still standing, even after knowing more than I did when I wrote it?

For the near future I have felt it best to cancel some meetings on the outside because of the overload of work that is left us with the retirement of the former supervisor. Even though by the terms of my employment contract I am limited in the number of hours I can be paid for in a year, and I am no longer allowed to volunteer if I use up those hours, yet I can still put in some more before the end of this year, and it would be much appreciated by my co-workers. I walked into the Catholic chaplain's office and took one look at the stack of paper work on his desk and gave him a hug and walked out with a stack of it amid his happy thank you's.

At the same time that our supervisor retired the Islamic chaplain took off and went to Nigeria on family issues and then came back with all kinds of health issues (so he claims, at least) and has been out for two months. This means that we have to cover for all of the Islamic services and recording of attendances, etc., etc., in addition to covering the work that our supervisor did before. We are hoping so much that the new man coming on will be a team member and take up all this clerical work required by Trenton. That would certainly be of much more help than a conflicting voice from the hyper-Calvinist camp. I hope by this update on affairs as they are, you will pray earnestly that God will lay His hand on it all and keep the door open for His own truth here in the prison.

Please don't get a mistaken idea of what I said about covering for Islamic services. We do not have to teach it or even supervise it, but the prison rules will not allow inmates to congregate without a staff member or volunteer being present. When I have to do such, I just stay in my office next to the chapel with my door open and continue to do my work.

We are presently studying in Christian Living classes from the Ten Commandments and how they touch every area of even our present living. There is a lively interest and much interaction as we learn to apply them. Isn't it an absolute mark of their Divine inspiration that they can be so concise and yet leave no area of life, thirty-four hundred years later, without clear direction? Thank God for His Word. I might just tuck in here a comment from outside the prison, and that is concerning how amazing it is that preaching on the Ten Commandments brings many Christians of today under a cloud. Perhaps they should impact our lives more than having two plaques on the front lawn?

Do you remember me telling you about the man from El Salvador who when I ask his beaming face if he loves Jesus he replies, "Oh, I love Him too much! I love Him too much!" At the last Bible study, he came in and beat me to it. He beamed up at me and said, "Do you love Jesus?" Oh my, how good it felt to be asked! I am not sure how much English he really understands, because many times he looks somewhat blank about what we are saying, but I can tell he really feels God's presence and that in turn brings more of His Presence.

It is a worthy prayer for us to remember all those souls, unknown to us, who are a part of the preparing Bride of Christ. "The foundation of God standeth sure, having this seal, The Lord knoweth them that are his." And God will certainly hear us when we pray for them without a name. Paul said, "God is my witness, whom I serve with my spirit in the gospel of his Son, that without ceasing I make mention of you always in my prayers..." And so, even if we do not know enough about them to pray in detail for their needs, God hears the mention of them by us, and it will have its reward.

As I work among men in prison, I never cease to marvel at how seemingly impenetrable some of them are to the simplicity of the Gospel, and then on the other hand, how rapidly others grasp the deep things of God. Even as I say that I remember that there were only two responses to which the Scripture says Jesus marveled. Mark 6:6— "And he marveled because of their unbelief..." And, Luke 7:9— "...He marveled at him, and turned him about, and said unto the people that followed him, I say unto you, I have not found so great faith, no, not in Israel." So, basically, things have not changed much over the years, for Jesus found the same condition that we find today.

I feel obligated to insert a reflection here after being with many of you in camps this summer. One after another has come and expressed how much these letters mean and how much they are enjoyed. I want to and I need to take all of those expressions and turn them right around and give them back to you. The reason is, that without your prayers I would be a total failure in ministering to men in prison. The reason that there are encouraging things in these letters is that God is answering your prayers. We are laborers together with God in this ministry, and you are just as important to it as I.

King Louis XIV of France was perhaps the most loved king of all ages. As the multitude gathered in the cathedral for his funeral, Massillon, the French preacher, arose and held up a little golden urn with a lock of hair from the late King Louis. For some time he just held it and gazed upon it until the crowd wondered if he had lost control of his emotions over it. Suddenly his voice thundered out, "God alone is great!" He is! All of us are but unprofitable servants doing that which is our duty to do. Prayer is absolutely just as vital as standing before the men in prison with a message to them. Thank you! Thank you, for holding us up in prayer before the Only Great God! He still answers prayer! Bless His name.

Years ago a very blonde young man with horrendous tattoos all over him came into the service on a Sunday night. He sat down against the back wall and listened. At the close of the service he came up and said, "Chaplain, will you pray with me? I want Jesus to come into my heart." With only a moment or two to pray, I did and then asked for his name and number. That week I scheduled him for a one-on-one visit and when he came into the room the beauty of Jesus was shining all over him in spite of the tattoos. He told me that it was the first Christian service he had ever been in, and that he had been raised a Muslim. He said that when we prayed, it felt like God reached down inside of him and took out everything bad and then moved in Himself. He said he felt like he got born all over again. He didn't have a clue that such is the Scriptural name for it.

I was telling that story shortly afterward in a camp. At the dining room table a man sat across from me and said, "So that was who God told me to pray for!" I said, "What do you mean?" He said, "I was out on the railroad tracks praying and God said, 'Pray for B——!' I told God I didn't know anyone by that name. God said, 'Pray for B——!' Now I know who it was!" Wouldn't you be thrilled if someday in heaven a former prisoner walked up to you and said, "Thank you for praying for me!" Thank you!

In His love,

William Cawman

12
"LET BROTHERLY LOVE CONTINUE"

October 1, 2019

GREETINGS TO YOU ONCE again as yet another month comes to a close. If it is anywhere near accurate that there have been 72,228 months gone by since the creation of the world. How quickly that number is being added to. If that number reflected the miles on your car, you would consider it as yet fairly low mileage, wouldn't you? Perhaps that might instill a bit more meaning into the Scriptural commands, "Redeeming the time, because the days are evil... Walk in wisdom toward them that are without, redeeming the time."

This past month I had the privilege again of taking a good black brother from the Fort Myers Rescue Mission into the prison with me for three days. He was with me three years ago with very good effect, for the majority of the men I preach to in the prison are black, and they certainly prick up their ears when they hear a black brother preach to them about the necessity of a pure heart as a second definite work of grace.

I must tell you about a couple of visits that we had one day while he was there. There is a man who is forty-two years old and has come to the prison just in the last few months. A week or two before our visit, as he listened to me teaching, he came to me and confessed, "Please pray for me; I have a terrible pride problem, and I need God to do something with it!" He was saying it with positive evidence that he had seen the serious horribleness of such in his heart.

Now a couple of weeks later he came in to see us. He looked at me and said, "Do you remember that I told you about that awful pride problem I had in my heart?" I assured him that I remembered. He said in essence, "Well, as I prayed about that I saw other deep sins in my heart that were just as ugly and I began to pray about them one by one. All of the sudden it dawned on me— it's not this sin or that sin, it's me that needs gotten rid of! I don't want anymore of J———!" It was said with such a spirit that both of us listening immediately felt like shouting! We both assured him that he was positively on the right pathway to full deliverance, and that he could do nothing better than cry to God for a clean heart.

He told us that the visit was so perfectly timed for the way God was dealing with his heart. He was obviously overwhelmed by what was happening on the inside of him and was perfectly in tune with it as well. Praise God! I believe we will soon have another witness to full cleansing in the Blood of Jesus.

Then our two precious sanctified men who work in the special needs area came in together. What a heavenly atmosphere we enjoyed for a half hour as they spoke of the continuing victory God is giving them right in the midst of their enemies and evil forces. The one is scheduled to be released in just a year and the other one is already feeling it. He looked straight at me and then pointed to the other man and said, "Chaplain, I just love this man!" I assured him that I did, too. Then he asked me, "What are you going to do with him when he gets out?" I told him that I had no plans for him except to let Jesus have all there was of him and direct him wherever and to whatever He would desire. They both agreed that such was exactly what they both would want, too. These two men would absolutely exemplify the song we sometimes sing, "'Tis burning in my soul; 'tis burning in my soul! The fire of heavenly love is burning in my soul!"

Then still another man came in for a visit who has been for a little while in my classes, but who I have not had a one-on-one visit with as yet. He catches one's eye as he is being preached to, because of the eager response he manifests. He told us his case. He has been somewhat of a Christian for several years and has a good wife and family. He is part owner of a car wash. He had made a friend, who was visiting with him, and the friend asked him if he could do him a favor and just go down the street a bit and bring him some drugs. He knew that his friend was suffering without them and reasoned that maybe it would not be such a bad thing if he would just do it that once— he is now in prison. He is suffering the consequences of a momentary bad choice, but along with it he fully realizes that he needed this wakeup call as he was drifting along pretty careless spiritually. I trust he will go all the way through with God because of it.

Since I often write portions of these letters throughout the month as things happen, I already have an update on the forty-two-year-old who had the pride problem. The week after writing the above, I was in KY in a convention and a volunteer was taking the class that he is in. He came in all aglow and gave the following testimony. He said that he was seeking the Lord to be sanctified and an officer grabbed his brand-new Bible from him and threw it down on the floor and kicked it across the room. He felt a sudden rush of anger come up inside of him and immediately went to his cell to pray and ask God to remove it. Suddenly he felt a cleansing power go all through him and he could say with certainty that he was sanctified.

When I returned the following week he came into class still aglow with it. I told him I had heard good news about him and he said, "Oh, it's wonderful! Just wonderful!" As I went on teaching the class he looked just like a hungry boy devouring his favorite dish. At the close of class time he said to me, "I was right with you in all of that! It's wonderful!" Thank God for another witness to the power of the Blood of Jesus to cleanse the heart from all sin.

I felt it on my heart this week throughout the classes to go back again over the steps from the sinful heart to full salvation through two definite works of grace. I tried to show the utter foolishness of believing that a Christian still lives in sin. I told the men that every once in a while, I become freshly aware of all the different doctrines they are exposed to and that I had no right to stand before them and declare that I was the one that was right, but I told them that God's Word is right. Every false teacher who professes to be a Christian claims the Bible as his foundation for teaching. But I told them there is a definite proof of whether they are teaching truth or not and that is to go back to the very purpose of Christ coming into the world. He came, John says, "that He might destroy the works of the devil." Every honest soul admits that sin is the work of the devil, and so if Christ came for the express purpose of destroying it, and yet a Christian can do no better than to continue in it, then Jesus Christ was a total failure in His purpose.

I then went on to explain again the work of being filled with the Spirit, which cleanses out all remaining sin but leaves the Treasure in an earthen vessel. I tried to be open and honest as to the nature of temptation and human errors, but also to the genuine work of heart holiness that puts an actual end to the indwelling of sin. I told them that when any confusion came up over different teachings it was always safe to take such interpretation of God's Word as would set us free from sin, rather than make excuse for its continuation either in practice or nature. Aren't you so glad that when we let God's Word interpret itself it makes complete and glorious sense? All doctrines that fall short of a holy heart and life end in a quagmire of contradiction to clear teachings in Scripture. God — His own Word declares — is not the author of such, and the way to heaven as outlined in our precious Bible is as clear as God Himself!

At the close of each of the studies, several men came and expressed their joy at hearing it that way. One man who has been such a disappointment because of his playing around with all the sinning religious doctrines, came and said to me, "Would you call me down? That got through to me tonight!" I will.

Also, please keep praying for my big Muslim gruff guy! Something draws him to come into the class before we start. Oh, how I long to see him find a loving Jesus instead of a dead Muhammad!

I want to thank you for praying for our new supervisor. I've told you often how God kept His hand upon the former one until the door stayed wide open without a single restriction for us to teach truth as it is in God's Word. God so far has abundantly answered your prayers. The new supervisor has been overwhelmingly supportive and appreciative of all that I am doing. He expresses it nearly every time I am around him. Please keep praying that when the inevitable happens and the inmates begin to try to pit his theology against what I am teaching, he will not react wrongly. I understand that he did get rid of some volunteers in the prison where he came from because he did not agree with their theology. Actually, he is not allowed to do so and it would be inconsistent unless he would also get rid of every other group except his own. I do not anticipate that, especially as you continue to pray for us.

Yesterday my wife was planning to come in for two of the classes and as I left the facility to go up front to get her, he was coming out with me to go to another facility. He said, "Which way are you going?" I told him I was going to Facility 1 but that I was going up front to get my wife first so that she could play the keyboard and teach the men some choruses. "Oh that's wonderful!" he said. Later he met us coming back from the study and greeted my wife and thanked her for volunteering and coming in.

I am spending quite a bit of extra time in the prison right now because during the two or three months between supervisors the clerical work really got behind. Several reasons contributed to that. Not only was there a missing body to keep up with that end of the work, but the Islamic chaplain made a sudden trip over to Nigeria and came back reportedly sick. He has been out for over two months and the last word was that he might be able to return by the end of October. I have heard that he is so bad that sometimes he is confused over where he even is. I just wonder what took place over there with him.

Anyway, that just adds all the more to our workload, as we have to record all of the documentation as to attendances at Jumah prayer, etc., on top of everything else. Then, we are approaching the High Holy days for the Jewish inmates and I spent quite a bit of time today placing them individually in each service that they are to attend. Then it has been quite a while since we had anyone with time to go through all the religious programs and remove those who are not attending, move those to another roster who have changed facilities, etc. You see, there is seemingly no end to the clerical work involved in today's chaplaincy, especially in a prison this size—actually three prisons in one.

Just in the last year there has been a literal explosion of enrollments in Odin worship. What the reason is, I don't know for sure, but today's Christianity leaves the soul of man so empty and void that there is an apparent attraction to these bizarre religious beliefs. I believe that if you would study the history of Christianity from the Day of Pentecost until now, you would find it true that every false teaching or cult that exists has sprung up during a weak period of the Church of Jesus Christ.

What a bulwark against all error is the fire of Divine Revelation, but woe be to the knowledge of truth when that fire burns low!

Will you help us pray for more fire right here in this prison? Thanking you for Him,

William Cawman

☩

November 1, 2019

THANK GOD FOR THE Blood of Jesus that forgives our sins and gives us divine life within. Thank God for the cleansing Blood that purifies our whole soul by filling us with the Holy Spirit. Thank God for *keeping grace!* It works! The brother that I wrote about last month, who found a cleansing of his heart after such a revelation of it that God so faithfully showed to him, is now being kept by the same cleansing Blood that set him free. It is a joy to watch a soul enter into the grace of God and then learn about it afterward. Have you ever seen someone sitting in the driver's seat of their new car devouring the operator's manual to see what all they have gotten? Well, I'm watching something very similar to that with this dear man. Consciously enjoying the inward working power of Grace, he is now all ears and eager face to hear more about living this glorious life. Give me any day a soul with a kindergarten understanding of holiness and a heart with zero resistance to further light, rather than a doctorate in theology with a mulish, heel-dug-in complacency— dead right, but dead!

This dear man is not dull mentally or spiritually and is just soaking up truth like a sponge. Naturally, he is facing the latter part of Romans chapter six, that of yielding his members instruments of righteousness, instead of instruments to the old man, and it would be totally unfair to him and to what God is doing in him to measure him by the standards of a person raised in a holiness home or background. But one thing is very obvious: there is no resistance to any new light upon his pathway. He says he just wants to be completely like Jesus overnight but keeps recognizing old response patterns trying to work back at him and he hates it. I'm just encouraging him to take everything straight to the Blood of Jesus and let God perfect all that is yet lacking. He said, "I really want that!"

After he left another man came in to visit and told me that he is really wanting to be completely right but that he is still struggling. Then he told me that he was working with the man I have just been telling you about and that he told him how he had found himself so full of sin and problems, but finally realized that it was not all those problems, but he himself that needed to be put out. He said, "When he said that it went straight to my heart, and I told myself I want what he has found."

A man who got out of prison a couple of years ago and then attended our church for a year or so, but didn't go all the way with God, is now back in prison again, and I hope and pray he really gets straightened out this time. He told me the other day that when he arrived back, he was in the waiting room and another inmate walked by holding a big Bible under his arm. He asked the inmate if Chaplain Cawman was still there in the prison. The man let out a string of oaths and profanity and replied, "I don't have a thing to do with Chaplain Cawman!" Neither does the devil he serves, thank God!

And then I want to tell you about another man who was in our prison from the very time it opened, and consequently, I worked with him for a number of years. He was in the classes and was doing so well, seeking a pure heart, and then was moved to one of the northern prisons. He is serving a thirty to life sentence for murdering a girl when he was but in his teens. At the close of thirty years they gave him a three-year hit. He served the three years and they gave him another one. Then they looked over his spotless prison record and realized they had made a mistake and so withdrew the second hit. He is now in somewhat of a holding pattern waiting for further direction from parole. In the meantime, they sent him back to this prison. I was visiting with an inmate the other day and looked up and of all things, there he was standing outside the office window smiling a great big smile at me.

I called him down and he told me all of the above and then said that he is earnestly seeking to be cleansed within as he knows there are still things in him that shouldn't be there. He then said that as far as his sentence and a date for being released is concerned he has committed it all into the hands of the Lord. As he left the room, he looked back with a big smile and said, "I'm kissing the rod!" Please pray that whatever time he has here he will pay the full price and be filled with the Spirit. You can imagine— no, you and I can't— what he will face after over thirty-three years of being locked up while still in his teens, when he steps out into the world of today. I will certainly do my best to urge him into all the fullness of God while he is here.

This afternoon I had another visit with him and he came in and sat before me like a hungry little bird, ready to devour anything I told him. After talking with him and listening to him for a while I am not really sure how far along he is with God, but one thing is for certain; he has it settled to go through with God and does not sense any kickback at anything God might reveal to him or require of him. I tried to guide him in taking everything he encounters to the Blood of Jesus and letting God show him whether he is just passing through a fiery trial of temptation or if there is any remaining sin in him.

He sat there with deep emotion and tears as he listened and assented to all I said. He is eager to leave thirty-plus years of prison behind him and come worship with us in our church. He said very plainly that he knows that what we are teaching and preaching is the true way, and he wants it. Please pray that God will open and close any doors to his future as He sees best, and that he will respond to it and find the beauty God has yet in store for him.

He told me about his visit a couple of days before by two members of the parole board. Before I relate it to you, let me make the observation that there are two scenarios I have observed in my short life that are equally pathetic. One is church members trying to handle other church members, and the other is sinners trying to handle sinners.

Our brother was called in before the parole officers and they began to grill him concerning his crime thirty-three years ago. They insisted for two grueling hours that he had more to tell them than what he had already said. Finally, he looked at them and said, "Gentlemen, I don't know what you want me to say. I have told you everything that there is to tell you. I am hiding nothing. I turned myself in from the beginning and told the whole truth from the start, just as it happened. I have nothing to add to it because I've told it all." They continued to pressurize him to tell them more. Aren't you glad that God does not do that when we come to Him for forgiveness? Pray for him. He was conscious of the Lord being with him through it all.

And then I must tell you an update on my big burly Muslim man. On a Wednesday afternoon he came into the Bible study room again on his way to the library to work as a paralegal. He shook hands with us both and then went on his way, but after the Bible study he met us in the hallway again and shook hands with my wife and then looked at me and said, "We need to talk."

The following week I put him on the list for a visit and when he entered the room I shook hands with him and he said, "That's partly what I want to talk to you about: that handshake." I at first thought he was going to withdraw himself from shaking hands due to his Muslim belief and especially from shaking hands with my wife, which is taboo among them. Instead he looked me in the eye and said, "Is something wrong? Have I done something? The last time you shook hands with me it wasn't the same. I thought you dropped my hand so quickly that I thought something must be wrong."

"Oh, no," I replied, "I don't have a clue what would have given you that impression. You will always be my friend. I pray for you nearly every day. I don't know what I would have done different to make you feel like that."

He quickly realized that I was sincere in it and that it was a trick of the devil to separate us, so then he said, "I really want to keep visiting with you. I really enjoy these talks and tell the brothers (his Muslim compatriots) that I really enjoy visiting with you. I want to keep up these visits." I assured him that we would do so as I wanted to keep visiting with him, too.

At present he is yet making an effort to reconcile Christianity and Islam, for having never known the reality of Christ living within, he is not yet seeing clearly. I told him that I would expect that he prays the five daily Muslim prayers, but then I asked him if he prayed besides that. He said, "Oh yes, of course I do pray the prescribed Islamic prayers each day, but many times in between those I really open my heart up to God and tell Him all about myself and the way I am and ask for His help."

I encouraged him to continue to reach out to God in those times of prayer and ask Him to reveal Himself to him. Then I told him about the Colombian man who a few years ago had been so unhappy with first Catholicism and then Islam, but that when I encouraged him to just seek to know God personally, he entered into a glorious reality of Jesus living within, and is still enjoying it. Some of you have told me you are praying for this man. Thank you! Please keep doing so as I believe God is answering those prayers. For some reason he really wants to talk with me and I will open that door as often as prudence will allow within the parameters of prison culture.

The Muslim chaplain is still out on sick leave. He went to Africa in June or July and has not been back since. We hear almost nothing about him except that he got Malaria while over there and is very sick. By now, I know it has to be something more than Malaria and I wonder what all he got into over there. At any rate, ever since he left it throws a lot of extra work on all of the rest of us, as we have to schedule all of the requests for Islamic services and then record all of the attendances, etc. And there are several hundred of them here in the prison. We have begun to temporarily schedule Imams from some of the other prisons to come down on Friday to help in the Jumah services, but whenever they cannot cover one of us has to be there.

We have also just passed through the Jewish holy days, Yom Kippur and Rosh Hashanah, with Chanukah yet to come, and we have twenty-some Jewish inmates. This also takes more time than is usual in the regular schedule as the Jewish chaplain only comes on Tuesdays. It is so sad to witness the utter emptiness of their worship since they did not open the door to their Messiah. The bondage of their laws will not even allow them to carry their driver's license in their pocket on their Holy Days. They aren't even supposed to wear shoes on their feet.

We had visiting Jewish rabbinical students come in to help with the services, and they could not drive themselves or even ride in a vehicle, so they had to get a hotel room nearby and walk under police escort to and from the prison. It was my turn to accompany them two or three times from the front lobby to the chapel and once as we started to leave the chapel with everything locked up behind us, one of them discovered a small piece of paper about the size of a credit card in his pocket. We had to return to the chapel, unlock the doors and secure his piece of paper in my office so that he could walk home clear with the law of bearing no burden on the Sabbath Day. All the while I was thanking Jesus for setting us free from the curse of the law and putting the Living Law within us, which is such a joy to keep.

With love and gratitude,

William Cawman

December 1, 2019

THIS LETTER IS COMING to you exactly twenty years after the first one written. I wonder just how many prayers for South Woods State Prison have gone up to the throne above in these twenty years? I know of a certainty that many of them have been and are still being answered, and so with deep gratitude I thank each of you in behalf of many men and in behalf of Jesus and His precious Blood for those prayers— every one of them!

One of the recipients of those prayers for many years now, was just moved from where he has been for quite some time in one of the northern prisons back down to the closest prison to the one where I labor and first met him. He wrote to me the following lines:

> "He showed me a pure river of water of life…"
> I am still decompressing from the sensory assault called praise at —— [the northern prison], but my spirit remembers a sweet verse of "flows from Emmanuel's veins…" I truly look forward to fellowshipping in spirit and in truth.
>
> Dear Brother, this place reminds me of Ezekiel's vision of the abominations in the temple in chapter 8. The professors— I hate to call them Christians— are more learnt in crucifying the Son of God afresh than exalting the Holy Jesus who saves to the uttermost. If not for the faithful Holy Spirit I would be swallowed up in despair and doubt.
>
> Brother, this has been, and is, the sweetest time in my life. Everywhere I turn are troubles, but they only make Jesus more worthy of praise. How sweet to trust in Jesus.
>
> Eighteen years ago today, I sat across from you and confessed, "Before I didn't know if I was saved. Now I know." I'm smiling as I remember how you almost jumped out of your chair.
>
> "Consider Him…" After 18 years I feel like I am just beginning to consider Christ. I thank Jesus for the simplicity that is in Him. If I couldn't simply exalt Christ above all I would fail utterly. I am smiling, thinking of how blessed it is to admit defeat, and be a failure, when it makes us always triumph in Christ. Amen.
>
> Dear Brother, I feel more and more like a stranger, every day

that passes. I cling to the promises of God in Christ Jesus, but the more I profess them the farther it moves me from those I tell. I'd wonder if it was the same out there... sigh; sin is deadly.

In spite of it all, Jesus is becoming more real to me every day. I don't have a single brother to encourage the way of holiness, but the Holy Spirit is more than enough... I can't help glorying in a Father who abides within... I am so grateful for Jesus manifesting to help me destroy self. Thank Jesus for all who love Him in Spirit and in Truth.

A man who has come to classes and Bible studies for years has been missing nearly all of them for some time. On Sunday night I accosted him as he came into the service and he said, "I've been too busy holding Bible studies." Another man told me that he went to one of them and that he was promoting once in grace always in grace so strongly that he didn't want to hear anything contrary to that. Then I received a request slip that he wanted to talk with me one-on-one. I prayed that morning, as did my wife also, that God would give me the anointing I needed to talk with him.

He came in and told me that he has only eleven months to stay in prison after all these years and wondered if I could direct him to a Christian-based shelter when he gets out. I looked at him squarely and said, "There is something I need to talk to you about. I understand you are having Bible studies on the tier and teaching that a person cannot lose salvation and be lost, once they have been saved. You know better than that, and someday soon you are going to stand before the Great White Throne and give an account, not only for adopting false doctrine yourself, but for teaching it to others. So now, how can I recommend you to a Christian shelter on the outside for you to go and promote false teachings there?"

His head began to wilt and he said, "I guess I never saw it like you are telling me. No, I don't want to give an account for teaching false doctrine. Can you put me back on the list for your classes again?" I told him I would gladly do so and would also bring him some sound teaching in a book that would expose such erroneous doctrine for what it really is. Please do pray for him. Surely God is trying once more to reach him before he goes out to wreck his life even further.

Another man then came in a wheelchair with no legs. He opened up immediately with this question: "Chaplain, —— [naming another inmate who also does his own deeply Calvinistic teaching and avoids me like poison] prayed a prayer over me and then told me he had saved me. Now I've moved over to this unit and I'm listening to your teaching and I feel I can trust you. Is it really true that that man saved me? I don't know if I am or not."

I said, "Now, there is not a man on earth that can save another man, including myself. Only Jesus can save us and He will if we really repent of our sins and ask Him to come into our heart." I then tried to point out the way to God, and he brightened up and said, "Oh, now I see what I need to do. I'm going to do that, because I really want to be sure that I'm saved." He told me that he was working in the Twin Towers in NY and about a year before they were bombed, he was going home from work and slipped off the edge of the subway platform and was run over by a train. He watched it cut his legs off and then he passed out until weeks later when he came to again in the hospital. I would judge that he is just now experiencing his first awakening spiritually.

I wish you could come with me for a visit to the man I wrote recently about who began to see all kinds of spiritual problems on the inside, but finally realized it was he himself who needed to die. As I sit with him and try to explain the holiness way, he just grasps it like a drowning man and never objects or kicks back at anything. He is just so eagerly eating up every bit of instruction that I have three books waiting to give him tomorrow. I am excited for this man. And thank God he is not entangled in a wrong marriage nor does he have any children, so it is almost a new start for him in his mid-forties.

I just must give you a few lines from our dear brother who was a third-generation Mormon, and is now in the prison system in another state after twenty years here.

> How truly joyous it is to greet you in the Holy name of Jesus. As I sit here writing in a crowded day room, at a steel table surrounded by loud profanity, perversity, and a blaring television, our Lord has me in complete peace, and full of an indwelling fire for Him. He certainly does "create a hedge," as you say, doesn't He? That inner fire is like a hedge in itself; it burns up all the possible distractions as if it were a hedge of fire on the outside. I just smile, and say the sweet and Holy and powerful name of Jesus, and greet you in that name. After all, He left the ninety and nine and pursued me in dayrooms just like this one, didn't He? Bless Him.
>
> Our God can be a hedge of fire, and yet also an inviting fire of warmth and refuge to a contrite heart. Yesterday, a brother with whom I've been meeting for several weeks (who 2 weeks ago changed his DOC record religious preference from "Pagan" to "Protestant" and has been attending church with me) sat down at this same dayroom table with me on one of those cold, round, steel disks attached to it, and asked what I was writing. It was a letter to ——, and I told him about them. Then he said he'd just spoken to someone who told him that unless he used the name "Jehovah" in his prayers, God wouldn't hear him. I asked him how it had struck him to hear that. It "bothered" him, he said. I asked him to compare that to how our discussion of Jesus Christ's redeeming Blood and salvation had struck him. He said, "pretty much the opposite." I told him: "there's a reason for that!" Then I read to him part of your Oct. 3rd letter. By God's providence I had it right there with me, because you were the next one I was planning to write to! My new brother and I praised God's mercy and goodness because He's put in us a soul-bell, and given us ears to hear it— and even caused us to feel "Bothered" when it's not there. I prayed with him that as brothers in Christ we can help each other stay focused on the

Lord, His Person, His Word, His ways, and be obedient to Him — attentive to what keeps that bell ringing, and immediately notice any actions or doctrines that leave it silent.

Isn't it precious that so often a person who was not raised around the language of a true Christian uses the very expressions and concepts that we have heard for years? I believe our language and what we have learned from our fathers in the faith is just right, and we need not be looking for new or improved terminology, for God and His work within the heart of man never changes.

Our new supervisor has been overwhelmingly supportive and cooperative and proves to be a very qualified leader, but, sadly to us, he has told us that he is not staying. He is still the supervisor of chaplaincy in the next closest prison and he wants to stay there. He says he was not told that the supervisor's position in this prison is totally clerical work, with all of the record keeping and legislation and answering of inmate complaints that it entails. We told him we knew that and had begged that they give us a secretary instead of another chaplain, but such did not happen. So I don't know just what we will yet end up with, but God knows, and that is enough.

I have taken several visiting pastors and their wives into the prison just lately and it has been a real blessing to the men. They love to hear new voices and I can't blame them, for I get tired of mine, too. We are planning to have services again on Christmas Eve and the men are looking forward to that. Please help us pray that in those services many will hear the call of God and let Jesus be born into their hearts. What a Christmas present that would be, wouldn't it?

Thank you again for all of your prayers this year that has passed by so quickly. How many more we will have, only God knows, but I want to be at my best for Him and His preparing Bride.

With love,

William Cawman

13
JESUS IS WORKING STILL

January 1, 2020

ANOTHER YEAR IS HISTORY as I write this letter to you. Where has it gone? This year past has not been the most tranquil year I have ever spent in the ministry to the prisoners. It has had seasons of wondering if the ministry was about to come to an end due to all of the political waves coming down from our state government, but thankfully to God and you who prayed, the year closed out with more of a sense of personal favor than I have ever experienced. There is the overall antichrist spirit that is growing stronger and stronger, but personally, the feared attacks have turned into very clear appreciation.

The area of concern as of now is not for me personally, but for anything "Christian." It becomes more of an uphill battle every week to get the classes together due to either the negligence of officers to let the men out of their cells to come, or else open hostility to Christianity. Meanwhile, the orders from Trenton are that they want us to hold weekly services for the heathen, the worshippers of Thor and Odin. They insist that they must have everything they need to do homage to these old Norse gods, while Christianity is becoming more blatantly ignored. Please help us pray that the men will be so filled with the Spirit of God that they will not take any wrong attitudes over it all, but just go deeper in God.

I must tell you something that really excited me just this week. I must lay a foundation for it first. If you haven't heard, let me tell you that a massive turning to God is taking place in the Muslim nations of Pakistan, Afghanistan, Iran, Iraq and the Gaza Strip. It is coming about by case after case of Jesus appearing in dreams to the Muslims in such appeal to them that they instantly forsake Islam and want to follow Jesus. Soon they will quietly, but with great risk, ask another who they suspicion might have had a dream, and before long a little underground band of dedicated followers is gathering in the night, pledging to each other and to God that they are willing to die for Jesus. Many of them have died, too, but others have been preserved miraculously. It is not only the common people, but ISIS members and Imams who also are having the dreams.

I will relate just one instance as an illustration of what is taking place. It is of a man by the name of Hassan, who was doing his best in Cairo to bring Muslims into a conversation and then introduce Jesus to them. He knew full well the risks, but he loved Jesus! Suddenly he was startled awake by a rough hand and orders to follow with the cold muzzle of a gun in his right temple. "Don't say a word." A masked voice whispered the command in the dark. "Get up, and come with me." The rough grip on Hassan's right arm shoved him along quickly, while his mind raced ahead to what was inevitably to follow— another Egyptian martyr.

"Up the stairs." A five-story climb was exhausting. "We have to jump off this building onto the roof of that one over there. It's the only way to get in." For the first time since leaving his apartment, Hassan looked squarely at his captor's face and declared he could not make it. "You can and you will." He did. Adrenaline (and angels) helped him make a magnificent landing below with his captor right beside him. The assailant seized Hassan's right arm again and forced him toward a hatchway in the abandoned warehouse. Hassan was sure he would never again see the night sky. He whispered, "Jesus, into Your hands I commit my spirit."

"Open the hatch door, and climb in quickly." The gun pointed that way. He hoped the scene wouldn't end too quickly, and once inside the gloomy structure, the plot took a startling twist. He stepped into a foreboding room, lit with a single candle, fully expecting his immediate execution. Ten obviously Muslim men stood in a circle and stared at him as he entered. They ordered him to sit down. When he complied, the menacing atmosphere changed instantly. The mysterious group smiled at him.

The man who had kidnapped Hassan spoke first. "We are imams, and we all studied at Al-Azhar University. During our time there, each of us had a dream about Jesus, and each of us has privately become a follower of Christ. For a time we didn't dare tell anyone about this. It would, of course, have been our own death sentences. But finally, we could hide it no longer.

"We each prayed to Jesus for His help to learn what it means to be His follower. Over time, He brought us together, and you can imagine our amazement when the Holy Spirit revealed that there are other imams who have found Jesus as well. We know you follow Christ. He led us to you."

The kidnapper finally explained the point of this clandestine encounter. "I'm very sorry I had to frighten you with the mask and the gun, but I knew it was the only way to get you here. It was just too dangerous any other way. I apologize. But now our question is, will you teach us the Bible?"

I have related all of that so that you can properly appreciate the excitement that I am experiencing to tell you that the dreams of Jesus have started among the Muslims in South Woods State Prison! But let me back up. Tuesday, Dec. 17, I went out to the minimum-security unit to answer a written request of an inmate to see a chaplain. He sat down across the desk from me and just started right in. "Chaplain, I need to tell you something. I have been a Muslim for fourteen years, but two weeks ago I had a dream. Jesus stood before me." Then he let me know that it was so powerfully drawing that he immediately left Allah and set out to follow Jesus. I then asked him if he was afraid when Jesus appeared to him. He pondered in deep thought before answering. "When I served Allah, I was scared of him. Now that I am following Jesus, well— it is a different kind of fear."

I said, "Do you mean a fear of losing Him or grieving Him?" "Yes, that's it."

I went on to tell him that if he will keep his heart open and invite Jesus to keep coming to him, He will. I told him that Jesus might not continue to come in dreams, but that he would sense a definite Light as to what he should do. He was deeply taking in everything I told him. I was visiting with him just before our class time in the minimum camp and so I asked him if he would like to stay for the class and tell the other men what he had told me. He did, and they were excited, too.

I have been telling all the groups in the prison, as well as my supervisor, and we are praying that it will just be the beginning of a landslide of turning to Jesus among the Muslims here. Now, are you excited enough about this to help us pray some more in? I hope so!

Now let me tell you something else that is often looked upon mistakenly. When a person feels they have prayed through and found a pure heart, and then later discover that there is still some hidden imperfection that needs to be taken care of, that person in so admitting this, takes a giant step forward, even though many would consider it a step backwards. Such is the case with the man who felt he got sanctified after the officer threw his Bible across the floor. He had a very severe physical infirmity which he felt he could not live with and so asked to have surgery. He told me all about it. It was a brutal affair, and more brutal than the physical was the treatment he received. The nurses were absolutely profane and vulgar around him. He felt several times during all of this that he was struggling with uprisings that were not yet like those of Jesus, and he was as honest as could be with me over it. I urged him to waste no time but bring those uprisings by name before the Blood and ask God to fill those voids with the Holy Spirit. Please do pray for him that he will not stop short until the refining Fire has completely done its work in him.

Would you please forgive this insertion into a prayer letter if I comment that the failure to endure the refining Fire is plaguing our churches, our pulpits, our mission fields, and our Bible colleges. Oh God, give us a revival such as William Booth prayed for in his song: "Send the Fire, send the Fire!"

I must share something with you that was so thrilling to me from Christmas Sunday night. We had a service in the prison before the one in our church and I preached to the men from the thought of leaving their all (their sheep) and going to find Jesus. I told these things about that: If they truly seek Him, they will find Him. When they find Him, they will know it. When they find Him, they will love Him. When they find Him, they will want everyone to find Him. And when they find Him, they will be ready for Him to come again.

At the close I asked my wife to dismiss in prayer. She stepped forward to the pulpit and said, "I need to say something first." Then she opened up her mother heart to the men before her. She told them we had sons that were the same age as some of them, and that she really cared about them and loved them and wanted to see them all make it. I could tell without a doubt that she was getting to their hearts and that it was coming from hers. It is possible that hardly a man in that room ever knew a mother like that. Afterwards an inmate passed by and shook her hand and called her "Mother." I just thanked Jesus with a melted heart for giving me such a wonderful wife and helpmeet!

I sent a Christmas letter, as I usually do, to the inmates who have left our prison for other ones. I asked this personal question to each of them: "How is it this Christmas time with your heart, my Brother? Is there anything or anyone that brings a cloud between you and the smiling face of Jesus? If so, may this Christmas day find it completely removed so that the Star that shone for the Wise Men can shine into your heart in cloudless splendor!"

Here is a response a few days later:

> What a genuine joy it is to my soul to have someone ask me if there is anything or anyone that brings a cloud between Jesus and I. My heart finds no comfort nor rest from any other "so-called" concerns over my welfare. Thank Jesus for natural affections, but they are like the flowers that bear no fruit: beautiful, even aromatic, but quick to wither... While I have few opportunities to fellowship, I do enjoy a liberty of God's presence that some monks of old would've come down off their poles and out of their caves, to experience. In the midst of a crooked and perverse generation I am finding Jesus in all. He is bigger, better, greater; more than all.

Again this year we had a Christmas Eve service in each of the areas. We begged the men that if they did not know for certain that Jesus had been born in their hearts to ask Him for it and not come into Christmas Day without Him. Our time is so limited with them in services like this. I often wish we could forget the clock and just settle in to seek God, but I know God understands the limitations and He is still able to send the Holy Spirit to follow up His work in them.

As we enter a new year my heart's desire is to see many men come to a genuine indwelling of Christ in them and then get their feet established in the way to heaven. There are distinct challenges to working with hearts that have never known even the barest beginnings of self-discipline and control. Oh, how we ought to thank God if we have been raised in a Christian home, or for that matter, in a home at all. But thank God that even in a dearth of such upbringing, God's grace can still make the wounded whole. Thank you for praying.

William Cawman

February 1, 2020

First of all let me follow up with a bit more about the man in prison who had the dream that started him following Jesus instead of Allah. I was visiting with him a few days after his dream and he said, "Chaplain, I need to tell you something. Sunday night just before church I was reading my Bible and the words just jumped out at me, 'This day is salvation come to this house…!' Then I went up to church and the man preached about that very verse. Does this mean that I am now a true Christian?"

I asked him if he felt that Jesus was living in his heart, and he said, "Oh yes, I'm changed from what I was!"

"Then," I said, "that is what makes a true Christian."

"Oh, thank you, thank you!" He wants to visit as often as we can, for he is now finding so much that he never found in Islam. What a tragedy that so many professors of Christ have given up the Pearl of Great Price until Islam appears attractive.

My wife and I spent the first two weeks of the year in Bolivia preaching twice a day to a very hungry-hearted and appreciative group of people. They so eagerly sent their greetings to the men in prison who were praying for them, and vice versa. One day soon all of God's great family will be gathered home and forever be one, and Jesus' prayer for that will be answered. Lord, haste the day!

I will tell you something interesting and heart-warming from Bolivia that the men in prison immediately recognized for what it was. A couple of weeks before the meeting down there one of our precious pastors and his wife were up in La Paz for her to consult with a doctor over some physical problems. After paying the doctor, they did not have money to spare for one of the better bus companies, so took a cheaper one.

As they were traveling through the mountains at night,

Pedro (the pastor) heard something break in the steering and the bus started swerving. He was sitting beside his wife with their baby girl on his lap, and behind them was their daughter of about ten years. Just as the bus started swerving dangerously and Pedro knew they were in for trouble, a young girl came up and said, "Let me help you with your daughter." She was meaning the ten-year-old behind them. Just then the bus rolled over on its side, just before going over a steep precipice.

Pedro and his wife and baby fell to the other side of the bus, which was now on the bottom, and seats and people came crashing down on them. They are still suffering from all the bruises they received. But the girl was unhurt, and when they turned to thank the girl who had helped her, she was nowhere to be found. When I told the men in prison about that they immediately brightened up and looked at each other and said, "It was an angel!" They were right— it was.

Last month I told you about a man who so responded to a revelation of sin in his heart and prayed it through that it would have appeared that he was sanctified. He later entered into a real valley of persecution, which revealed to him that he was not yet completely pure within. Please keep praying for him as he is earnestly and intelligently seeking to be completely filled with the Spirit. You see, it is ever so important that these men, as well as all men, find more than a correct theology regarding purity of heart. They must be "filled with the Spirit," or the spot, be it ever so small, that is not filled will soon reinfect the whole, or as the Bible so succinctly puts it, "Know ye not that a little leaven leaveneth the whole lump?" Holiness teaching, holiness professing, holiness singing— well, it is all good, but without holiness of heart no man shall see the Lord, either here or hereafter.

I also told you that our supervisor, who came to replace the retired one, has been doing an excellent job and has been very cooperative. However, he does not want to stay here, but wants to continue where he was before. A new man is to come soon to take his place. He comes from a northern prison that is very small and has only about thirteen men in service on Sunday night, so this will be quite a change for him, to say the least. Please pray that he will be just the right person for the job and that the work can go on as God would have it to.

Recently a man returned to this prison after being gone from it for a number of years to one of the northern prisons. He was an earnest seeker after God before he went away, and still is. He is a firm believer in holiness of heart, but as yet has not been able to fully claim it for himself. I'm not just sure what all of his struggles are, but he is always right in tune with the truth. He murdered a young girl when he was but a teenager and received a sentence of thirty to life. He did the thirty and was given a hit of three more. He did the three and again was given a hit of three. Then about the time they sent him back to this prison, they realized they did not have solid grounds to keep giving him more time, so they rescinded the second three and sent him back before the board. He was gone for several days, fully expecting to be released after meeting with them.

All of the sudden I looked across the compound and there he was, back again. As soon as I could, I scheduled him for a visit and he told me that they had given him three more years, part of which he has already done. I asked him what the reason for their decision was and he said that they grilled him with questions and he told them that he had no more to say without making something up. He told them that he had turned himself in and had told the truth from the beginning. They were not satisfied and said he was hiding something from them. They gave him three more years because they said he could not pinpoint the trigger that made him commit the crime.

I told him that no matter what the outcome was, he had done the right thing by simply telling the truth. I told him that eventually truth always comes out on top, and he fully agreed and said he was not angry about it, but was accepting it as from God. Please remember him in prayer that he will find a fully satisfied heart and that soon. He has been in prison now from about nineteen years of age to fifty-four, and will be fifty-six when he gets out, provided they don't give him more time yet. By the time a man has spent that part of his life in prison, he is a poor candidate for release if not completely filled with the Spirit of God. He has lived a structured life for most of his existence— told what time to get up, go to bed, what to eat and when, where to go, etc., etc. The insecurity of being thrust from that into a world of smorgasbord choices is completely overwhelming, and more than most men can handle.

Now I have a very exciting answer to prayer to share with you. Last fall our local church pastor who had been with us for almost fourteen years and who was very loved by all of us, felt the Lord leading him to finish his time here and move to another church. He had been very faithful not only to the church but in taking some of the services and studies in the prison when I would be away in meetings. The men in prison also respected him very highly and loved him. As a result, I cancelled most of the meetings abroad through the end of the year, but not sensing a clearness to continue to do so, we were looking to the Lord to supply us another pastor.

Rev. Philip Hessler and his family came to visit us and went into the prison with us as visitors in the month of November. There was immediately a mutual bond between them and the men in prison. After much prayer on both sides, Bro. Hessler answered the call and will be coming, Lord willing, to pastor our church.

Before he left to go back and close up affairs where they had been, he and his wife and two oldest daughters took the orientation course and became registered volunteers in the prison. When I returned from Bolivia, several men told me how much they loved him, which made my heart so happy. To all of you who were aware of our need and helped us pray, thank you! Now just pray that the Lord prospers their closing out of affairs where they are so that they can soon come to us. They have six daughters and one son, and we are so happy God is leading them this direction.

A few months ago, I mentioned briefly a man who had been working in the Twin Towers in NYC a year before they went down. He had been on his way home from work and had accidentally stepped off the platform of the subway train and was immediately run over by an on-coming train. He watched as both of his legs were cut off and then he passed out until in the hospital. As strange as it may sound to us, this middle-aged man had apparently had no thought of God previous to the accident. He is just now awakening for what would seem the first time in his life to spiritual realities.

On the tier where he was for a while, there is an inmate who professes to be a teacher of truth and righteousness and holds Bible studies on the tier. He came to my classes for a season, but found my teaching to be "false doctrine," and never attends anymore. He got ahold of this hungry-hearted man and put him through his program, then they moved the man to another facility. I have had two or three visits with him and then he stopped me on the way out of Bible study this past week and asked me the question, "How can I know I am covered by the Blood?" We had been discussing the Passover in Egypt and applying it to our need of knowing we are covered by the Blood. He went on to say, "When I was over on tier —, —— saved me; but how can I know he saved me?"

I said, "No one but Jesus can save you; I can't nor anyone else. Only the Blood of Jesus can save you and wash away your sins. You get alone with Jesus and pray to Him and tell Him you are sorry for your sins and ask Him to come into your heart. When He does, He will wash away your sins in His Blood and then the Spirit of God will let you know that you are under the Blood." "Oh, okay, I will do that." Friends, this man did not come from Bolivia or China or Papua New Guinea; he grew up in "Christian America!" Perhaps no darker mission field exists anywhere in the world than across our back fence. May God awaken us to the need next door!

The Jewish inmate who has been a continual source of turmoil for years, because of his special needs and because of who his father is, was recently moved to a Federal prison. Everyone breathed a sigh of relief to see him go. I only wish he could have found his Messiah before he left here, but pray that still he will do so.

And then our Muslim chaplain is finally back after months of illness of some sort. They said he got Malaria in Africa and that started off a list of other problems which needed surgery, etc. I have wondered just what all he did get into over there. He came back to us a skeleton of his old self, but seems to be gaining some ground now. One thing I know for sure, and that is, I don't have any interest in traveling to Africa or anywhere else out from under the protection of the One and only True God! False gods have nothing to offer against the demonic powers of those nations where such has been turned loose. At least, now that he is back, it lightens the administration load for the rest of us.

I am disappointed with my last visit to my big burly Muslim. I was so hopeful that he would come to the Light and become a big burly Christian. He had told me he really wanted me to keep calling him down and that he was telling the other Muslims he really enjoyed talking with me. The other day I scheduled him again and it was not the same. At the close of the visit I asked him if he wanted me to continue calling him and he said, "I don't care; it's up to you, but not unless you want to." Once again, I was reminded of how many souls there are all around us who at their first encounter with Jesus trembled like Felix, but got over it and never trembled again. It is vitally important what response a soul gives to the first ray of Divine Light. Probably had Saul of Tarsus braced himself to go on and finish his present errand, he would have never faced Light like that again. Pray that I will know for sure whether the Lord wants me to pursue him or not. I would have loved to have him for my brother!

Thank you for your prayers,

William Cawman

March 1, 2020

LAST NIGHT I JUST finished the prayer letter for February 1 and then went into the prison today and had such a precious visit that I will write about it before I lose any of it. It will have to go into the March letter even though I am writing on Jan. 27. You see, if you keep praying there will be more to write about!

For years I have mentioned an inmate who has been living the life of holiness without a flaw for at least seventeen years. He is the one who is a double murderer and is serving a thirty-year sentence without a plus or minus. He is now nearing the end of it and today, as we visited and I looked into his radiant face, he told me the following:

His brother, who he is very close to, lost his wife about a year ago after a long illness. He is getting married again to a woman in his church who lost her husband. He is moving into her house and so told our brother that he can have his old house, which is a mobile home about twenty miles from our church. Then he learned from his cousins that when their grandfather died, he left all of the grandchildren an inheritance. It is not a huge amount, but sufficient to get him started very comfortably upon his release. Then an aunt died and her children, his cousins, were discussing what to do with her car and one of them said, "Well, —— is going to need one when he gets out of prison," so they took it and parked it in the driveway of his house. With all of that news the Lord spoke to him very clearly and said, "Now you see, I am taking care of you, but don't forget that when I led the Children of Israel into the Promised Land I gave them houses they did not build, and vineyards they did not plant, etc., and I said to them, 'Beware that thou forget not the LORD thy God.'"

Then, he told me something else that really warmed my heart. He said that he learned of a legal provision for a sentence like his, which allows no early release for good behavior, etc., in which money is available upon release. He investigated and then filled out all the paperwork and as soon as he finished, he felt a cloud and the Lord spoke to him and said, "Am I not enough to take care of you?" He instantly tore the paperwork to shreds and felt a wave of God's favor sweep all over him. I said to him, "Now, brother, there is a grand lesson for you; don't ever walk under a cloud! Wherever you plan to go or worship or be employed, walk only in the Light and God will keep you in the center of His sweet will."

We will surely miss him when he leaves the prison, but I believe God has something special for him when he gets out, too. Pray for him!

And I had another visit with our dear brother who, as a Muslim, had a dream in which Jesus appeared to him. He is eagerly learning all he can about his new life. He said to me, "I'm just blown away by this God thing!" Then he asked me if, when Jesus forgave his sins, He also forgave all the sins he committed while he was a Muslim. I assured him that God's forgiveness covers every sin we ever committed, and he replied, "Oh thank you! Thank you!"

He had another question: the girl that was killed along with others in a recent helicopter crash— what about her soul? I explained to him about the provision in the atonement by which a soul is covered until that moment when they commit their first willful sin. He seemed so relieved over that.

I couldn't help wondering (or might I know better?) if ever there was a soul filled with such wonder and delight over entering the Muslim religion as this man is in coming out of it into the light of the Gospel.

Do you remember the man who plunged in with what seemed to be all of his heart after an officer grabbed his Bible and kicked it across the floor? I had another visit with him today. It is very often so, that when a person with no reality of grace in their background makes a conspicuous plunge at the Pool of Bethesda, we may think they went farther than they actually did. It would have sounded like this man found a full deliverance from inward sin after that episode, but time has revealed that the Refining Fire is still at work in him. Malachi certainly spoke the truth when he asked, "But who may abide the day of his coming? and who shall stand when he appeareth? for he is like a refiner's fire, and like fullers' soap: And he shall sit as a refiner and purifier of silver: and he shall purify the sons of Levi, and purge them as gold and silver, that they may offer unto the LORD an offering in righteousness." Many people have had an encounter with Jesus, but so few stand still long enough for the Fire to do its refining.

Today he told me that he has been hoping that when he went to classification next, they would downgrade his sentence and allow him to go out to a halfway house. Instead they assigned him to stay right here for the two years remaining on his sentence. He said he was disappointed and felt very angry about it for awhile, until he realized that God allows things sometimes that we might not want.

I said to him, "Now, let me talk to you about that. First of all, we cannot take away anything from God, for He never changes, and the Bible says that God is love."

"Oh, yes," he replied, "I believe that completely."

"Then," I said, "Maybe God sees that you would be better able to really come into His full image by staying right here where He has been helping you. Do you realize that halfway houses are literally hellholes? I've never heard anything good about them. God knows that if you are just changing localities and environments, you will not settle down to this one thing necessary, and so He has been good enough to leave you right here."

With a huge smile he replied, "I needed to hear this! I know what I need to do."

I then began to explain to him very simply why there are two separate crisis experiences in being conformed to the full image of Christ. He listened intently and then said, "I really want that!"

He then told me that he has been talking to his mother about all that he has been learning from our classes and that she is really getting help from it as well. He said he told her that God is not angry with us, but with the sin that dwells in us. He said that was a huge relief to her and that she is also getting closer to God through what he is finding.

He hugged me tightly and thanked me and said he was going to seek after the fullness of the Indwelling Spirit until he finds it. Please do pray for him, as I believe he is a genuine seeker after all of God.

Then another man came in who wanted to see me, as he was leaving the next day. I asked him how he was getting along and he said that it was pretty good until just a couple of days ago. Just before his release the mother of two of his children told him that she is seeing someone else, and it left him shaken and depressed. He looked at me with fear in his eyes and said, "Chaplain, I'm afraid to go out." I asked him if his being there was drug related and he said it was. I then asked him if he felt he had moved on past that danger. He said that up till now he felt he had, but he was afraid he was going to go out and feel so depressed that he would be in danger again.

I began to emphasize how important it is to really have the Spirit of Jesus dwelling within us and that we are not safe anywhere without it. I asked him if he had ever really had the assurance that his sins were forgiven. He said he hoped so. I told him that if they really were, he would know it, and that he needed to spend the rest of the one day he was here really asking God in earnest to come into his heart, to tell Him that he could not live without Him. I asked him if he knew what I was saying and he said he did. I then told him that I might not see him again before he left, but that when he knows he is saved to write to me back in the prison and let me know. I trust he will follow through on it.

Our new supervisor is supposed to begin at the end of March. Please pray that he will prove as helpful and cooperative as the temporary one we have had. The last few months have been very blessed with his supervision, and we hate to lose him.

We continue to experience many inconveniences as to our Christian services, such as failure to call them out, failure to unlock the doors and let the men out, etc. Meanwhile, our state government is insisting that we provide regular services for American Indians and Buddhists and other such. The irony is that American Indian "religion" is not a religion at all; it is simply an ethnic culture. An Indian can be any other religion at all and still participate in the tribal ceremonies and carry on. It is clearly evident that, as we have said before, the antichrist is not anti-religion; it is anti-Jesus Christ.

I would like to request special prayer for the inmate I have written about a few times over the years, who was sent to another prison for several years and recently returned. He has been a seeker after a pure heart for some time, and has no desire to turn back from it, but the last little while I have noticed in his countenance what appeared to be discouragement or depression. I talked with him today and he freely admitted that he is struggling. He is the one I have mentioned before who has a thirty-to-life sentence. He served the thirty and was given a three-year hit. He served the three years and was given another three-year hit. Then they realized that there was no valid reason for the second hit and so they revoked it and scheduled him to see the parole board again. He came from there rather discouraged as they mercilessly grilled him to get him to say what they wanted to hear, but which was not the truth. He seemed to be victorious over that for a season, but lately prison life has just been wearing on him, with unfavorable cellmates, etc. I can certainly understand why it would be so— nothing but prison from nineteen years of age to fifty-three years. During the whole thirty-four years so far in prison he has not had any infractions of the rules or charges against him, but still he is there.

Please do pray that God will get him through all of this victoriously. I tried to talk to him about the Scriptural admonitions such as the words of James: "My brethren, count it all joy when ye fall into divers temptations..." and Peter's words: "Wherein ye greatly rejoice, though now for a season, if need be, ye are in heaviness through manifold temptations: That the trial of your faith, being much more precious than of gold that perisheth, though it be tried with fire, might be found unto praise and honour and glory at the appearing of Jesus Christ."

I said, "I am not being insensitive to your trials. I feel deeply for you, but God has promised grace for all of this and it is wrong to not claim it." He replied that he knew that was the truth and he was not giving up. He said he feels like he is in a tunnel right now and I told him that tunnels are shortcuts to the other side of the mountain. He smiled at that.

I am still faced over and over with the disappointment that as men are leaving for parts of New Jersey, and especially the northern areas, I do not know of any churches that I can recommend them to. At one time they were scattered all over the state, but today this is a dry and barren land when it comes to genuine churches, let alone holiness ones. Please help me pray that God will use some of these men to go out into these desolate places and start a fire there.

And so, since the needs are so many and God is so big and able, let's pull on heaven for some more miracles bigger than our needs! Have you ever had the most exciting experience that even while you were calling on God to work out a miracle you suddenly discovered to your surprise and amazement that He had already answered, but in such a way you never dreamed of that it took you off guard? What a God we serve! Let's not disappoint Him by asking too little.

In Christian love and thankfulness for all you are doing for us,

William Cawman

14
A WHOLE NEW APPROACH

April 1, 2020

> *"God is still on the throne, and He will remember His own; Though trials may press us and burdens distress us, He never will leave us alone!*
> *"God is still on the throne; He never forsaketh His own; His promise is true; He will not forget you— God is still on the throne!"*

ISN'T THAT GOOD NEWS in these troubled times? It seems there is not a single area of any of our lives that this "present distress" has not affected. We are praying not so much that God will straighten things out, but that He will be able to accomplish His will in His all-out effort to prepare a Bride for Christ's soon return. Oh, that our nation and many other nations would heed the warnings and wake up to righteousness.

Perhaps none of us were aware of how strong the anti-Christ spirit had overwhelmed our nation until it began to be exposed. Now it is baring its teeth and showing its fangs alarmingly. You may have noticed the picture just recently of our President surrounded by ministers praying for him. To whatever degree any or each of them really had contact with the true God, the very scene aroused the unmitigated wrath of the evil minds in our government. They were furious!

According to Jesus' warnings, we may as well expect such and while so doing, we are going to need the grace and beauty of holiness of heart to refuse to allow a proper righteous indignation to become even a shadow of carnal attitudes toward those thus minded. A godly preacher in my young life used to say that holiness was designed for the last days. We surely need it, don't we?

When the restrictions began regarding the virus, volunteers were told not to come into the prison. Then they banned contact visits. About that time we went away to a revival meeting and before returning I was informed that part-time chaplains were asked not to come in and that all religious services were cancelled. So a couple of days later I went into the front office of the minimum unit camp and got access to a computer and wrote the following letter and sent it to each inmate in my Bible studies and classes:

> I am writing this letter to you since for the present I am not able to come into the prison with all the precautions regarding the Coronavirus.
>
> I want to encourage you to look to Jesus for all your needs and to be sure you are fully right with Him and His Word. We don't know why God allows some things in our lives, but we do know that if we take it rightly, He will use it to strengthen our connection to Him. Perhaps He is preparing us for even greater trials as the day of His appearing draws closer.
>
> For many years our Brothers in the Lord have suffered persecution in other countries that we know nothing about. They have fulfilled the Scripture which says of them, Re 12:11 *And they overcame him by the blood of the Lamb, and by the word of their testimony; <u>and they loved not their lives unto the death.</u>* We have had a long, comfortable season to seek after the Lord and get ready for His return, and yet so very many are still not ready for what is coming. We have had such a comfortable lifestyle and

such a favorable surrounding in which to call ourselves Christians, that our love for Jesus might not stand up to the same persecution others are enduring.

God loves everyone just the same; He has no favorites. Therefore, He might just allow our comfort level to be shattered so that we wake up and seek Him with more than lip service. If He does, it will be just another side of His great mercy. 2 Peter 3:8-12 says: *But, beloved, be not ignorant of this one thing, that one day is with the Lord as a thousand years, and a thousand years as one day. The Lord is not slack concerning his promise, as some men count slackness; but is longsuffering to us-ward, not willing that any should perish, but that all should come to repentance. But the day of the Lord will come as a thief in the night; in the which the heavens shall pass away with a great noise, and the elements shall melt with fervent heat, the earth also and the works that are therein shall be burned up. Seeing then that all these things shall be dissolved, what manner of persons ought ye to be in all holy conversation and godliness, Looking for and hasting unto the coming of the day of God, wherein the heavens being on fire shall be dissolved, and the elements shall melt with fervent heat?*

Certainly, seeing that these prophecies will soon come to pass, we ought to be more in earnest to be ready for that Great Day than anything else in the world. Getting out of prison is not nearly so important as making it to heaven. Escaping the discomforts of this life is insignificant compared to escaping the fires of hell for all eternity.

So, while you are deprived for now of church services and Bible studies and classes, spend time alone with Jesus asking Him if all is well with your soul. You will be ever so glad you did when that time comes, and maybe soon, when as the Bible prophesies, everything about us will be shaken. Right now we are getting a little taste of what is to come. Our economy is shaking terribly; our medical system is shaking; the hearts of many are shaking with fear and anxiety. Let us rise up and pray through into the presence of God and then move among men about us with a trust and confidence that will cause them to ask where our peace comes from. Remember the Scripture that says: *For God hath not given us the spirit of fear; but of power, and of love, and of a sound mind.* 2 Tim 1:7

Let me encourage you with a few verses from Philippians 4: *Rejoice in the Lord alway: and again I say, Rejoice. Let your moderation be known unto all men. The Lord is at hand. Be careful for nothing; but in every thing by prayer and supplication with thanksgiving let your requests be made known unto God. And the peace of God, which passeth all understanding, shall keep your hearts and minds through Christ Jesus.*

God is still in control, and when this storm passes, may it find each one of us stronger in the Lord and in our love for Jesus! Spend time in God's Word, knowing that after all the thoughts of men are over with, we will all be judged by that Word. Reach out for the highest and deepest conformity to Jesus Christ that you find promised in that Holy Word and then ask God to fulfill it in you. He knew all about this very hour when He shed His Blood for us!

In Christian love until we can meet again, William Cawman

The start date of our new supervisor has been postponed now until April 13, due to all the restrictions in place at present. Please do continue to pray that he will be a man that God can use to further His cause here among these men.

There are times when I find such a need of God's wisdom to know how to handle a particular situation. A few months ago I noticed a young man who had signed up for one of my classes. He showed all the telltale signs of a very rough background which had marked him visibly as a misfit even in today's bankrupt society. In a week or two I noticed that another young man who looked almost like him also started attending the class. Then I discovered that they were twin brothers. They would sit in the back row of the class and talk to each other and I could tell that their interest in the class was very low. They were there for each other.

I looked up their whereabouts and found that they were in two different housing units in the same facility. That is actually against the prison protocol, but I would not have done anything regarding them if that was all there was to it. But I knew they were breaking the prison rules to attend class for the purpose of visiting with each other. I went to the sergeant and told him my observations and the next day they moved one of them to another facility. I promptly re-enrolled him in the class in that facility and both of them quit attending.

Even though I knew I had done the right thing, I felt badly that I had lost the opportunity to try to show them a better way. I did have a personal visit with each of them and they both agreed that their past lives were not what they wanted for the future, but it takes more than wishing to change things. Their home life had been extremely dysfunctional to the degree that they hated their parents for it. I don't want to ever come to a state of mind that seeing a soul slip through my fingers doesn't give me grief of heart. Pray for them.

With love and gratitude, and a plea for your prayers,

William Cawman

May 1, 2020

AS YOU COULD EXPECT, it would be a novel if I would tell you of what is going on in the prison this past month, for I do not know and have no desire to make something up. As a matter of fact, let me insert here a personal note that I am not trying to preach to others: I don't read novels! Recently I picked up a missionary book in the back of a church where we were for meetings and started to read it. I soon discovered that, as interesting as it was, it was not factual. It was a novel. I lost interest immediately. I have a big enough imagination myself. I do not need to borrow one from others. So there, now you know that much about me, don't you?

Anyway, since I have not been able to go into the prison the whole month of April and since I get no news whatsoever from inside, I will send you a copy of the letter that I wrote to the men in my classes and Bible studies. I brought to my home a list of all their names, numbers and locations in the prison so that I could at least keep in touch with them during this time, even if it is a one-way communication.

Here is what I sent in to them mid-April:

To my students and Bible Study members, Greetings to you in the love of Jesus.

I felt it on my heart to send you an update from a more refreshing source than the daily news. I want to report to you that GOD IS STILL ON THE THRONE! I saw a church sign that read: "Forecast: OUR GOD REIGNETH!" I am not fanaticizing or being insensitive to the current situations. I am looking unto Jesus; not this present world.

In Genesis chapter fifty we read that when Joseph's brothers came to him after their father's death and were fearful of his action toward them, Joseph said to them: *Fear not: for am I in the place of God? But as for you, ye thought evil against me; but God meant it unto good, to bring to pass, as it is this day, to save much people alive.* Now, let's look at the present situation through that viewpoint.

We are in the midst of a worldwide pandemic. There is no question but that it is real, and we are doing right to try to prevent it from spreading farther. As obedient Christians we will do our best to cooperate with our government in trying to stop the spread of this disease. Consequently, that is why I write you this letter instead of being able to come in and learn of God together. Sometimes we do not rightly value the privileges and opportunities God gives us so mercifully and lovingly until they are taken away from us.

But it is also very evident that behind the Covid-19 epidemic, there is another disease germ that is far more deadly. We are experiencing the rise of the anti-Christ who is revealing himself through world leaders in taking advantage of this to exercise and practice control and herding of the populace. It has been coming for some time and there have been faithful prophets who have raised their voices in warning, but too often they have been ignored just as Israel ignored the prophets in their day. We have been warned of the damaging effects of advancing technology. Ignoring such warnings, we have become addicts of a constant tidal wave of information, much of which is completely designed to brain wash and manipulate. We have lost our ability to think for ourselves. We have sold our thinking power to the ceaseless influx of news from an anti-Christ, anti-establishment, destructive media. The news media is in total control of us, and we are largely unaware of our danger.

I say all of this to warn you and to beg you to step out of line with this program and get into vital contact with our loving God. You will thank Him for all eternity if you will take the warning and spend less time, in fact, no more time than is necessary, listening to the news, and listen for the voice of that Great God who is still on the throne and in control of all that is going on. I believe that you have in your worship hymnals the words of this song:

"This is my Father's world, And to my listening ears
All nature sings, and round me rings The music of the spheres.
This is my Father's world; I rest me in the thought
Of rocks and trees, of skies and seas—His hand the wonders wrought.

"This is my Father's world. The birds their carols raise;
The morning light, the lily white Declare their Maker's praise.
This is my Father's world. He shines in all that's fair;
In the rustling grass I hear Him pass; He speaks to me everywhere.

"This is my Father's world. Oh, let me ne'er forget
That though the wrong seems oft so strong, God is the ruler yet.
This is my Father's world. The battle is not done;
Jesus, who died, shall be satisfied, And earth and heaven be one."

And so, while the world all about us is suffering physically, financially and emotionally, God is ruling over it all and getting a Bride ready for His soon return. He is not baffled; He is not under Satan's control, but is controlling Satan. Let me give you evidence of it. Churches all over the country are resorting to new and different means to come together for worship and God is using it to His glory. One church had everyone park in the parking lot and they sent the service out over the sound system. A man was walking by with his dog and the dog, seeing all the people and being a lover of people, came over to see them all. The man came to get his dog and heard the service. He stopped and listened all the way through and then said, "I didn't know that is what you were teaching here; I'm coming back!"

On Easter Sunday morning we had our service the same way; in the parking lot. Our church has been there for fifty years, and the next-door neighbor who farms 300 acres around the church has never once come inside. That morning we were singing with great joy, "He lives! He lives! Christ Jesus lives today; He walks with me and He talks with me along life's narrow way. He lives! He lives! Salvation to impart. You ask me how I know He lives? He lives within my heart!" Those neighbors were out on their deck grilling their dinner and heard it! When I saw it, I just wanted to shout it all the louder; "He lives!" Isn't it comforting and re-assuring that He lives?

All across the country are reports that God is being glorified over what the devil intended for evil. Isn't our God perfectly adorable? The Scripture tells us in Ps 76:10 *Surely the wrath of man shall praise thee: the remainder of wrath shalt thou restrain.* That promise lets us know that if there is any of this turmoil that God cannot use to His glory, He will shut it down. Do you see? OUR GOD REIGNETH!

And so, for now we are unable to meet together in worship services and Bible studies and classes, but just look up and ask God to let His glory be seen through it all, and when the entire battle between right and wrong is finally over, the whole wide

world will bow the knee and confess that OUR GOD REIGNETH!
With love and prayers, William Cawman

Just when and to what degree the doors will open again for us to go in and have classes only God knows at this point. But isn't it so comforting and reassuring that *He knows!* There is an expression that I often heard during my high school days that I haven't heard for a long time. Back then it was a very derogatory statement. It was always directed to what today is labeled a "nerd," and it was thusly expressed: "He's just a big know-it-all!" I am not saying this in any sense derogatorily, but Dear Friends, God is the *big know it all!* Hallelujah! And since He knows it all, the sum and total of my knowledge is to know that! What a stress reliever! The old Methodist Hymnal has the words: "Oh that the world might taste and know, the riches of His grace; the Arms of love that compass me would all mankind embrace!"

Please do remember (and I know many of you are) the men during this lockdown time. I do not know to what extent they are even locked down inside of the prison, for as I said, I have no word, but I'm sure it has brought a whole new set of trials and discomforts to them. A few of them are grounded and settled, and I have no fear for them straying away from the path of holiness, but still they need and would want our prayers. Many of them, however, are not yet made perfect in love, and many of them are not yet even born again, and they are in great danger of either taking wrong attitudes or of giving up under this long deprivation.

God alone knows if conditions for ministry will ever be the same as before all this happened, but we do know that whatever He allows, it will work for the furtherance of His kingdom if we stay in perfect step with Him through it all.

I would also ask you to pray especially for the babes in Christ. The one in particular is the Muslim who had Jesus appear to him in a dream and immediately began to follow Him. He has been so open, but open without a background of Christian teaching. He is so vulnerable to falling prey to the Calvinistic teachers among the inmates, who will without a doubt press their "doctrines of devils" down his throat. Please pray that the very same Jesus who appeared to him will continue to appear and guide him away from such and into the pathway of Light.

In Jesus' parable of the sower, the very first cause of failure to bear fruit is due to the birds of prey that come and snatch away the seed before it has a chance to take root. Oh, how vividly Jesus portrayed in this exactly what happens to so many new babes in Christ. Could I share my heart with you over this? I find it a temptation that I must resist, to maintain a righteous indignation against these thieves and robbers without allowing Satan to take that into his kind of hatred for them. Not that he hates them; oh no, he loves them; but he would like me to fall into the snare of the Church of Ephesus and, while hating their evil, lose my love for them. Wrong attitudes for the right cause or for truth, render the one taking them just as wrong as what they are opposing. My children used to quote a little ditty (from where they obtained it, I don't know): "Here lies the body of Jonathan Gray. He died while defending his right of way. He was right— dead right— as he sped along; but he's just as dead as if he were wrong." Thank you, my children, I want to always remember that!

Right now, while the world is undergoing an awakening at least in part, isn't it strange that "social distancing" is preventing us from door to door visitation? What a reminder we need that "For my thoughts are not your thoughts, neither are your ways my ways, saith the Lord. For as the heavens are higher than the earth, so are my ways higher than your ways, and my thoughts than your thoughts." We have to keep learning this, but God keeps right on knowing what He is doing. Let's stay in tune with Him!

With love and gratitude,

William Cawman

June 1, 2020

No, THIS TIME AGAIN it is not news from the prison, but news about the prison. There are still a number of active cases of the virus in the prison and several have been sent to outside hospitals. The twenty-four units in the prison are in a constant update as to which ones are quarantined and which ones are in isolation. The one encouraging factor is, that it should not continue indefinitely because in a place like that it is more than likely there is 100% exposure, so that should get them all in or over it more rapidly— at least I hope so.

I finally did get to meet my new supervisor on Wednesday, May 27. He told me that there are as yet no religious services and no school classes. Social workers come in once a week and he comes in for short periods. They did call me in, however, to take a Covid-19 test to clear me for when I do return. How foolish is that? The day after the test I could have been exposed and it may be months yet before I can return. They do not project anything at this time, but more than likely religious services will remain cancelled until maybe Fall.

I did then go into the front office and obtained access to a computer so that I could print out the location of all the men still enrolled in my classes and Bible Studies. Numbers of them have been moved to different units because of the quarantining, etc., so I wanted to be able to address letters I am writing to them correctly. I have been trying at least once a month to send each of them a letter by going into the prison post office and dropping them off in the inmate mail. That way I do not have to pay postage to send them.

I have sent you two of the letters and here is the one I just sent in to them.

> To my students in all classes: Greetings to you each one again in the continuing love of Jesus.
> It is a good time to remember the words of David: *Thy praise*

shall continually be in my mouth! I have told some of you before how my dear father, a man who I never saw commit a sin in my whole life, yet suffered much under the attacks of Satan. Thank God, he found victory through the Blood and made it through to heaven without a cloud or doubt about it. He has been there in the presence of Jesus and beyond the attacks of Satan now for over thirteen years! I wonder what all he has experienced of: *Eye hath not seen, nor ear heard, neither have entered into the heart of man, the things which God hath prepared for them that love him.*

One night last week I had a dream about him. I dreamed that we were in a good service and as I passed by him he looked up at me and said, "I don't know what it's all about, but I feel Satan tormenting me over something." In my dream I passed on by to another seeking soul and God spoke to me and said, "Go back and tell your father that it is time to look up and praise Me." With that I woke up and my first thought was, "I will worship the Lord in the beauty of holiness!"

Now, my dear brothers, are you worshipping the Lord in the beauty of holiness? He is worthy of your total devotion, your total trust, and your total obedience, isn't He? Let's be sure we are giving it to Him.

Now the Scripture says: Heb 10:19-24: *Having therefore, brethren, boldness to enter into the holiest by the blood of Jesus, By a new and living way, which he hath consecrated for us, through the veil, that is to say, his flesh; And having an high priest over the house of God; Let us draw near with a true heart in full assurance of faith, having our hearts sprinkled from an evil conscience, and our bodies washed with pure water. Let us hold fast the profession of our faith without wavering; (for he is faithful that promised;) And let us consider one another to provoke unto love and to good works:*

You see, there is a qualification for worshipping the Lord in the beauty of holiness. We must come to Him (1) with a true heart. It is a mockery to try to praise God when our heart is knowingly not right with Him. The Scripture also tells us: Ps 66:18 *If I regard iniquity in my heart, the Lord will not hear me.* And so it is clearly necessary that our heart be right with God before we can rightly worship Him. (2) with a clear conscience. This means that we cannot come to God and worship Him if we are not fully right with our fellow man. Mt 5:23,24: *Therefore if thou bring thy gift to the altar, and there rememberest that thy brother hath ought against thee; Leave there thy gift before the altar, and go thy way; first be reconciled to thy brother, and then come and offer thy gift.* (3) in full assurance of faith. Heb 11:6: *But without faith it is impossible to please him: for he that cometh to God must believe that he is, and that he is a rewarder of them that diligently seek him.*

Now, when you come to worship and praise God in heaven with this Scriptural preparation, every enemy, every circumstance, every battleground, is under your feet, for God will give you victory when you exalt Him with a pure heart. Satan loves and will even help you to complain about your circumstances, or your injuries, or the injustices done to you, or others around you, etc., but he will turn and flee when you rise up to praise God with a true heart. Let the praises of God ring out from SWSP until the devil has to flee the territory he thinks is his. Let's claim SWSP for Jesus!

My wife and I are presently in a revival in Beechwood, IN and we are trusting Jesus for more of His love and grace and sweet will. Will you men please remember us in your prayers? I know you do, and I thank you. I told some people that I don't know that there would be another pastor in the whole world that has as many prayers prayed for him as I do. I feel humbled by that, but I thank you! Please pray that I will love Jesus more than I have ever loved Him before.

Did you know that love is more than just an emotion? It is a deeply planted commitment of the will, and therefore it dwells in a part of us that is capable of stretching larger and larger, without any limit to it. Wasn't God good to give us such a capacity and then to fill that capacity with something as precious as love to grow there? Even human love is a gift from God, and it is precious too; but the divine love that is shed abroad in our hearts by the Holy Ghost is infinitely greater and deeper than human love.

You see, love is something we as humans have, but something we can lose. Many people have lost their love for God and for everyone else except themselves, and they are living a miserable self-centered life. Many more people are losing their love in times like this when we are under the chastening rod of God with such afflictions as Covid-19. But God never loses His love, because it is not something He has, but rather it is what He is! GOD IS LOVE, John tells us. Why wouldn't everyone want to love Him back?

As I sit here writing to you, I look out the window at the beautiful green lawns all around us. I see the trees with their new coating of soft green Spring leaves. The sky over head is deep blue with lovely white puffy clouds floating over. The sun is shining so softly and the air is full of Spring. Flowers are blooming in every color of the rainbow. And then my mind remembers what Peter told us: 2 Pet 3:10-14: *But the day of the Lord will come as a thief in the night; in the which the heavens shall pass away with a great noise, and the elements shall melt with fervent heat, the earth also and the works that are therein shall be burned up. Seeing then that all these things shall be dissolved, what manner of persons ought ye to be in all holy conversation and godliness, Looking for and hasting unto the coming of the day of God, wherein the heavens being on fire shall be dissolved, and the elements shall melt with fervent heat? Nevertheless we, according to his promise, look for new heavens and a new earth, wherein dwelleth righteousness. Wherefore, beloved, seeing that ye look for such things, be diligent that ye may be found of him in peace, without spot, and blameless.*

What manner of persons ought ye to be? Let's you and I study diligently to know the answer to that, shall we? We cannot for now meet together to study God's precious Word, so I will give you Peter's question to study. And be sure that the answer you arrive at will have the full, blessed smile of God on it! Certainly also, *Seeing then that all these things shall be dissolved...*, it is no time to set our affections on this old world, is it? It is soon to perish and vanish away, so let's be sure we are laying up treasures above.

Let's also pray much for our nation and for the world during this present affliction. God has us under the chastening rod, and let's pray that many will wake up and call on God who never would have done so otherwise. My wife just said to me yesterday, "With God, no experience is ever lost." He knows just how heavy to afflict us that we might be partakers of His holiness. Let's not pray like spoiled children that God will take away the punishment, but rather that we will allow it to do its work. It will be worth all it costs to make it to heaven, won't it?

With much love and prayers, William Cawman

I received a letter from an inmate who was moved to another prison a few years ago and he was responding to the letter I had sent, because I not only send it to the men in this prison, but also to several others who are now in other prisons. This letter was from the Colombian man who was gloriously saved in 2015 and then sanctified a while later. He has been through the virus.

> Yes, the virus got me, all of me, except my soul. One month later, I am still weak; it takes great effort just to keep a conversation up, but the prudent hermit in me somehow relishes the excuse to remain silent. I can attest to every single symptom reported by many, except a prolonged cough. Mine was rather sporadic, in little bouts, kind of timid. Fatigue, however, defined my month long experience; each time I stood up, I felt the immense force of gravity and the incommensurable weight of the mixed nitrogen, carbon dioxide, sulfur dioxide, and many rare gases in our atmosphere. In contrast, the oxygen I hardly noticed. (Does my environmental science background emerge here?)
>
> One day, fortunately just one, I felt that the time for departure arrived. Despite my best efforts, and I have forty-nine years of training doing just that, I filled my lungs with air without being able to retain much of it. Exhausted, I was joyful. My inner thoughts overwhelmed my life with thanksgiving. Grateful for the family that nurtured me and loved me, and grateful for many people I met, especially those who remained when all

others deserted, I felt that life had treated me extremely well, much better than I deserved. That day I felt the power of spiritual forgiveness, the presence of the risen Christ, who loving me first drew me to discover His reality, to know Him, to know His Spirit, and I also felt hope and assurance that everything was well. I thought of Job, "What, shall we receive good at the hand of God, and shall we not receive evil?" I said farewell with great peace despite my distress. However, God had other plans for me: air began to fill my lungs, and after a long night, dawn surprised me with new life. Ah, the power of thanksgiving. If that intimate experience and awareness of my mortality is an indication of my future experience of departure, then there is nothing to fear. I feel privileged of having experienced life, but above all I am awed by the corrections officer who first dared to preach me the gospel, and by YOU, the chaplain who endeavored in prayer that I may be saved, and saved to the uttermost...

With love,

William Cawman

15
EVEN IN TROUBLED TIMES

July 1, 2020

YOU MIGHT WONDER, AS I also do, just how long this present situation is going to last. About three weeks ago, my new supervisor called me and said, "I can't believe I'm telling you this, but they want you to come back to work; they want to start up religious services again. They are telling me that you can have nine men for thirty minutes."

I said, "And who chooses the nine men?"

He said, "I don't have a clue! Why don't you come in Monday and we will try to get some details."

But before Monday came he called again and said that it was put on hold till further notice. Thus far there has been no further notice. These decisions come from the State capital, not from the local prison. Please help us pray that God's will be done in it all.

And so, once again I will just send you a copy of the most recent letter I am sending to the men in my classes and Bible studies. At least that way you might be able to back up the letter with your prayers for the Holy Spirit to make it effective as only He can.

To All My Brothers in Prison:

Greetings in the precious love of Jesus! This is now the fourth time I have had no other way to communicate with you than by letter from the outside. It seems that only God knows when this present distress will end and we can again be together to study and learn of God and to worship Him above all.

I trust that each one of you are finding new grace from His never-failing supply of all that we need. When God first created Adam, He did not create him with cravings and emptiness that caused him to long after something or someone he could not find. For a brief period, God allowed him to feel the need of a helpmeet, but then God supplied that need also.

The reason that Adam was so complete as to have no longings after something he did not have was that immediately after creating him, God breathed into him the "breath of life," and that very "breath" was abundantly everything he needed. That "breath" was simply another term for the Blood stream of Jesus imparted to him. And so God designed every particle of Adam as a dwelling place for the Blood stream of Jesus to abide.

Now, you and I and every other person born into the world since Adam are born without that Blood stream of Jesus flowing through our nature, making us complete and satisfied. Consequently, we early in life begin to crave that missing element. We try and try to satisfy our longings and incompleteness with the things we see and feel and taste around us, but it falls pathetically and tragically short of bringing satisfaction to us down deep inside. The mercy of God to us did not allow anything else that He had created on earth to satisfy us. Only Jesus can truly satisfy.

As you should well know by now, Satan is the enemy of God and all righteousness and he is the enemy of man as well. If he cannot keep a hungry soul intoxicated with the things of earth around him, he will then come as an angel of light and try to give him a religious outer garment. But he is the arch-enemy of any soul who would dare to open their heart to the call of Jesus and allow His Blood stream to be imparted into them. What a thief and robber this enemy of righteousness is! He does not care at all how religious a person becomes as long as they do not open their heart to the "breath of life" which comes in to abide where once the dominion of sin reigned. No church, no religious program, no person on earth, can impart the "breath of life" into another soul. "In him was life; and the life was the light of men." Jn 1:4.

But, don't despair! Even though you cannot produce life from yourself, nor gain it from any other person, God's Word tells us: Rev 3:20 *Behold, I stand at the door, and knock: if any man hear my voice, and open the door, I will come in to him, and will sup with him, and he with me.* 2 Cor 6:17,18 *Wherefore come out from among them, and be ye separate, saith the Lord, and touch not the unclean thing; and I will receive you, And will be a Father unto you, and ye shall be my sons and daughters, saith the Lord Almighty.* 1 Jn 1:9 *If we confess our sins, he is faithful and just to forgive us our sins, and to cleanse us from all unrighteousness.* 1 Jn 1:7 *But if we walk in the light, as he is in the light, we have fellowship one with another, and the blood of Jesus Christ his Son cleanseth us from all sin.*

Many other Scriptures could be quoted which show that if we will do our part (underlined portions), God will be faithful to impart to us that satisfying portion of the Blood of His Son, cleansing and filling us with the very same "breath of life" that He breathed into Adam in the beginning, thus making us just as fully complete as he was.

Many false teachers in this day proclaim that there is absolutely nothing we have to do to be saved; that Jesus paid it all. That is a half-truth, which ends up a lie. Jesus did what He did for us without our help or permission. When He died for us, He was fulfilling God's plan given to Moses way back in the wilderness of a high priest and an offering for sin. In Exodus chapter 24:3-8 we read a brief account of that first Day of Atonement. In that account Moses took the blood of the bullock into the Holy Place all by himself. No one went in with him and no one helped him. When Jesus died on the cross no one helped Him offer Himself. Jn 10:17,18 *Therefore doth my Father love me, because I lay down my life, that I might take it again. No man taketh it from me, but I lay it down of myself. I have power to lay it down, and I have power to take it again. This commandment have I received of my Father.*

But go back to Exodus 24:7,8 and notice: *And he took the book of the covenant, and read in the audience of the people: and they said, All that the LORD hath said will we do, and be obedient. And Moses took the blood, and sprinkled it on the people, and said, Behold the blood of the covenant, which the LORD hath made with you concerning all these words.*

You see, the blood Moses took into the Holy Place did nothing for the sinners outside until after they had made a covenant with God to obey all that He said to them. Then Moses took the other half of the blood and sprinkled it on the people telling them that it was the "blood of the covenant."

So you see, when Jesus gave His life Blood on the cross for us, the world was rotting in sin. They did nothing to add to His sacrifice. But after He had ascended into heaven and sprinkled His Blood on the Mercy Seat in heaven (see Heb 9:11-24) He came back and then presented Himself and His Blood to Thomas (see Jn 20:27,28). He now stands alone as our Great High Priest. He has completed the work of redemption for us, but not until you and I have entered into a covenant with God— *All that the LORD hath said will we do, and be obedient.*— does that Blood have any saving effect upon and in us.

May the Lord lead each of you into that blessed relationship with Him where His divine nature, His divine Blood stream is flowing through your nature. When it does, it comes in with power to live above and without sin. Read 1 Jn chapter 3 and you will find what this Blood stream that flows from the riven side of our Redeemer does for us when we actually allow it to flow through us. Verse 9 says: *Whosoever is born of God doth not commit sin; for his seed remaineth in him: and he cannot sin, because he is born of God.* Multitudes of religious teachers flatly contradict this written Word of God and tell us that we cannot live without sin. They are telling the truth! They cannot! But If they would only let the "seed" of Jesus Blood come in to abide they would find that: *But as many as received him, to them gave he power to become the sons of God, even to them that believe on his name: Which were born, not of blood, nor of the will of the flesh, nor of the will of man, but of God.* Jn 1:12,13.

My brothers, are you living only the outward form and struggling to try to be a Christian, or are you living under the Power of a son of God, with His Blood stream flowing through your nature, cleansing you from all sin and giving you a life of complete victory over it? The never-failing Word of God declares plainly that such is available. Multitudes of Blood washed souls bear witness to the absolute truth of it. So for the sake of your soul and the sake of the shed Blood of Jesus, don't try to live without the fulness of that same "breath of life" that God breathed into Adam when He created him.

With much Christian love until such time as we can meet again, William Cawman

Meanwhile, I can pray and so can you. Thank you for doing so. Here are a few lines from an inmate who is now serving time in PA but receives the letters that the men here do. The men in the prison here are not allowed to write to me on the outside, but he is not under that restriction being in another state.

Dear Bro. Cawman,

Since the lockdown we've been doing all bookwork, no groups which is great. I have a lot of time to read my Bible. I hope you are both rejoicing in the Lord. We may never get this quality time to spend in His Word. You & Cindy can have devotions all day, pray, meditate on His Holy Word.

Thank God for His patience and longsuffering with us and with this rebellious country. I've been able to speak with several souls down in the hole and share the Gospel of Jesus Christ with them. (2 Pt 3:9) God is faithful to every soul.

I appreciate everything you've done for me, but especially sharing a full salvation from all sin and entire sanctification. What a mighty God we serve.

I pray that I might have a real burden for lost souls... I pray for everyone. This time is proving to be beneficial to my soul. I'm rejoicing in this lockdown as it is refreshing to dive into His Word and meditate on the truths. Glory to God! What a privilege we are given in this country to have access to read our Bible anywhere.

Please do help us pray that soon the doors will open again to carry on with God.

William Cawman

┼┼┼

August 1, 2020

MY SUPERVISOR INFORMS ME that plans are being made to try to reopen religious services, but that it may be a while yet. And so, once again I sent the letter below to the inmates in my classes. Since I cannot report on the classes you will just have to attend with me by reading the same that I sent to them. Thank you for praying for us.

To My Students in SWSP:

I greet you once again by a letter, which is the best we can do for now. I trust and pray that the past few months have drawn you closer to Jesus, even though Satan would like to have you get farther away from Him. Just how soon we can again resume classes and Bible studies, I have not heard as yet, but hopefully soon.

My wife and I just returned from a camp meeting in Marysville, OH, and a few days later we found that a number of people who were at the camp tested positive for the virus. I was tested just this morning, July 27, in the prison lobby and so will wait to see what the results of that test are. If I have it, I am feeling quite well in spite of it?!?

I don't know how many of you have come down with it, but it seems that maybe few people will escape being exposed to it by the time it is all over with. However, even if any of us escape coming down with the virus, we are still being affected in many ways by the political and financial and social waves that it has created. What a strange world we are living in compared to just a few months ago!

I was praying for you all again in my prayer closet this morning and something came to my mind that I want to share with you as you and everyone around you tries to cope with the strange things that are happening.

Most of you know that my daughter, Debbie, has now been in Africa for almost fourteen years. Many of you have also heard at least a part of the story of her life before she made it to Africa. There is one moment of that time that I want to tell you about, but for those of you who have not heard her story, let me just give you a brief account that surrounds the moment I want to share with you.

I will give you here her own written testimony of how she was called to Africa:

I was about five years old the first time I remember God's hand on my life. We were in a normal church service; no special services in progress that I remember; but God was able to get a little wiggly girl's attention and focus it on a sinful heart. As we knelt to pray, I asked the Lord to make my black heart white, and for the first time in my life, I knew the joys of sins forgiven. I never remember saying "no" to the Lord, but I did not continue in a consistent walk with the Lord until just before my ninth birthday. Numerous times in those four years, I would realize that I had sinned or had grieved the Lord, and always my tender heart ran to the Blood of Jesus for forgiveness, but the summer I turned nine, God began dealing with my heart regarding a life-time commitment to be a Christian. He asked me if I was going to continue trying to ride the fence and running to the altar on little guilt trips, freeing my conscience but never making a choice for Jesus. He showed me where that path would lead me – I would not stay in the church living a clean life, but that path would lead to a road of sin and heartache. I made a choice that summer to live my life always for Jesus, whatever the cost might be. The Lord saved me the last night of camp-meeting that summer, and I can honestly say I have never spent a night outside of the fold of grace since. About a month later, the first Wednesday night of August, during a missionary meeting, God called me to be a missionary to Africa. I felt then, and feel today, God has given me the highest privilege on earth; I am unworthy, but oh, so happy!

When she was fifteen years old, God promised her that she would be in Africa by the time she was thirty. She graduated from high school and then took an intensive course in nursing and then went to Bolivia on a missionary internship. While there, she began to experience very severe headaches, but upon return went directly to Bible College to prepare as a missionary. Several times during her college years she crashed physically and had to come home. Finally, a doctor diagnosed her problem as a very severe case of Lyme's Disease. For the next several years she fought a losing battle with all kinds of effects of the disease. She lost control of her eyesight. She lost control of her bladder and had to be in a diaper. She went into deep spells of mental depression as black as midnight. Many days she could not even get out of bed, the pain and depression were so great.

One day in the middle of all this she felt just enough better to come out of her bedroom for family worship. I had prayed, then my wife prayed, then Debbie started to pray with these words: "Jesus, You taught us in the Lord's Prayer to pray, *Thy will be done in earth as it is in heaven.* In heaven, Your will is done with delight. Jesus, I believe I have been willing to go through this deep valley of suffering, but I'm not sure that I have been doing it with delight, but if You will help me, I will!" By this time we were all in tears. We were watching the beauty of a fully surrendered life and will just go deeper under trials almost unbearable.

Leaving many parts of this story out for sake of space, she finally went into spasms of intense pain that caused her legs to twist up backwards until it felt like her heels were touching her head. They were giving her medication enough to put an elephant under, according to the doctors.

One night the pain was so severe that she felt she could bear it no longer. She was now twenty-nine and was bedfast in our home. She looked up and asked Jesus to just take her home. God replied that He would if that is what she chose, but if He did there would be many hearts in Africa that would not hear the Gospel. She again looked up and said, "God, if You truly want me in Africa, You will have to do something." God said, "I told you when you were fifteen that you would be there by the time you are thirty."

On the Sunday night of January 15, 2006, she wanted to go to church. Her mother got her a walker and she hobbled into church walking on the tops of her toes because they were curled back under her feet. I was in a meeting in Guatemala. As the church was praying, she started into a spasm. The pastor and people gathered around her and once again anointed her with oil and prayed for her and her feet went out straight. Two days later it dawned on her that she was healed! She turned thirty on July 29 and went to Africa in early September and the Lyme's Disease has never come back. The doctors told her it was as much of a miracle that her organs weren't fried from the medication as that she was healed of the disease.

What a God we love and serve! But— let me to back to the point in all of this that bears a message I want to leave with you. "God, I am willing to suffer Your will, but if You will help me, I will delight in it!"

My Dear Brothers, are you delighting in all that God is allowing in your life just now? If you are just enduring it, or getting through it, you are missing a gold mine of blessings from God.

Let me share one more incident with you from my own life. As you know, on November 20, 2011, God suddenly took my dear wife of forty-one years home to heaven. The following day I was walking through our home not even wanting to be there. It seemed the light had gone out. Suddenly I stopped in the middle of the living room floor and looked up into the face of Jesus. With my will (not my emotions) I said, "Jesus, I belong to You, and I choose to embrace what You have allowed in my life." As soon as I said those words, rivers of love and grace began to pour through and through my entire being. I found the truth of those words of an old song: "He'll sanctify to thee thy deepest distress." I don't know how God does this, but we know that because Job refused to sin and charge God foolishly during his great affliction, God blessed him with twice as much as he had before.

Please don't misunderstand me; I am not serving God so that He will give greater blessings; I am serving Him because I love Him. But I have found and seen in others that when we choose to joyfully embrace whatever God allows or sends into our lives, it proves to be the very channel through which new grace is given that we never knew before.

This was our devotional reading in family worship for July 23:

"Why have ye not received all the fullness of the Holy Spirit? And how may we be anointed with 'the rest of the oil?' the greatest need is to make room when God makes it. Look around you at your situation. Are you not encompassed with needs at this very moment, and almost overwhelmed with difficulties, trials, and emergencies? These are all divinely provided vessels for the Holy Spirit to fill, and if you would but rightly understand their meaning, they would become opportunities for receiving new blessings and deliverances which you can get in no other way. Bring these vessels to God. Hold them steadily before Him in faith and prayer. Keep still, and stop your own restless working until He begins to work. Do nothing that He does not Himself command you to do. Give Him a chance to work, and He will surely do so, and the very trials that threatened to overcome you with discouragement and disaster will become God's opportunity for the revelation of His grace and glory in your life, as you have never known Him before."

Brothers, Satan is totally baffled and defeated when we see in everything God allows into our lives nothing but another blessing from His hand. Once while reading the Book of Job I got about halfway through it and suddenly stopped. It is absolutely certain that it was Satan that afflicted Job; but in 19:21 he cried out, *Have pity upon me, have pity upon me, O ye my friends; for the hand of God hath touched me.* I stopped and said to myself, Job, don't you know that was Satan that brought all this about? Then it dawned on me that Job had his eyes so fixed on God that he didn't give Satan credit for anything! What a secret to continuous spiritual victory over sin, the world and the flesh!

Men, let's have victory through Jesus! He died to give it to us. He shed His Blood for this very reason! Let us look everything that comes in the face and then say, "For this, I have Jesus!"

With much Christian love until we can meet again, William Cawman

When we are able to open again, I have heard that there will be regulations that could drastically alter the way we have done things before. I have heard that there will be no text books allowed (for what reason that would be? Or maybe I misunderstood?) and that handouts would be done in some other way, so I don't know what the future holds for us. Whenever I begin to have too many wonderments about it all, I have to remember that God opened this door to begin with and that it was entirely His idea, not mine. So He can order it as He sees fit. He does all things well, doesn't He? We will trust and obey!

With thankfulness to God and you who are praying,
William Cawman

September 1, 2020

WELL, A LOT HAS happened since the last letter I wrote to you. In case you need a fresh reminder that our God answers prayer, let me tell you what He did in answer to your prayers. Many of you will remember that some time back I seemed to be in the crosshairs of the supervisor in Trenton. It really appeared that my ministry in this prison would be finished. I sent a prayer request concerning all of this and I know you prayed. Then we had the Covid-19 episode and no part-time chaplains or volunteers have been allowed in since early March. During that time the new supervisor of our local prison started his duties here and I know that the Catholic chaplain told him what all I did when I was there. Early in August my supervisor called me and told me that that same man in Trenton had notified him that I was to return to work August 10. As far as I know, no other part-time chaplains were called back. I refuse to believe anything other than that God answered your prayers. Thank you.

So now that I have been called back in, let me tell you what else is happening. First of all, I am praying to God for a fresh anointing for this part of God's great harvest field. I cannot coast on past methods, or past anointing even, but am asking for a deeper passion for these men than ever before. I beg you to pray for me. I don't want to fail one single soul that God has opened the door again in order to save.

Every Monday morning we all have to spit in a tube until we produce a tidal wave that reaches a mark on the tube. Then we have to screw a second vial onto it to release blue liquid into our sputum. Then we document and label it and it goes in for testing. How long this will last we don't know, but you can imagine it is not what I consider a really very spiritual part of ministry.

At the same time that I was called back the man from Trenton came down and held a meeting in which he said he wanted us to come up with a plan to give every man a chance to have a service at least once a week. However, he said, "Please take note of the word I am going to use concerning it— the word is p-e-n-d-i-n-g." He said it still had to clear the governor's desk before we could actually start. Two weeks have gone by and we have heard nothing further. My supervisor told me today that his feeling is that the issue is not a top priority with our governor.

Since there are to be no volunteers allowed the rest of the year, whatever services are cleared to happen, it will be up to my supervisor and I to conduct— that is, the Protestant ones. I told my supervisor that I would just have to cancel most of my scheduled meetings for the rest of the year and stay by him, and he really appreciated it. If we are not cleared to hold services, then I will just go through all the names of the men in my classes and visit with them one-on-one as often as I can.

If we do hold services, they have told us it is to be limited to twenty-four inmates plus one chaplain, and they want each inmate to have an opportunity once a week. So you can see we will be pressed to do all of that plus the regular chaplaincy functions. We may never have just the same curriculum as in the past, so it is almost like starting all over again with most of it.

During the time the prison was undergoing the virus, many of the men were moved from one facility or one housing unit to another, thus making it necessary to reassign many of them. On top of that, on Sunday the thirteenth of September three thousand six hundred inmates with less than eight months yet to serve are going to be released. Never before has such an influx been sent back out into society all in one day. I'm not sure exactly how many from our prison will be among that number, but it will be several hundred anyway.

Over the past nearly twenty years I have written often about the inmate who was serving a thirty-year sentence but has for all the time I've known him, lived a wonderfully sanctified and victorious life. He has finally completed his time and is looking forward to coming to church and hopefully with some of his family. We are looking forward to it, too, needless to say. There is one man, however, who is not looking forward to it. That is the man he has worked side by side with for years, and that in the sweetest of Christian harmony. This other brother is the one who told me some time back that he had a problem: his face was hurting from smiling so much! He is really going to miss the one and only man he has been able to have complete fellowship with. I visited with him and told him that my wife had prayed that morning for God to raise up another man he can have such fellowship with. He just beamed and said, "Oh, tell her thank you! Thank you!" Will you pray for him, too?

Nearly all the men I have visited with so far since coming back have expressed to me how much it meant to them to get the letters I sent in while absent. Some of them were allowed to have times of fellowship in the courtyard or in the dayrooms, but they surely missed the services and Bible studies.

There is another man I would request a special interest in your prayers for. I am not exactly sure how long I have tried to help him, but he is just as needy as ever before. Many years ago he would come faithfully to classes and Bible studies and would seem to do well for a while, but then he would fall prey to the teachings of Calvinism and drift back into sin. Once or twice during these years he has been released on parole, but then came back again with fresh charges.

Once while out he became enchanted by a seventy-two-year-old woman with Lupus. He was in his fifties at the time and she was sending him one hundred dollars each month. This man has been married and has a living companion that he is divorced from, and he knows full well that any other woman is forbidden, but he was really struggling to give her up. I talked very straight to him and asked him if he was going to allow her to be the price of his soul. He broke down and prayed and seemed to get a fresh start, but then once again drifted into spiritual laziness and excuses. He told me that when he goes to the Calvinistic teachings, he feels comfortable and at peace, but when he comes and listens to me telling them that they can sin against God and be lost forever even though once saved, he feels scared.

I called him down and visited with him again. At first he

tried to put on a front as though all was well with him, but I know him well enough to dig down beneath his front. He began to get honest and confess his sinful behavior and shameful spiritual poverty. I said to him, "J——, you are now sixty-six years old and you have played around with God for your whole life. If you are ever going to make heaven, you are going to have to make a willful turn around and never go back again. You are going to lose your soul the way you are going."

I related my own years of spiritual poverty and how God helped me to set my will to be different, and then how He came and delivered me from that wilderness and set my feet on a heavenward pathway from which I have never and will never turn back again. Well, Hallelujah! I feel a shout coming from way down deep inside right now! *I know* there is a way out of such a wilderness!

All of the sudden I visibly saw him again plunge under conviction. We went to prayer and after I prayed, he prayed. Then he promised that he would go back and start resisting all that has hindered him and really seek God. I will not leave him long without a follow-up. I cannot let this man go, for God and God's family did not let me go. As he left, still deeply convicted and tearful, he said, "Thank you, Chaplain Cawman, for never giving up on me."

My new supervisor worked for almost twenty years in the federal prison system, but was forced to retire as they require it at age fifty-seven. He is now sixty-one and has been in one of the smallest state prisons in the interim. I am thankful that he is so far being very solicitous of any help I can give him and believes that we are there to see men saved. With so many uncertainties as to when and how far we can go in resuming services, I told him I would just concentrate on visiting the men one by one. He looked me in the eye and said, "That might even do more good than the services." That is exactly what I had observed over the years past. You might also remember him in your prayers.

It has been several days since I wrote what is above. Just

today, I suddenly received a message from the assistant administrator that the plan to release thirty-six hundred inmates passed the senate, but the assembly took it off of their agenda and they don't meet again until eight days after the planned release date, so the release is on hold. I immediately began to be aware of a stir in the administration area. I walked across the hall to where several social workers and office workers were eating their lunch and asked what they thought about it. They were livid. They had been working for months to get all the release documents in order, to find locations for the men, and to get them their physicals so that they were cleared to leave. Furthermore, the inmates have already been notified. I began to wonder, why was all this planned and worked toward before it even passed congress? Is this just one more index as to the disruptive and lawless state our nation is in? I talked to one of the sergeants who is very friendly to me and he says he doesn't know what is going to happen now.

Anyway, God is not perplexed nor confused nor baffled, so we will stay in His will and keep doing all we can to minister to these most needy men.

Today among the inmates I visited two of them were Spanish, one from Guatemala and one from Mexico. The one from Guatemala conversed in a mixture of Spanish and English, but mostly Spanish, and that through his mask. I tried to do the same and found it most interesting. His family is still all in Guatemala and they are all Catholics, but he has found something far better. He testified to me, "I love Jesus. I love Jesus. He change my heart!"

The other one from Mexico told me that he really didn't realize he was doing anything so bad until he ended up in prison. Now he says he looks back and sees the awful dark hole he was living in. He is now walking in the light and says he will never go back to that dark hole. He is almost finished reading his Bible for the second time and is finding so much light and help in it.

Another man today told me that he really loves the Lord

but that he is not happy with his slow mind. He says he tries so hard to memorize Scripture and to remember what he has read, but he just loses it. I told him that Jesus asked us to love Him with all the mind we have, not the mind of an Einstein. He smiled and looked so relieved over that. He has been taping little Scripture verses all over his cell to try to remember them. I told him to keep it up, but above all to ask Jesus to fill him completely with His own Spirit. I asked him if he remembered when he was full of the devil and he readily agreed. "Then," I told him, "Jesus wants to fill you even fuller with His Spirit."

So many of the men are still trying to be Christians instead of letting Jesus come in and live His life out through them. There is a man who is serving a life sentence and who is supposed to go serve another one in another state when this one is finished. That's pretty grim, isn't it? Anyway, he has been coming to Bible studies and has been very vocal and seemed to have a good testimony in part— that is, when he testified instead of trying to preach to the others.

Yesterday, as I sat with him and asked him how he was doing he just opened up and got honest. "Chaplain, I'm struggling." I said, "Are you struggling with Satan or are you struggling with sin inside of you?"

"It's sin inside of me." Now we could really get down to business, and he seemed to be open to it. Do you see why I feel the private visits are many times more productive than services? One thing is coming through clearer and clearer, and that is that for the present God has me shut in with these men. One of the sergeants said to me yesterday, "Chap, I'm glad you are back!" May the Lord's will be done in the days ahead.

With love,

                                          William Cawman

16
CARRY ON!

October 1, 2020

What a joy it has been to find that many of the men during the time we were not able to be with them, say that they kept up their prayer life and Bible reading, and when I ask them if they are finding the Power within to live above sin, they say they certainly are.

I have been going through the lists for all three facilities as well as the minimum-security camp and assigning the men one by one for a visit. Just today (I'm writing this now on September 14), I was visiting with men out in the minimum camp and got a call from my new supervisor. He said, "I want you to visit a man out there that I talked to the other day. I prayed the sinner's prayer with him and he accepted Christ into his heart. I think you are the one to follow up on it."

I went to the unit where he was housed and asked for him. He seemed most ready to be followed up on and wanted me to visit him again soon. I urged him to seek and ask to be completely filled with the Spirit of God. I told him that if he left any door open in his life to something he knew wouldn't please God, the devil would immediately drag him back into sin again. He was very responsive and bright and I will certainly see him again soon.

I thank God that my new supervisor has bonded with me really well and seems so in harmony with seeing men get right with God. He comes from the Christian and Missionary Alliance and I told him that my wife and I are using A. B. Simpson's devotional, *Days of Heaven on Earth,* in our daily family devotions. With such a cooperative supervisor and a wide-open door for the rest of this year, I feel warmly bound to put my best into letting God use me to accomplish all that He has opened this door for.

One of the men I put on the list the other day was a thirty-year-old man from Brazil. He does graphic art designing and has been back and forth to this country. The last time he was here he was accused of a murder and put in prison with a life sentence. He called his mother and she said to him, "Son, you have said several times that you really wanted an experience with God that would give you the power to live right. Maybe God is allowing this for that." He readily agreed and began to seek God. He told me that he wasn't interested in just trying to live better, but that he wanted a real experience with God. He said that as he sought the Lord, God answered by coming into his heart and giving him just what he had been wanting.

But he said he couldn't understand why he had a life sentence for something he didn't do. He just took it to the Lord and committed himself and his sentence to Him. In a little while the prosecutors came in and told him that the DNA didn't match and so he was going to be released soon.

He had been over in the industrial building working when it was time for his appointment with me. Since he is going home soon he hadn't been going to many of the appointments set for him, but his officer told him he thought he should keep the appointment with the chaplain. As he told me his story he concluded by saying, "I really feel deeply that I owe something to God. I want to find what He has for me."

I said, "So you are going back to Brazil, right?" He said he was. I told him I knew of some missionaries down there who were building a Bible School for the purpose of training pastors and Christian workers. He immediately brightened up and said, "I would love to go there! I know God has something for me."

I said, "No doubt something besides graphic design, right?"

"Right!"

I am presently working on getting connections between the missionaries and him for when he is released very soon.

As he left the room he said, "Chaplain, this was ordered by God. I'm so glad I came down to see you today." Pray for him that he will follow all the way with God.

Well, the inmate that I have mentioned to you again and again over the past twenty years was in our church Sunday! Was he ever drinking it in! Let me give you just a glimpse into the catastrophic life change he is going through. Immediately after the preaching and dismissal, he said to me with a huge smile, "Every time that little girl (she is about seven months old and a very active member of our church who has not yet developed her volume control) said something, it went clear through me—'You're free! You're free!'" Do you realize that he had not heard a baby's voice for thirty years?

He certainly desires your continued prayers as he seeks out God's will for him from here out. We are so delighted to have him in our church, but he is also greatly missed by those he left behind who were in harmony with his love for Jesus and the holy way to heaven. Please pray for him as he carries a real burden for the many he left still in prison. He is corresponding with a number of them and pray that God will anoint those letters with help from above.

I have been reminded again, as I visit with man after man, of the precious Scripture that says, "Nevertheless the foundation of God standeth sure, having this seal, The Lord knoweth them that are his." Hidden away in places we would never think about are souls who are responding to that "true Light, which lighteth every man that cometh into the world." God knows every one of them by name and just where they are. I am finding some of them among the men I have been visiting with.

Now there are two Scriptures that I believe go together well. One of them is the one just quoted about the Lord knowing them that are His. The other one says this: "The secret of the LORD is with them that fear him; and he will shew them his covenant." You might ask how they fit together? Well, many people in the world today can talk ever so fluently about their "Christian" life, but every once in a while, someone begins to testify and a little bell begins to ring down inside of the heart in which Jesus dwells. What is happening? The Lord is sharing what He knows about that soul with your own heart. It is much like an introduction—"Here is your brother!" Oh, how I love it when God shares His secret with me.

Here is one just yesterday: "Chaplain, I've always known the way, but now I know Him! He is living in me!" Oh, that I could somehow pry open the blinded eyes of so many others so that they could also see Jesus! While telling you of these that I am finding, let me say that Jesus is not coming back in the Rapture for only Elijah! He still has seven thousand which are not bowing the knee to Baal!

The powers that be up in Trenton gave us orders now to begin opening up for services. They have termed it a "soft opening," and instructed us to provide a thirty-minute service for each inmate who desires it with a limit of twenty-four at a time. Just how to schedule such, and with only three chaplains and no volunteers, we planned to meet on Monday, September 21 to come up with a plan.

Monday morning my supervisor called me and said there would be no staff meeting because of the following reason. He and his wife had been trimming branches out of a tree on Saturday and a branch fell right across his mouth and knocked him unconscious to the ground. His wife got him to the hospital, bleeding profusely, and they took x-rays and said he would have to go to Cooper Hospital in Camden for a plastic surgeon to put him back together.

But what was really upsetting at that point was that the x-ray showed some sort of mass on his brain. They were quite alarmed and his wife immediately called a number of people from their church (Christian and Missionary Alliance) and they began praying for him. When he got to Cooper they took another x-ray and the mass was gone! Thank God, He still answers prayer!

My supervisor told me the staff meeting would have to wait as he looked like a combination of Donald Duck and Hitler. I said, "Well, at least it didn't knock your sense of humor out!"

So I have been continuing to schedule the men enrolled in Sunday services for private visits until we can have a staff meeting to decide just how to proceed with services. They are calling another part-time chaplain in, because with three facilities to cover each week with services, two of us cannot handle it all. Because of the restriction of twenty-four men at a time, I sat down and counted how many men were in each of the twenty-four tiers so that we could schedule them according to those numbers. They do not want us to have the services on Sundays as it would require them to pay a chaplain overtime to come in on Sundays, where the Sunday services have always been mostly held by volunteers, who cannot return for possibly the rest of the year.

Hopefully our supervisor will return soon and we can finalize a plan, send it to the administration for endorsement and then up to Trenton for their approval. You see, this entails a bit more than a local church board meeting.

I was visiting with an inmate and one of the sergeants knocked on the door and came in. He wanted to know if there was preparation work they needed to do for the reopening of the services. I told him about the supervisor's accident and that because of that we had no firm plan yet of just how we are going to hold all the services. He understood but said to keep him informed so that they are not taken by surprise.

Now... could I share a little detail with you? Have you ever read that God can make the wrath of man to praise Him? Have you ever read that He can set a table before us in the presence of our enemies? Have you ever read that He can turn the devices of the wicked back upon their own heads? Well, not even a year ago, the future of our ministry in the prison seemed rather shaky. The Christian services were being ignored and pushed around in such a blatant way that it was obvious that we were not wanted. Even from the head offices in Trenton there were vibes that perhaps our ministry was drawing to a close.

Then came the dreaded (and most dreadfully taken advantage of, by the news media) Covid-19. It closed down religious services completely for over six months while the virus ran through the ranks of the men in prison, killing a very few, making seriously sick a few more, giving others a slight sickness, and the majority nothing at all. Now we are experiencing no new cases and so they have ordered religious services to start up again. The atmosphere is totally changed! Everyone seems to be anticipating and eager to cooperate with the reopening until I move about the prison feeling just as much wanted as a few months ago I felt the very opposite!

God knows what He is doing, doesn't He? Old Satan, Obama, Hillary, Nancy, Chuck, CNN and all the combined forces that are threatening our beloved nation with extinction are no more than a flea before an elephant to our God! Hallelujah for the power of the Blood of Jesus! It loses nothing by the rage and insults of men and devils combined. Let's sing with renewed zeal and fervency, "It has never lost its power... It will never lose its power!"

Now in light of all that and the emotional explosion it just drew out of me, would you please pray for a fresh outpouring of anointing and power to fulfill whatever God has had in mind in turning this tide into a new open door right on the very grounds it seemed to be closing? Just how long the present door will stay as it is, God alone knows, but I feel a deep urgency to work while the day is. Please pray that a harvest of souls will open their hearts to the very God who is giving them this opportunity. That God, doubt you not, is not Allah, nor Buddha, nor Santaria, nor Thor, nor the Virgin Mary, although we have all of those and more on board, but the God who is rich in mercy enough to open a door that seemed to be closing is JESUS CHRIST, the ONLY BEGOTTEN SON OF GOD!

Thank you so much for continuing to pray for this little corner of the last great harvest field.

William Cawman

November 1, 2020

WHAT A DIFFERENT MONTH this has been and I have so much to tell you about it. Thank you for all of your prayers for us during this time of unprecedented changes in the prison. We have felt them and God has been answering them. Thank you, again!

I will start with an update of the events outside of chaplaincy which are having a huge impact on our ministry right now. I would never have imagined, when I started ministering here in 1998, that things could be so totally different from what they were then. And those changes are coming so fast and furious that we hardly recover from one alteration until another is thrown at us. So that you will know how to understand and pray for us effectively (which we desperately need) I will try to trace the trail of changes, mostly from just this year.

When the prison was first erected— which is actually three prisons within one compound— a chapel was provided in each of the three facilities which would hold about fifty men. The very first Sunday night when church was called out, over two hundred men showed up for the service. They started at that point to divide each facility into two groups and hold two services each Sunday night. That was soon found to be inadequate and since it was at the same time decided to abandon mess halls in favor of men eating on their units, they remodeled the mess hall in each facility into a chapel that would easily hold two hundred.

For a number of years we had an ideal program for all of our religious services. We had a large room which could be used for Sunday services and Friday Jumah prayer, and could also be used during the week for Bible studies and classes. In one corner of it was a chaplain office where we could hold one-on-one visits with the inmates. We had library cabinets with religious books and reference books so that the men could come down and study. We had a designated officer for both first and second shifts so that we were covered all day and all evening.

Then, for whatever reason (or probably for lack of reason) the post was abandoned, and ever since, the only time an officer is there is for Friday Muslim service and Sunday night Protestant Worship. We begged, we pled, we gave out our strong reasons why we needed our chapels back, but to no avail.

Then with the turn of this year, Sir Covid came to visit us. We were shut down for seven months while they tried to deal with getting it under control. Finally, on August 10, they sent me word that I was to come back because they wanted to provide religious services again for all the inmates who desired it. It took about two more months for them to decide just how we could hold services safely, and in the meanwhile, I just took advantage of the hours I had accumulated during the shut-down to visit with the men one-on-one. What an opportunity that has been. When a man is alone and no one of his peers around to have to protect his image with, he becomes much more honest as to where his problems really are, and I found such needs expressed as had never been before. I will try to tell you of a few after I finish this journal.

Finally, plans were approved by the State government office for us to have a thirty-minute service for up to twenty-four inmates and one chaplain, once a week. Since no volunteers are allowed back in yet, this whole provision has to be accomplished by the chaplains. We asked the administration if we could simply call out the services and let come who may, but they would not hear to it and so we had to take the time to enter all the names of men who had before gone to Sunday night services into the appointment rosters for the new time slots. Many of the men who would have come on Sunday nights have work assignments during the week, so we knew the numbers would be much smaller.

But because of the need for distancing, thank God, we got our chapels back! We started it off, but as we anticipated, only a few men came at first. It is a major endeavor to communicate any change of schedule to 3500 inmates and about 600 officers. We are now in our third week of trying to get this up and running and...

Here's the "and..." Again, for whatever reason or lack thereof, a decision was made to collect all of the inmates who had less than eight months yet to serve, and release them all on one day! It was going to mean that out of our prison alone, over four hundred inmates would be returned to the streets in one day, not to speak of the rest of the prisons in the state which would bring the number up to several thousand. Never— never before has there been such a thing even thought of! Couldn't they have been released a few at a time over a longer period so as to give society time to absorb them? I confess I see the whole thing as just one more peek hole into the larger chaos we have capitulated ourselves into as a nation. This was scheduled to take place on September 13, and for weeks ahead the social services department and parole boards were overwhelmed with getting them ready to leave.

The inmates had all been notified and processed. The families had been alerted and arrangements made as much as possible. Then it came up before the State legislature and passed in the Senate, but when it came before the Assembly, it was taken off of the agenda. Overnight, the word came down that the release was off. My suspicion would be that the senators were hearing too much apprehension from the public, and rightly so. It was promised to be revisited again in October for a November release.

And so now we are scheduled for the day after the Election, November 4. In order to accomplish this as smoothly as possible, inmates who are to be released are being moved to one housing unit while the ones in that housing unit are moving other places in the prison where the vacancies are left. So after all of our labor to update the appointment lists for men to come to services, we will have to do it all over again after the release is accomplished. And who knows how long it will take to fill up the vacancies again with men from county prisons, etc.?

Now, while and in the midst of all this bedlam, we are still trusting and believing God to win more souls from out of it all for His kingdom. Yesterday we received orders from Trenton that on the day the men are to be released, all of us as chaplains are to cancel everything else and prepare for a long day of helping with their exit. I have written up a brief little pamphlet to hand to them and we are requested to say a prayer and give something besides hand sanitizer and a mask to each of them and tell them goodbye. It will remain to be seen just what they will do with themselves as the streets are suddenly flooded with several thousand men trying to find their way back into society as useful citizens. Please help us pray that God can use it to sober many of them up and turn them around, as opposed to Satan welcoming them into his agenda for the uncertain times ahead.

So much for that, and I apologize for taking so much space to tell you, but really it is a huge issue that is impacting our efforts to carry on an effective ministry here just now. When they called me back in I was thrilled with the new open door; I still am— but "there are many adversaries!"

I am still working my way through the list of men on visits, but of course I don't have the time I did at first, as we have to conduct the services now as well. The response to the services after so long without them is very rewarding.

I visited with a man for the first time who has but one week left before getting out (not in the mass release). I found a very serious young man who considers his time here a merciful awakening to the course he was taking. He told me he wants a real relationship with God. He said, "You know in the Book of Acts how the Holy Spirit came down on the disciples and filled them with Himself? I want that!" I said, "The reason you want that is because the Holy Spirit is on the other end of this creating that desire within you. Just give yourself over to God without a fear and you will not be disappointed."

He has a young wife at home who is pulling for him and wants him to make good. I told him he has too much in his favor to sell out to anything else. He wanted to know where he could find a good church. When men ask me that I tell them that I do not tell anyone that they need to go to the church I go to in order to get to heaven, but that I know why I go there. He smiled and asked me for the address. I gladly gave it to him and hope to see him soon.

In a recent letter I told you again about a man I have mentioned over and over for years who makes a good start and then falls prey to either the sinful life about him or the TV evangelists who instruct him that it is perfectly normal and acceptable to live in sin. Then he will come back to me and get serious again and make another start and repeat the cycle all over again. Can I give up on him? Did God and others give up on me when I was going in circles myself?

The other day he visited with me again. It didn't take long for him to get honest and admit he had been falling down over card games and getting angry at those about him. I began once again to face him with the seriousness of how he was playing around with God. I told him that God was not obligated at all to help him when he would in turn just throw it away and go back into sin. As I talked very straight to him I could see his countenance withering more and more and then he began to stand up on the inside and take hold of what I was saying to him.

Suddenly I noticed him just shiver all over and then said, "Oh wow! Could we pray?" As we prayed he broke down and once again asked God to forgive him and then sat there half stunned with what he was feeling inside. I said, "——, God has spoken to you once again. You need to let this be the last time you go back into your sinful ways. You know better. You know what is right and what is wrong. You know what you need to do to rise up and walk with God. Take a hold of His hand right now and settle it and then keep it settled every moment to obey God. You will not go very far down that pathway until you sense Him coming to your assistance." He was reluctant to leave the room, but I happen to be a living witness that there is a God in heaven that can deliver from the briars of a wilderness wandering, and I will continue to follow after him.

And then there is another man almost in the same condition that I have been working with for about the same number of years. He has been in and out of the prison, just as has the first man I told about. As we visited again for the ???'th time, he too seemed to be sensing the seriousness of how far he had gone in wasting his privileges. He told me that he cannot trust himself. I told him that might be the truth, but that if he would put his trust in God, there could come a turnaround that would set him on a new pathway forever.

Could I relate something to you that I have been convinced of and which never ceases to humble my own heart? I shamefully look back on twenty-five years of wandering in a wilderness of unbelief, spiritual laziness, and broken vows to God. I did not do it in the same venue as many men I work with. I never went into the outward sins of the present world. I lived a wilderness experience on a church pew. I know full well the addictive power of spiritual failure. "But God!" Aren't you glad those words are in our precious Bible?

Almost forty years ago God broke the chains of that spiritual failure as I rose up with a determined will to let Him do it. Shortly after He delivered me I felt God lay it on my heart to tell the whole story in a church way out on the west coast. When I had finished, a dear saint came up to me and said, "Don't think that God won't ever use those years you are calling wasted." I said nothing but rejected it in my heart. How could He? But to the utter humbling of my heart, God has taken again and again the ashes of my forgiven and surrendered past and used it to let me know He has a way out for others, no matter the chains that bind! I can look into the distraught countenance of a man thus addicted and put out my hand to him and say, "Come, friend, 'I know a Fount where sins are washed away. I know a place where night is turned to day. Burdens are lifted; blind eyes made to see; there's a wonder working Power in the Blood of Calvary!'" I know One stronger than the chains of any wilderness. I know a Power greater than years of spiritual defeat. I know Him. His Name is Jesus! Hallelujah!

In love,

William Cawman

December 1, 2020

NO MATTER THE TURMOIL in the world around us, this letter will be kept free of politics, so help me, God! When Jesus told us about these things that are happening right now, He told us to "look up!" And so, we will! God is still on the throne and He is still getting a bride ready for His soon return, and I can see positive evidence of that among men in prison. Can you imagine going to sleep one night on a two-and-one-half inch piece of foam covered with hard plastic; that laid on a steel platform bolted to one corner of the ten by twelve room, with a like beauty rest in the opposite corner of that cell, and then waking up in heaven? Oh God, please give us more ready souls inside of this prison, for Jesus' sake and to the honor of His precious Blood!

I have written however so many times (and again last month) about an inmate who has been so unstable and up and down spiritually that he is literally addicted to spiritual failure. So was I, just in a differently shaped form. But I was very encouraged today in visiting with him. He told me he has been finding power to turn away from sin and also a love for the Word of God. I talked to him about how the devil— now enraged— will do all he can to tempt him back through one of his formerly weak areas and that he must settle this like his life depended on it if he is going to continue to live clean. I told him that as he keeps his will engaged to turn from wrong and follow God, he will soon find a delight in help coming from heaven to his aid. He said he was already sensing that. Please pray for him. Somewhere in the pathway of spiritual failure there must come the last of the failure, if we are to rise up and take a new pathway. Pray that he will.

I also went to visit with a man who had turned in a written request, saying that he wanted an opportunity to speak to a chaplain "about his spirituality." I found a forty-one-year-old hungry man, ready to take anything I would tell him. I discovered something all over again— when a person is really hungry spiritually and ready to walk in the light, there is a magnetic pull on the heart in love with Jesus who is trying to help him. I wish I could meet more like that and feel it more often, but thank God for the one here and there.

It was such a joy to try to point him to the loving arms of Jesus. I told him that he needed to thank God for his desire to know Him, because that meant that God was on the other end of that desire, giving it to him. I told him there was no way in the world that God would plant in him a desire to have a relationship with him and then hold it from him. Then I told him what I often tell seeking hearts, "Simply look up to Jesus and say, 'Jesus, I believe You died for me. Whatever it was that You saw I could become that made You willing to die for me, here— I want to become that!'" I will certainly follow up with him soon.

In a service this month I had two so very opposite reactions to the Word preached. I was preaching to them on the two "ifs" of Deuteronomy 28. "*If* thou shalt hearken diligently unto the voice of the LORD thy God, to observe and to do all his commandments which I command thee this day..." and "But it shall come to pass, *if* thou wilt not hearken unto the voice of the LORD thy God, to observe to do all his commandments and his statutes which I command thee this day..."

At the close of the message a very small-framed Mexican man just burst forth in emphasis to the truth, having obviously enjoyed it. Another man who I have encountered for several years and believe him to be completely possessed with the demon of Calvinism, came up with open Bible and said, "You just taught all these men that the grace of God and His blessings depend on our keeping the law. Paul says we are not under the law. Grace is the free gift of God."

I replied, "You may leave now." I have done my best over and over to point him kindly to the Scriptural teachings, but I have also noticed for years that Calvinism, willfully believed, renders one totally unteachable and arrogantly defiant of truth.

The next day I was relating this to my supervisor and he looked knowingly at me and said, "I think I know who you are talking about; ——?" It was. He said that the same man had also requested an interview with him and told him that he would like to set up a relationship of iron sharpening iron. My supervisor told him he didn't think that was an appropriate relationship between a chaplain and an inmate, and then he asked him if his strong theology had kept his life in order. At that he went silent.

I had asked him the same thing perhaps a year or two ago with the same result. It is absolutely astounding how carnal ego can rise up to instruct others when so in need of sound teaching itself. Paul encountered the same thing in Romans 2:17-23. Apparently, the carnal mind is just as imbecile as it was two thousand years ago. Oh, how wonderful to be entirely rid of it!

For twenty-two years we have had a service for the men on Christmas Eve. It has been one of the highlights of the year. We would get together a good group of volunteers and visitors and try to make it a very special time for men who are so sorely missing family and home as at no other time in the year. This year we will not be able to do anything very special and I know the men are going to really miss it. My supervisor and I are planning to have a short service during the regular weekly time slot for each area at the beginning of the week, but the time limit is thirty minutes per service and that for only twenty-four inmates. Please pray that the God to whom a day is as a thousand years will anoint the services to the spiritual good of the men.

All signs are certainly pointing to our time being short. Oh, that we can yet get as many into the fountain as possible before we can work no more.

I received another very encouraging letter from the former Mormon who is now serving time in Michigan. He wrote that quite a few of the men had contracted Covid-19 and that he had finally tested positive but had no symptoms whatsoever. He actually ran six miles the day he tested positive. He told of how hard it was to go through quarantine in a cell day after day, but he said it gave him more time to be alone with Jesus.

I don't know if I ever told you this, but some time back he was tested along with some others and was one of the few who passed for the purpose of training seeing eye dogs for blind people who cannot afford to pay for them. It is a very worthy program for men in prison. He first had to be trained himself, and then he is given a dog that lives right with him in his cell for several months as he trains it. He is just getting ready to train his fourth one.

As you are probably aware, our present trend in government is more zealous to foster any type of false religion than to support the true God. Consequently, since no volunteers are allowed in just now, we chaplains each have to take two half-hour slots each week to see that other groups have a chance to meet if they care to. We each take a morning and first open the chapel to the Jewish inmates, then another half hour for miscellaneous groups, viz., Jehovah's Witnesses, Buddhists, and Odinists. Usually at least one or more Jewish inmates will meet, but very often the others do not bother to come when it is called out. Of course, we do not have to conduct anything or participate, but we just have to be nearby in order for them to congregate.

One morning I was sitting in for the Jewish inmates and there was a black man who obviously was not Jewish at all. He totally monopolized the session with his arguments that a man does not have to have a Jewish mother in order to be a Jew. Of course, this is one of the tenets of the Jewish teachers. He argued that Rahab was not a Jew but was in the line of Jewish decent, and that Ruth the Moabite was not a Jew even though she was the grandmother of David. I just listened but thought he did have a valid point. He told the other men that "these shepherds who are over us just don't like my looks!" He is a first-class troublemaker and I have been told by the Islamic chaplain that he was just as much trouble when he was a Muslim!

Now, it would be easy to just avoid such a case, but perhaps he is really only saying that he has not found what he is looking for? I am asking God if He would have me pay him a visit and ask him if he is open to hearing about a God that can satisfy him and help him to find something worth living for. It is easy to feel drawn to a person who is already nearly living by Christian values, but it very well could be that the greatest needs around us lie beneath some very unlikely exteriors.

The Master's last commission to the final hour of earthly time was, "Go out quickly into the streets and lanes of the city, and bring in hither the poor, and the maimed, and the halt, and the blind. And the servant said, Lord, it is done as thou hast commanded, and yet there is room. And the lord said unto the servant, Go out into the highways and hedges, and compel them to come in, that my house may be filled. For I say unto you, That none of those men which were bidden shall taste of my supper."

What a calling! What a challenge! They are all around us—the broken, the maimed, the dysfunctional, the marital casualties, the drug-destroyed minds. But they are souls for whom Jesus shed His precious Blood just as much as for you and me. And so when I meet one of these almost bizarre personalities I pray that God will give me the compassion of Jesus and let me see them through His eyes. Is anyone today more "messed up" than the demoniac Gadarene? Yet Jesus had time for him and He changed him, too, didn't He?

Let me tell you something about a man that I don't think I've ever written about before. He is a very quiet man with a charming smile who has attended Bible studies and classes faithfully for a number of years. For a few years in the middle of the time I've known him he was sent to another prison and then came back again. As far as I know there was no reason for that except what they call an administrative move.

Going back a number of years (I don't remember how many) he embraced and sought after the experience of heart holiness. Ever since then, whenever I call him in, I marvel at the keeping grace of God. And by the way, I marvel at it in my own life also! I asked him again just a few days ago, "Are you finding a fullness of the Spirit in your life that is keeping you from all sin?"

With a beaming face that reflected no hesitation or uncertainty he said, "Oh, yes! I am!" As far as I know there would be little if any support or outward help for him to so live in his circumstances, but GOD!

I love the words of the last verse of a hymn that says: "Be Thou exalted, O Spirit of power; dwelling within our hearts to keep us from sin." Thank God for sending such a One to abide within us, and do so forever! Hallelujah for our Jesus and His Holy Spirit!

It is extremely rare for a man to come out of prison without the fullness of the indwelling Spirit of God and stay true to whatever he found of God in prison. A man who has been out for only a few months now says that coming back into society from a structured prison life is nothing short of shock. If there is anywhere within or without a handle that Satan can still get ahold of, be assured, he will grab it with a vengeance. The sooner he can knock a man out and back into his way of life, the surer he is of causing him to fail forever. He wants to get them to fall backwards before they learn the first secret of spiritual warfare, and by so doing he virtually inoculates them against ever trusting God's grace again.

And so, at the close of another year, I want (and they want) to thank you, each one, for your prayers. And then could I request that we get a fresh grip on God and pray that whatever time we still have to work with these men, many more will go through a personal crucifixion of all sin and be filled completely with the Holy Spirit. Nothing short of that will enable them to live the wonderful life Jesus died to give them, and prepare them for heaven.

William Cawman

Members of Schmul's Wesleyan Book Club buy these outstanding books at 40% off the retail price.

Join Schmul's Wesleyan Book Club by calling toll-free:
800-S$_7$P$_7$B$_2$O$_6$O$_6$K$_5$S$_7$
Put a discount Christian bookstore in your own mailbox.

Visit us on the Internet at
www.wesleyanbooks.com

You may also order direct from the publisher by writing:
Schmul Publishing Company
PO Box 776
Nicholasville, KY 40340

www.ingramcontent.com/pod-product-compliance
Lightning Source LLC
Chambersburg PA
CBHW071736150426
43191CB00010B/1601